From **Command**
to **Community**

CIVIL SOCIETY:
Historical and Contemporary Perspectives

Series Editors:

Virginia Hodgkinson, Public Policy Institute, Georgetown University
Kent E. Portney, Department of Political Science, Tufts University
John C. Schneider, Department of History, Tufts University

For a complete list of books that are available in the series, visit www.upne.com.

From
COMMAND to
COMMUNITY

A New Approach to Leadership Education
in Colleges and Universities

Edited by
Nicholas V. Longo &
Cynthia M. Gibson

TUFTS UNIVERSITY PRESS
Medford, Massachusetts

Published by University Press of New England
Hanover and London

TUFTS UNIVERSITY PRESS
Published by University Press of New England
www.upne.com
© 2011 Trustees of Tufts College
Manufactured in the United States of America
Designed by Doug Tifft
Typeset in Quadraat and Quadraat Sans by Michelle Grald

University Press of New England is a member of the Green Press
Initiative. The paper used in this book meets their minimum
requirement for recycled paper.

For permission to reproduce any of the material in this book,
contact Permissions, University Press of New England, One Court
Street, Suite 250, Lebanon N H 03766; or visit www.upne.com

Library of Congress Cataloging-in-Publication Data
From command to community : a new approach to leadership
education in colleges and universities/
edited by Nicholas V. Longo and Cynthia M. Gibson.
     p.   cm. — (Civil society: historical and contemporary
perspectives)
Includes bibliographical references and index.
ISBN 978-1-61168-023-2 (cloth: alk. paper)
ISBN 978-1-58465-970-9 (pbk.: alk. paper)
ISBN 978-1-61168-014-0 (e-book)
1. Community leadership—Study and teaching (Higher)—United
States.
2. Civic leaders—Training of—United States.
3. Community and college—United States.
I. Longo, Nicholas V. II. Gibson, Cynthia M.
HM781.F76   2011
306.43'20973—dc22

                                        2010051600

5 4 3 2 1

||||||||||||||||||||||||||||

CONTENTS

||||||||||||||||||||||||||||

PREFACE

Ten years ago, we had yet to meet one another but were traversing similar paths on which the ideas for this book were born. One of us was a program officer for a national foundation interested in increasing youth civic and political engagement. The other was the director of a new national initiative to mobilize college student participation in public life.

Neither of us experienced a dearth of advice from a range of colleagues, experts, and others who had strong opinions about the best way to achieve these rather lofty goals. Many of these suggestions centered on encouraging youth voting or community service; others advocated more civic education and issue organizing.

All of these ideas were well founded and eventually found their way into our— and many others'—efforts to ignite youth civic engagement. Missing, however, was the notion of young people as leaders in the communities in which they were serving, working, and being educated.

In fact, among the people who suggested that we focus on "youth leadership," most, when pressed as to what they meant, explained it in ways that reflected the traditional notion of the old, top-down, charismatic leader who leads the way— the "Great Man." As a result, they often urged us to consider offering things like leadership forums, seminars, and even camps that would train young people in a set of leadership skills, most of which were centered on public speaking, management and organizational theory, and fundraising. Those who did well in these areas or programs, it was believed, would be good leaders.

In the years that followed, however, we both saw the world moving in other directions. In addition to noting global events that had exposed the superhero model as somewhat flawed, we found ourselves spending more and more time listening to the voices of the next generation of college students and their changing definitions of leadership in democracy.

This new generation of young people who had grown up with technology—and the practices and values that come with it, including collaboration, transparency, and diversity—wanted more participation in the decisions being made in their institutions, their workplaces, and their communities. They were losing trust in bureaucratic institutions—including higher education, foundations, and government—and making their voices heard in other ways, namely, through their computer touchpads. They weren't interested in charismatic leaders showing them the way anymore; they wanted to do it themselves or in partnership with others.

According to a poll by Peter D. Hart Research Associates, for instance, nearly 65 percent of young people surveyed saw ordinary people as being better equipped to solve their problems than authority figures or experts. They were also more likely to have ambivalent, even negative feelings about formal leadership, preferring horizontal arrangements where everyone's a leader. And they wanted leadership to reflect that notion. As one student involved with a civic leadership program at Miami University explained, "I've learned that, yes, I could lead a group of people, one me and all the rest followers, I could do that." The student continued with the conception of leadership which permeates this book: "But how much better would it be if it was a room full of leaders."

Those and many other experiences like them prompted an array of new questions in our minds. What did a twenty-first-century leadership model look like? Was there a relationship between civic engagement and leadership in a rapidly changing, globalized world? How would we prepare young people to practice this new form of leadership? And given the role of higher education in preparing young people for leadership in all sectors—public, private, and nonprofit—how can those institutions transform their approach to leadership education in ways that better reflect the challenges and trends in our world?

Those were the questions with which we both found ourselves grappling as we began conversations for this project in 2007. Fortunately, the McCormick Foundation was also interested in them, generously providing us with an exciting opportunity to convene a national symposium in May 2008 dedicated to exploring these issues. Hosted by the Center for Information and Research on Civic Learning and Engagement (CIRCLE) at Tufts University, the Harry T. Wilks Institute at Miami University, Illinois Campus Compact, and Public Allies, the event at Miami University in Ohio brought together more than forty-five participants, including students, professors, and program directors from thirteen colleges and universities, and leaders of several national and state nonprofit organizations who are involved in some of the most innovative efforts in the country to enhance youth leadership through civic engagement, engaged scholarship, service, political activism, and civic learning.

This book summarizes the experiences, insights, and recommendations from this group, as well as offers essays from a set of recognized and emerging leaders in other sectors about the need to clarify a new definition of leadership education—one focused on developing student leadership through civic engagement in colleges and universities. Authors also underscore how a new definition of leadership education is not only a set of programs, courses, or skills, but an ethos that should extend across disciplines, departments, and individuals to permeate the way in which entire institutions function. That ethos is one that values the transparency, authenticity, collaboration, action, and interactivity that are fast becoming the hallmark of a new global society—one that young people are embracing and one with which older, more traditional institutions are grappling.

This new ethos is part of a shift from command and control to community and reciprocity in leadership—a change that is documented throughout this book.

Our ability to grapple with this project collectively is the result of help from a host of collaborators, colleagues, and friends. We'd first like to thank the McCormick Foundation for its generous support of this work, and especially the leadership provided by John Sirek and Andrea Jett. The Kettering Foundation, in particular David Mathews, John Dedrick, and Maxine Thomas, also helped seed the ideas for this book. We are grateful to the planning team from the 2008 symposium: Abby Kiesa and Peter Levine with CIRCLE, Kathy Engelken and Ericc Powell with Illinois Campus Compact, Paul Schmitz with Public Allies, and Angela VanHorn, Sarah Woiteshek, and Stephanie Raill Jayanandhan with the Wilks Leadership Institute at Miami University. We also got helpful feedback and encouragement from Dick Cone and Nan Kari, along with John Schneider from Tufts University and Phyllis Deutsch from the University Press of New England. This project is the product of the collective vision of this group, the participants from the symposium, and many others, not least of whom are the talented authors who contributed superb and lively chapters to this book.

As we move further into this new century, there's no question that a new world is beckoning—one that will require the ability to work across cultural, economic, and geographic boundaries; to be comfortable with technology and the transparency, fluidity, and speed that comes with it; to focus on action and results; and to recognize the assets of everyone with a stake in an issue.

That's why we believe there is no better time for higher education to think differently about leadership and to create opportunities for young people to apply their leadership models in organizations and communities around the world. Anything less risks alienating a whole generation of young people: a new generation eager and able to work for the common good and prepared to serve as leaders now and for years to come.

Cynthia M. Gibson and Nicholas V. Longo

Defining the New Leadership

Cynthia M. Gibson and Nicholas V. Longo

Introduction
The New Leadership

Ask almost any group of people what they think of when they hear the term "leadership," and they are likely to respond with words and concepts that reflect some version of the "great man theory": one charismatic individual (usually a man) to whom others look to "show them the way." A quick perusal of books about leadership on Amazon.com or at any local bookstore, in fact, underscores how entrenched this notion of leadership has become in the American psyche, with nearly every cover featuring the pictures of well-known business or political experts and text promising to let us in on the secret of what makes a "great leader." Not surprisingly, that usually translates into being a superhero—someone who is independent, magnetic, comfortable with authority, and unafraid to make tough decisions.

Recently, however, there's been a new way of looking at leadership—one that reflects the global society in which we live and the new set of skills needed in an interconnected world. It also flows from a growing disillusionment with traditional top-down, hierarchical leadership models that dictate to, rather than work with, real people in real communities trying to find solutions to real problems.

Given that young people have been at the forefront of this movement—due, in some part, to their embrace of technology, which is driving more transparency, collaboration, and global awareness—it is not surprising that colleges and universities have been experimenting with and, in some cases, incorporating fully into their curricula, a new approach to leadership education that embodies these values. At Duke University, for instance, the Hart Leadership Program merges civic engagement activities with a leadership curriculum that integrates local and global community immersion experiences with academic study. A central tenet of the Hart Program—the first endowed undergraduate leadership program in the country—is the notion of "adaptive leadership," whereby leadership is viewed as a collective enterprise, rather than as top-down, and as an ongoing iterative learning process that stresses inner reflection coupled with external and collaborative action.

At Spelman College, the Center for Leadership and Civic Engagement offers young women the opportunity to participate in leadership programs that are based on the experiences of African American women leaders and that include an intergenerational mentoring program. Miami Dade College, the largest community college in the United States, offers "student ambassadors" work-study positions supporting service-learning courses on campus. At Providence College, as part of the first undergraduate major in public and community service studies, students are required to participate in a yearlong practicum in which they serve as "Community Assistants," liaisons between nonprofit organizations and service-learning courses. Bentley College—a business-oriented institution—recruits community-minded students to campus with an innovative scholarship program and then places them in leadership roles in service-learning programs. The University of Massachusetts Amherst's Citizen Scholars Program gives a cohort of students the chance to take five service-learning courses focused on community service, civic leadership, and social change. Similarly, Stanford University offers an interdisciplinary, yearlong capstone through which students develop engaged scholarship with community partners. Tufts University provides summer fellowships to students for engaged research projects on local, national, and global levels through its College of Citizenship and Public Service. At the University of Denver's Center for Community Engagement and Service-Learning, students learn community-organizing skills. And Miami University of Ohio offers funds for interdisciplinary "think tanks" focused on catalyzing public and community leadership in the academic curriculum, as part of the Wilks Leadership Institute.

While organized differently to address the unique culture of its campus, each of these programs is part of a growing effort in leadership learning that emphasizes "relationship over position" and "action over attainment" (see chapter 6). A student who participated in a two-year program at Miami University, which asks students to study the impact of globalization on southwest Ohio in conjunction with participation in a civic leadership project, explains the change that sometimes occurs as a result of seeing leadership education as a component of civic engagement: "In the beginning I had a very narrow perception of a leader as an individualistic, 'in charge' person who pulled or pushed others along with them. Having a better understanding of the way communities are structured and function, I now see leaders do not necessarily have to be out in front of an issue, but rather, need only to stand by their own convictions and [be able to] work mutually with other leaders in their efforts" (quoted in Longo and Shaffer 2009, p. 154).

This student—and thousands of others—are part of a new wave of new leadership that recognizes the latter as less a matter of position and income and more one of action and public purpose. It emphasizes collaboration and horizontal arrangements in which everyone is a leader, rather than part of a hierarchy. It is also more bottom-up than top-down, and it is inclusive in welcoming diversity in all its facets. In short, there is a shift from an old style of leadership to a new one—from command to community.

This shift in the notion of leadership is hardly an accident. It is the direct result, many believe, of significant cultural transformation, especially the advent of and adaptation to innovative technologies that have revolutionized the way in which people communicate, learn, and work. Today, knowledge and information can be absorbed and distributed instantaneously and in ways that allow for more voices to be included in what were once more narrow domains of experts and professionals. Technology has also driven a shift to a more globalized society and economy in which poverty, substandard education, access to health care, climate change, and other public issues are the world's problems, not just those of individual countries.

Given these extraordinary changes, it is hardly surprising that young people (and increasing numbers of older adults) have and will most likely continue to have very different notions of leadership. Specifically, leadership is understood as something that is measured not by individual accomplishments or personal success, but whether and how civil society and communities are served. The most prominent difference between Baby Boomers (roughly, those born between 1943 and 1960) and Millennials (roughly defined as those born after 1980), for example, may be the latter's experience of growing up in a technology-driven world. Technology facilitates communication with large communities of people, including people working in groups to solve problems—faster. This approach to problem solving flows from young people's disillusionment with traditional, top-down, hierarchical leadership models that dictate to, rather than work with, people in communities in order to address problems (Hart, 1998). Millennials are also impatient with bureaucracy, focused on the practical, and skeptical of closed-door processes (Friel 2007; Tapscott 2009).

More than any other generation, Millennials are also eager to "make the world a better place" (COP 2008), signifying a distinct departure from their Gen-X predecessors, who were often accused of being "apathetic" about political and civic involvement (Tapscott 2009). During the 2008 election cycle, for example, about 23 million of the 122 million voters who cast ballots were under the age of thirty—representing at least 60 percent of the increase in voter turnout that year (CIRCLE 2009).

That is just the beginning, says Tapscott (2009), who calls the Millennials—whom he terms "Net Gen"—a "political juggernaut that will dominate 21st century politics in America" (p. 244). Already, they are one fifth of overall voters, and by 2015 they will be one third of the voting public. He and others believe this generation will radically change (and is already rejecting) conventional notions of civic and political engagement. Specifically, he cites the "we vote, you rule"

(p. 259) ethos that has arguably dominated American politics. As a result, young people are calling for more interaction with politicians and advocacy groups, monitoring their actions, contributing ideas for their agendas and activities, and insisting on transparency. In short, this generation is demanding a new era of civic and political engagement—what Mobilize.org, a national group of Millennials who encourage their peers to become more civically and politically engaged, calls "Democracy 2.0" (Mobilize.org 2007).

This new approach to civic engagement, however, is not just the purview of young people. As Matt Leighninger (2009) notes, scholarly research and public opinion data confirm the larger public's changing attitudes toward authority and the erosion of trust in traditional institutions and leaders. Daniel Yankelovich, who inspired many people to rethink their views about citizenship in *Coming to Public Judgment* (1991), now argues that "In recent years, the public's willingness to accept the authority of experts and elites has sharply declined. The public does not want to scrap representative democracy and move wholesale towards radical populism, but there will be no return to the earlier habits of deference to authority and elites" (cited in Leighninger 2009, p. 2). Some studies, such as the 2008 Civic Health Index, an annual publication of the National Conference on Citizenship, have confirmed that there is "overwhelming support for laws and policies that would support greater citizen engagement" (cited in Leighninger 2009, p. 2).

These new attitudes and capacities were dramatically evident during the 2008 election, but at the local level, it has been clear for some time that citizens are interested in governing, and less willing to be governed, than ever before. In small towns and cities across the country, ordinary citizens are coming together to demand a voice in community decisions and are engaging in a wide range of civic experiments to help their communities (and their leaders) function more democratically and solve problems more efficiently.

Leighninger and others believe that the proliferation of these civic experiments, and the conditions that have produced them, signify the end of the era of expert rule, in which elected representatives and designated experts made decisions and attacked problems with limited interference, and the beginning of a period in which the responsibilities of governance are more widely shared. As a former mayor and the first chair of the Democratic Governance Panel of the National League of Cities notes, "We seem to be moving toward a different kind of system, in which working directly with citizens may be just as important as representing their interests" (Leighninger 2009, p. 2). Other legislators and elected leaders have begun to agree, arguing that they will not be successful if they continue to ignore citizens' desire to help solve problems that need fresh ideas—ideas that they believe could and should come from "real people" who face those issues every day. In short, those who have traditionally controlled decision-making processes now recognize that to have real impact, they need not only public buy-in but also public weigh-in (Gibson 2008). That means, in turn, that leaders need to be able to listen effectively, collaborate, be comfortable with diversity, and promote transparency.

Colleges and universities have taken notice of these trends, with a significant number of them offering a panoply of programs and curricula focused on promoting and practicing civic engagement, service, and community problem solving. Today, for instance, Campus Compact, a national nonprofit promoting the civic purposes of higher education, has grown to more than 1,100 member campuses served by thirty-five state offices. A recent survey by the organization (2007), in fact, found that

- One third of all students were participating in service and service-learning courses annually
- Thirty-four percent of institutions take activities like service-learning and engaged scholarship into account in promotion and tenure decisions for faculty
- Ninety percent of these institutions' strategic plans specifically mention instilling in students a sense of responsibility to their community as an important student outcome

Moreover, there are centers of service-learning and civic engagement at nearly 80 percent of colleges and universities that are members of Campus Compact, along with majors, minors, and a new career track for directors of community engagement in higher education (Campus Compact 2007). There is also significant financial support for community engagement, including federal funding through the Corporation for National and Community Service; a growing number of refereed journals dedicated to service-learning and community engagement; an international research association that recently held its tenth annual conference; and countless conferences, books, and new initiatives by national and international associations in higher education.

In recent years, some institutions have taken steps to embed service and civic engagement even more deeply in their academic cultures by requiring courses or experiences for graduation, creating full degree programs, and establishing institutes on these issues. A smaller, but significant, number have begun to consider faculty's civic participation—through engaged scholarship, teaching, and community problem solving—as a factor in tenure and promotion decisions and in awarding research grants. As a reflection of these developments, in 2006 the Carnegie Foundation for the Advancement of Teaching established new indicators for assessing the civic dimensions of colleges and universities. The voluntary community engagement classifications, developed by a national advisory board, include three categories: curricular engagement, outreach and partnerships, and curricular engagement along with outreach and partnerships.

While all of these are promising advances in honoring civic engagement and citizenship as one of the three legs of the academic stool (the others being employment skills and knowledge), there is not yet a solid basis on which to rest the notion of *leadership* as integral to higher education, especially leadership *through* civic engagement. To date, most efforts to increase youth civic engagement and youth leadership have been mutually exclusive, reflecting what has been a tendency to decouple the two activities in theory and in practice. Leadership education has also traditionally been the domain of business or other professional schools, along with divisions of student affairs, and focused largely on developing individual-level skills such as public speaking, management, supervision, and networking. Even when there are attempts to meld civic engagement and leadership development, these frequently are seen as add-ons or are relegated to freestanding centers outside the core university infrastructure.

This leads to the questions raised in the preface, which we are asking in this book. Why is a new model of leadership important in the twenty-first century? What is the relationship between civic engagement and participation in leadership, especially in today's rapidly changing, globalized world? And finally, what role should higher education play in transforming a traditional approach to leadership education into an approach that better reflects the challenges and trends in our world?

Time for Change, Say Students, Faculty, and Public Sector Leaders

To address these issues in a more thoughtful way, in May 2008 the Center for Information and Research on Civic Learning and Engagement (CIRCLE) at Tufts University, the Harry T. Wilks Institute at Miami University in Ohio, Illinois Campus Compact, and Public Allies hosted a national symposium on redefining leadership education in higher education, as mentioned in the preface. Supported by the McCormick Foundation, this event brought together more than forty-five participants from thirteen colleges and universities, along with leaders of several national and state nonprofit organizations working to enhance youth leadership.

The symposium was one of the first events in the country to attempt to clarify a new definition of leadership education—one focused on developing student leadership through civic engagement in colleges and universities. Prior to the event, participants completed an in-depth survey asking for their perspectives, experiences, and insights as to the formulation of a new definition of leadership education, about the advantages of melding civic engagement with a leadership development approach, challenges to incorporating this approach within higher education, and the best examples of how this approach is being implemented in colleges and universities across the country.

The results underscored both the complexity and the promise of this approach. Every participant expressed a desire to see higher education change in ways that reflect a deeper understanding of and commitment to a notion of leadership that approaches the challenges of the world not just by considering them in the abstract but also by "rolling up our sleeves and getting involved," as one program director said. "In the process of doing this, we model for each other how to do the work. That is the essence of leadership."

Nevertheless, there is still a tendency for higher education to focus primarily on theory rather than practice. That approach, participants said, is shortsighted and inadequate for facing new, global, and increasingly complex issues. When higher education does recognize the importance of experiential learning in leadership development, it still tends to focus on developing individuals' personal skills (for example, public speaking, time management, and résumé building) rather than on their ability to address real-world problems and issues through consensus building, strategic planning, and action in collaboration with others, in real communities. The latter, participants said, is essential to understanding that leadership now has a public purpose — one that strengthens democracy and goes beyond individuals' "standing out in the pack" and being recognized.

Participants also underscored that a new definition of leadership education is not only a set of programs, courses, or skills. It is an ethos that should extend across campus and that values transparency, authenticity, collaboration, action, and interactivity.

Some participants argued that when institutions such as higher education ignore these shifts, they risk losing their relevance. (As examples, they pointed to the newspaper industry and other domains that have historically served as important arbiters of knowledge but that are now facing potential demise.) Their concern echoes that of others who have claimed that, despite an all-time high in college attendance, higher education may be "losing its monopoly on knowledge," due to the Internet's rise as a "container and a global platform for knowledge exchange between people." That interactivity, they assert, is fundamentally absent from many colleges and universities: "There is a widening gap between the model of learning offered by many . . . universities and the natural way that young people who have 'grown up digital' best learn," said one college program director.

Without an understanding of these changes and, more importantly, opportunities for young people not only to learn about leadership but also to experience it in real-world communities where they can make a difference, higher education may increasingly be seen by young people as merely a path to a credential rather than as a place of meaningful and useful learning. In contrast, when students are invited to engage in, rather than react to, their education; when they are listened to as much as they are lectured to; when they are encouraged to discover for themselves and be creative, rather than memorize the teacher's information; and when they are allowed to collaborate among themselves and with others outside the university walls, they will be more likely to obtain the skills, confidence, and knowledge that will be critical to leadership in the twenty-first century (Tapscott 2009).

This new leadership ethos extends to faculty and administration: both are already facing the same kinds of scrutiny and accountability with which other institutions and fields (for example, journalism and politics) are grappling and which technology is driving. Young people will sit up and take notice when faculty are rewarded for efforts to involve students in active, community-based problem solving; when administrators are encouraged to speak publicly about the importance of civic engagement as fundamental to future leadership; and when trustees are asked to do more than attend meetings periodically.

Practicing the new leadership, however, will be noticed not only by students; the larger public — for better or worse — is also better able now to assess the value of colleges and universities in their communities. Those institutions that embody the values and ethos of the new leadership by promoting and participating in public problem solving will be more likely to underscore the civic mission on which they were founded and once again function as important leaders in civic life. In turn, they may be better equipped to mitigate perceptions that they are "out of touch" or isolated from "the real world" — images that have contributed to decreases in public funding, threats of local taxation, and questions about the role and relevance of higher education more broadly. By speaking publicly about the link between leadership and civic engagement, higher education not only helps to promote these models but also sends a message to the public that it is responsive to community needs and committed to contributing more meaningfully and directly to public problems and issues at the local, national, and international levels.

Everything Old Is New Again

Participants in the national symposium noted repeatedly that because a melded view of leadership education through civic engagement is relatively new, it will require explanation, education, and promotion across higher education, which has traditionally been slow to adopt new practices and curricula changes without evidence that changes will enhance student scholarship and institutional advancement. Many in the field will need to be convinced that civic engagement as leadership education and development is feasible, while others will want more explanation of why the two should be linked in the first place. Even among those faculty and administrators who may already be supportive of this approach, there continue to be questions as to how it may be implemented to help meet educational standards and goals. Students want to see how other students have transformed their views about the new leadership into solid action that has led to results in communities.

What may appear to be new, however, has deep roots in higher education, roots which have sometimes been overlooked but which are worth reiterating. Many colleges and universities, for example, were founded and established with a civic mission. In 1749, Benjamin Franklin wrote that the "ability to serve" should be the rationale for all schooling and for the secular college he founded, the University of Pennsylvania. This was a mission to which other colonial colleges, including Harvard, William and Mary, Yale, Princeton, Columbia, Brown, Rutgers, and Dartmouth adhered, based on their desire to educate men "capable of creating good communities built on religious denominational principles" (Harkavy 2004, p. 6). Land grant universities, established through the Morrill Act in 1862, also stipulated "service to society" as their primary mission, as did urban research universities founded in the late nineteenth century. Today, universities continue to pay homage to their civic mission in their rhetoric and published materials. Alexander Astin (1997, cited in Harkavy 2004, p. 8), found that random samples of the mission statements of higher education institutions, including research universities, tend to focus more on "preparing students for responsible citizenship," "developing character," "developing future leaders," and "preparing students to serve society," than on private economic benefits, international competitiveness, or preparing people for the labor market.

Others point out that the citizen-centered leadership emerging in higher education is similar to the style of leadership advanced in the 1950s and 1960s by the Highlander Folk School, a learning center for the civil rights movement, which put the idea that "we are all leaders" into practice. Highlander helped to empower an impressive array of civil rights leaders, including Fannie Lou Hamer, Ella Baker, Septima Clark, John Lewis, Bob Moses, and many others (Preskill and Brookfield 2008).

Its most notable student, Rosa Parks, attended a workshop at Highlander the summer before initiating the bus boycott in Montgomery, Alabama on December 1, 1955. In contrast to the common misconception that Parks was a poor seamstress who ignited a movement as an individual by refusing to give up her seat on a segregated bus, Parks was, in fact, the product of an amalgam of community-based educational experiences stemming from her work as an executive secretary of the National Association for the Advancement of Colored People in Montgomery, Alabama, and as a community leader. Several local organizations, for example, pooled their resources to help Parks attend a Highlander workshop on school desegregation because of her track record. The opportunity was transformative for Parks. "At Highlander, I found out for the first time in my adult life that this could be a unified society, that there was such a thing as people of different races and backgrounds meeting together in workshops, and living together in peace and harmony," she later reflected (Horton 1998, pp. 149–50).

Similar to the leadership model currently being developed by a new generation of young people, Highlander also minimized the importance of positional leadership and technical expertise, instead focusing on the capacity of ordinary people—often with little formal education—to define and then solve problems collectively. Thus, the workshops held at Highlander were based on the concept that all participants could be contributors, with the greatest leadership potential existing in the group and not any single individual. "Our desire is to empower people collectively, not individually," Horton writes (1998, p. 157).

The citizen-centered approach to leadership also has a rich literature that spans decades. It is sometimes overlooked, and current generations may be unaware of it. But it is a powerful foundation on which to base current attempts to promote the new leadership model. In 1996, David Mathews, president of the Kettering Foundation, described the importance of "leaderful communities" that make leadership "the responsibility of the many" (Mathews 1996, p. 9). In a synthesis of twenty-five years of research, Mathews agreed with the view of current generations that the challenges we face require a new conception of leadership that includes people from every facet of a community contributing their talents. "It is time for citizens to strike out in new directions and refashion our ideas about community leadership," he writes. "We need some leadership in changing our concept of leadership" (p. 17).

Political theorist Benjamin Barber also has attempted to change dominant conceptions of leadership and citizenship, arguing that in a strong democracy there is a need for strong citizens, not strong leaders. Barber's point is that when leadership is defined by charismatic individuals, the result is disempowered citizens. Paraphrasing Lao-tzu, Barber writes: "Strong democratic leadership is leadership that leaves a citizenry more capable when the leader departs than when he arrives. It is leadership that can boast: 'Now that he is gone, we can do this ourselves'" (1998, p. 100). Barber ultimately measures the success of democracy not in finding great leaders, but in no longer needing them.

Likewise, Harry Boyte (2004, 2008) has argued for a notion of citizenship that, like that of Barber and Mathews, sees citizens as the cocreators (and the real leaders) of democracy. As students in higher education become cocreators, as opposed to customers or passive learners, Boyte (2008) points out that they develop "the broader set of capacities and skills required to take confident, skillful, imaginative, collective action in fluid and open environments where there is no script." Boyte states that developing these leadership skills, which he refers to as "civic agency," is "the great challenge and promise of the new century."

Participatory and relational leadership models have also emerged over the past four decades from scholars and practitioners in the field of leadership studies (Goethals and Sorenson 2006; Preskill and Brookfield 2008). These conceptions vary from the seminal work of James MacGregor Burns (1978), who devised the notion of "transformational leadership," which treats leadership as a dynamic process for both leaders and followers that is connected to a larger purpose and higher levels of morality, to the "servant leadership" model developed by Robert Greenleaf (1991), which focuses on seeing leaders as people with a desire primarily to serve others. Both theories have influenced generations of leadership scholars and practitioners (Bass and Riggio 2006; Spears 1998).

Most recently, Ron Heifetz, founding director of Harvard's Center for Public Leadership, has emphasized the connection between leadership and public problem solving. In defining leadership as "mobilizing people to tackle tough problems" (1994, p. 15), Heifetz offers an important counterbalance to the more individualistic notions of leadership. Specifically, he conceptualizes leadership as distinct from authority and argues that the "adaptive work" needed today is the process by which leaders address problems that cannot be solved using technical expertise alone. These problems, Heifetz contends, cannot be confined to the few; rather, they require mobilizing the talents of many, on all sides of an issue, to work collaboratively.

In addition to the theoretical aspects of citizen-centered leadership, there is also a considerable literature about its pedagogical practice. The process of teaching adaptive leadership, for example, is well chronicled in *Leadership Can Be Taught* (Parks 2005), a work that describes the "case-in-point" method of teaching used by Heifetz and his colleagues, in which relationships and activities in the classroom form the basis of leadership education. "Perhaps the central strength of this work for today's world," Parks writes, "is located in its laser-beam focus on the systemic, interdependent reality of which we are each a part and within which each of us has the opportunity, therefore, to exercise leadership from wherever we sit" (p. 255). This approach, which has been described as "an improvisational art" (p. 208), is therefore "well tuned to the aspirations of the democratic impulse throughout the whole of our shared commons" (p. 255).

There has also been a growing emphasis on what has been termed "the social change model of leadership" (Higher Education Research Institute 1996). The social change model—with a focus on leadership as a process rather than a position—has been especially influential in the design of student affairs leadership programs, along with other more relational and ethical models identifying leadership with positive changes (Komives, Lucas, and MacMahon 2007; Roberts 2007).

Building upon the results of these programs, a report for the Kellogg Foundation argues that, "colleges and universities provide rich opportunities for recruiting and developing leaders through the curriculum and co-curriculum" (Astin and Astin 2000, p. 3). In calling for greater attention to leadership development in higher education, *Leadership Reconsidered* declares: "If the next generation of citizen leaders is to be engaged and committed to leading for the common good, then the institutions which nurture them must be engaged in the work of the society and the community, modeling effective leadership and problem solving skills, demonstrating how to accomplish change for the common good" (Astin and Astin 2000, p. 2).

Change Is Happening

Auspiciously, change is happening on campuses across the country, including in the institutions represented at the symposium, which embody the notion of the "new leadership" and its inextricable link with civic engagement. Examples from these institutions are included in the chapters that follow, beginning with the first section of the book, which attempts to define the new leadership and what it looks like in the context of higher education.

In the opening essay, Alma Blount, director of the Hart Leadership Program at Duke University, points out that although undergraduate leadership and civic programs have proliferated in recent years, they are often shunted to the sidelines rather than integrated into the curriculum. That is not the case with the Hart Leadership Program, where leadership and civic engagement have been intertwined since its inception in 1987. Blount suggests that this program can serve as a template for integrating twenty-first-century leadership education into higher education overall, and she provides rich insights from her own teaching experiences that emphasize public problem-solving work and "leadership for public life." Blount also illustrates how such curricula and programs work best at institutions that embrace a civic mission at all levels. As she notes, "The real-world ambitions of our students, the practitioner profiles of our faculty, and the applied research culture of our home institution, the Sanford School of Public Policy, have helped us avoid the land-of-abstraction, 'just follow these steps' syndrome that sometimes drives leadership programming."

In the next essay, Edward Zlotkowski, a leading voice nationally for institutionalizing service-learning in the disciplines, makes the case for the essential role of student leadership in the future of service-learning. Writing with student coauthors Katelyn Horowitz and Sarah Benson, Zlotkowski challenges "the still prevalent stereotype of youth civic indifference" and offers an alternative view that sees students as "active partners rather than passive recipients." This idea, the authors note, was central to *Students as Colleagues: Expanding the Circle of Service Learning Leadership* (Zlotkowski, Longo, and Williams 2006). That publication outlined four primary areas in which student civic leadership can develop: students as staff, students as reflection leaders, faculty-student partnerships, and students as engaged scholars, all of which have the potential to shift students from relatively passive vessels for learning "into a force for more substantive academic and civic engagement."

The essay then describes one such program at Bentley University, a business-focused institution that is home to the Bentley Service-Learning Center (BSLC). The authors describe the Center's program as one that uses the seven c's of the "social- change model" of leadership development: congruence, collaboration, controversy with civility, common purpose, commitment, citizenship, and consciousness of self (Higher Education Research Institute 1996). They also discuss some of the problems that can arise when student leadership is not sufficiently integrated into a service-learning program. The chapter concludes with some observations on the implications of rethinking the role of student leadership, along with a call for giving students the opportunity to work "with faculty," not just "for faculty." The authors write, "we do not *need* to regard the notion of students as colleagues as radical—despite the reluctance of the academy to change."

The next section of the book puts leadership and civic engagement in higher education into historical and contemporary context. Matt Hartley, associate professor of education at the University of Pennsylvania, and Ira Harkavy, associate vice president and founding director of the Netter Center for Community Partnerships at the University of Pennsylvania, provide a historical overview of higher education's civic mission. They describe the early civic impulses of colleges and universities; a civic reemergence in higher education, partially led by students, in the 1980s; and the shift from volunteerism to service-learning (service that is tied to curriculum). Drawing upon their collaborative partnerships in West Philadelphia, they argue that "democratic, problem-solving service-learning focused on concrete, universal problems that are manifested in a university's locality is a promising approach for developing effective civic leadership and for realizing the democratic purposes of the civic engagement movement."

In the next essay, Kathleen Knight Abowitz, Stephanie Raill Jayanandhan, and Sarah Woiteshek, from Miami University, begin by noting that while leadership for social change has become more popular in the academy, the idea of leadership *practiced in and for community and public life* has received less attention and focus in higher education *leadership* initiatives. The authors call for and define public and community-based leadership in higher education that reflects the growing movement among colleges and universities to rededicate themselves to the public good and a civic mission. They also outline some practical suggestions for enacting that kind of leadership in higher education, along with the kinds of skills essential for educating leaders for public life. A core component of the model is civic action, particularly action that involves citizens who are able to convene, deliberate, inquire, collaborate, and act with the intent to improve life for fellow citizens in their communities and the larger society.

The understanding of community-based leadership that the authors are promoting involves both "leadership education situated within real places and cultural contexts, in the regions in which colleges and universities are located," along with the "pedagogy and curricular design" of leadership programs. This conception of leadership is "a shift from the dominant conventional belief system that the task of leadership is to set a vision, enroll others in it, and hold people accountable through measurements and reward" (A Small Group 2007, p. 10). Rather, the authors propose that leadership, in its most essential form, is "convening people and framing conversations that enable participants to become responsible and committed to shared action."

The final essay in this section reminds us that although leadership education for public purpose has been around since the time of the ancient Greeks, in higher education we are still struggling to develop robust curricula and programs with this focus. Kathy Postel Kretman writes about the lessons she has learned for making "leadership learning for public purpose part of the mainstream educational experience" as director of Georgetown University's Center for Public and Nonprofit Leadership, which is putting leadership education into practice.

Kretman also writes about her experience as the director of *CivicQuest*, one of thirty-six university-based leadership education initiatives funded in the 1990s by the Dwight D. Eisenhower Leadership Development Program established by the United States Congress in the Higher Education Act of 1965. Kretman, along with several other project directors and leadership scholars, eventually prepared a report on the findings from the thirty-six projects. *Democracy At Risk: How Schools Can Lead* called for a twenty-first-century model of leadership that is collaborative, inclusive, participatory, and change-oriented. The report argued that there is no better place to prepare young people for civic engagement than the schools, beginning in kindergarten and continuing through postsecondary education, and that these kinds of approaches can be introduced by faculty and administrators at colleges and universities without great difficulty. Furthermore, they do not require large investments of human capital or money, but they do require an institutional commitment from the top and faculty "willing to get out of their comfort zones and academic silos; to take risks; and to model collaborative, creative, and courageous leadership." In sum, the Eisenhower Leadership Group concluded that "leadership can be learned, and that a collaborative and participatory approach motivates students to be interested in and capable of doing the work of leading social change. . . . In the next millennium it is [leadership education] that will be key to progress — in the workplace as well as the nation at large" (Eisenhower Leadership Group 1996, p. 12).

The third section of the book offers concrete and in-depth examples of new leadership education models at specific colleges and universities. These essays are unique in that many have been written in a collaborative, "wiki" style that reflects the new leadership model being highlighted in the book; that is, students have collaborated with professors and program directors. Representatives from each of the programs described in this section also participated in the aforementioned 2008 leadership symposium (including one of the student coauthors). Thus, the authors, many of whom are students or recent graduates, have firsthand experience with the curricula or programs discussed and with the national conversation from which this book emerged.

In the first essay, three of the most highly regarded programs that put student leadership at the center of civic engagement on campus are described, with lessons culled from their collective efforts. Tania Mitchell and Virginia Visconti from Stanford University, Arthur Keene from the University of Massachusetts Amherst, and Richard Battistoni from Providence College forcefully argue that "a sustained, developmental, curricular approach to civic engagement, one that attempts to build on the single course, single experience civic or service learning opportunities that shape most students' college years, is better able to engender new civic leaders." The authors then offer examples of these kinds of programs: Stanford University's Public Service Scholars Program, the Citizen Scholars Program at the University of Massachusetts Amherst, and the Public and Community Service Studies Program at Providence College.

With deep experience in developing these programs, each of which was originally founded more than a decade ago, the authors describe how each program is organized, builds community, and contributes to the understanding of the new leadership. In analyzing the programs, the authors find that student voice, community collaboration, engaged scholarship, and a commitment to reflective practice are "four fundamental principles that help produce students with an enhanced civic identity and the skills necessary for relational, action-oriented leadership." The essay concludes by acknowledging the many challenges to the creation of these types of student leadership programs on campus and by calling for more longitudinal research evaluating the impact of sustained, developmental, cohort-based programs.

Another important leadership education model involves multilayered leadership and civic engagement programs, with college students acting as civic "coaches" for K–12 students. In the next essay in the third section of the book, students, faculty, and staff describe the civic leadership approach taken at the University of Denver, which is rooted in the model of organizing developed by Saul Alinsky, a pioneer in community organizing who founded the Industrial Areas Foundation (IAF). The "messy and energizing, frustrating and rewarding" writing process that the authors experienced offers a glimpse into the reality of student organizing efforts, through five narratives by students involved in an innovative civic leadership program called Public Achievement. This is an internationally recognized program working with youth in schools and communities throughout the United States, and in Turkey, Northern Ireland, eastern Europe, South Africa, Israel, Gaza, and the West Bank.

Out of these narratives emerges a definition of civic leadership based on the concepts of "self-interest," "power," and "politics." The authors conclude by sharing concrete ideas for developing this type of leadership in higher education, based on their practical experiences with community organizing. These include building relationships using self-assessment, one-to-one interviews, and house meetings; selecting and researching issues using power mapping and community-based research; and acting for sustainable change using public action, critical reflection, and public evaluation. They remind us that ultimately, becoming a public leader is not an academic exercise, but one in which students build public skills through "real-world struggles and the taste of failure and success."

The Jonathan M. Tisch College of Citizenship and Public Service at Tufts University is the focus of the next essay. In describing perhaps the only institution in the United States with a college dedicated to civic engagement, Elizabeth Hollander, Kei Kawashima-Ginsberg, Peter Levine, Duncan Pickard, and Jonathan Zaff present elements of Tisch's programs that not only enhance the leadership capacity of students through a concerted series of civic engagement and experiential learning opportunities, but also create a strong civic culture across the university community (including the larger community of which the university is a part). An important aspect of Tisch's program ensures that students and faculty are carefully oriented to the geographical communities surrounding Tufts and are trained to work respectfully and effectively in partnership with community organizations. Student leaders are also expected to create, lead, or influence specific programs for civic education at Tufts and to influence the whole campus culture to be more "civically promoting," which, in turn, should help to cultivate student leaders for civic engagement. In this essay, the voice of one such student leader is highlighted.

Although it is comprehensive, the model leaves important questions as to whether students' levels of civic engagement increase as a result—and more important, whether and to what extent the university's civic culture plays a role in civic development. Using longitudinal surveys of students, surveys of community partners, focus groups, and a network-mapping tool, the authors describe how they attempted to measure these variables, what they found, and how Tufts is reshaping its leadership programs based on these findings. Although there is much more to be done to demonstrate outcomes in this area—one that is admittedly challenging—the Tufts team has put a stake in the ground by offering other scholars and practitioners some ideas for future research and assessment regarding civic engagement and leadership education.

In the final essay in this third section of the book, Decker Ngongang of Mobilize.org, a national organization working to engage Millennials and support their leadership in civic and political life, reminds us that while prestigious private institutions such as Tufts, Stanford, Duke, or Georgetown, which are incorporating innovative leadership education into their curricula, programs, and policies, are important because of their reputation and ability to set the standard for other higher education institutions, these are not the types of campuses where most students are enrolled. Today, more than 43 percent of college students attend the more than 1,100 community colleges in the United States (American Association of Community Colleges 2010), and this number is growing amid economic distress and the increasing desire for a college education.

Beginning with his own story of moving from a career in finance to becoming an advocate for civic leadership at community colleges, first through Generation Engage and now through Mobilize.org, Ngongang argues that community colleges are fertile ground for community leadership. He also describes innovative programmatic examples from his work with Central Piedmont Community College and Miami Dade College. In a sharp rejection, common among Millennials, of hierarchical models of leadership, Ngongang discusses his realization that "community leadership was not predicated on a degree or intellectual capacity; rather, the foundation of community leadership is *the application of perspective and experience.*" Concluding that for too long we have focused our civic opportunities on four-year universities, Ngongang argues that infusing community colleges with leadership education should be a national priority.

The last section of the book attempts to answer the question, "What does this all mean, especially for the future?" with essays that focus attention on leadership education through the lenses of international education, public service, and community organizing. Adam Weinberg, Rebecca Hovey, and Carol Bellamy, from World Learning, host of some of the most prominent study-abroad educational programs in the world, point out that leadership education in the twenty-first century cannot ignore the global risks, opportunities, and realities of an interconnected world and must provide the knowledge and vision necessary to resolve critical issues that the global community will face. Using the SIT Study Abroad programs in Uganda as a case study, they argue that a model of international education is needed that acknowledges the diverse global community in which institutions are based and learning takes place. By linking leadership and international education, they propose an alternative approach to both based on recognition, reciprocity, and responsibility to others.

Specifically, the authors refer to a "global ecology of learning" in which students learn through deep cultural immersion in communities—a process that can give students insight into how societal problems are constructed, perceived, and resolved through the actions of local citizens. Noting that study-abroad programs that are based on this ecology framework can "energize student learning while also invigorating higher education," they call for an internationalization of undergraduate education as a way to think about and act upon leadership development as a dimension of moral responsibility and democratic, civic engagement in an increasingly globalized world.

Addressing another area of increasing need, Paul Light, professor at New York University's Wagner School of Public Service, calls for a new appreciation of public service as integral to leadership in the twenty-first century, especially among higher education institutions. Despite the growth in service-learning and volunteering across college campuses, Light cautions that these are insufficient training grounds for meeting the demands that leaders, especially those in government or other public service arenas, will face. As evidence of current curricular deficiencies, he points to courses in which "citizen engagement is rarely discussed, leadership and ethics are mostly reserved for a week or two of discussion, cultivating diversity is a continuing challenge, and innovation is mostly considered a subject for on-the-job training."

Students, Light adds, also receive little instruction on the need to manage the highly complex networks of state and local government agencies, nonprofits, and businesses now involved in delivering the "extensive and arduous enterprise for the public benefit" that Alexander Hamilton considered the essential function of service and part of his design for a well-executed government. This new skill set, Light argues, is essential not only for lifelong careers in government but also for students who are interested in any level of public service. The chapter culminates with Light's vision for a more robust public leadership curricula—one that he believes should include public service history, ethics, social innovation, volunteer management, and other topics and skill sets that are central to leadership in the twenty-first century.

In the final essay of this section of the book, Stephen Smith offers his advice to colleges and universities for educating a new generation for effective leadership. A former student leader who helped to mobilize Harvard's well-publicized living wage campaign and organized many activist campaigns and national service conferences, Smith reflects on his experiences as a community organizer since graduating. In a challenging essay from a voice of the Millennial generation, Smith describes the lessons he has learned since "getting [his] hands dirty" as an organizer in Chicago with one of the leading organizing groups in the country, the Industrial Areas Foundation (IAF), and offers a wide range of practical recommendations for colleges and universities.

Smith notes, for instance, that he has learned that all people are created equal, but that not all community work is created equal, and recommends a focus on self-interest, mutuality, and regular evaluations. He reminds us that good leadership is relational and that mentors matter, and he recommends the kind of one-to-one meetings championed by the IAF, along with building institutional support for faculty and staff mentoring of students. Finally, he concludes with a key lesson that some might see as contrary to the more deliberative and inclusive approaches often fostered by his generation: teaching tension is essential. Smith observes that tension can strengthen public relationships and has been at the center of some of the most inspiring and promising historical and contemporary organizing work. He also includes recommendations that reinforce some of the trends among young people's approach to leadership described earlier, calling for a diversity of voices on campus, transparency in administrative decision-making, and service-learning courses that teach organizing knowledge and skills.

This book concludes with some thoughts as to what steps higher education can and must take if it is to meet the challenges that confront us locally, nationally, and globally in the preparation of future leaders. These recommendations were collected from all the authors in a fashion that reflects the new approach to leadership outlined in the entire book: rather than stipulating what we, the coauthors, think are the "best recommendations," we asked all those with deep experience to weigh in and participate. The result is a collection of innovative and, we hope, inspiring thoughts and ideas that will spur even deeper interest in advancing new models of leadership education in colleges and universities.

REFERENCES

American Association of Community Colleges. (2010). Fast facts. Retrieved on May 31, 2010, at http://www.aacc.nche.edu/AboutCC/Pages/fastfacts.aspx.

Astin, A. (1997). Liberal education and democracy: The case for pragmatism. In *Education and democracy: Re-imagining liberal learning in America*, ed. R. Orrill, 210–11. New York: College Entrance Examination Board. Astin, A., and H. Astin. (2000). *Leadership reconsidered: Engaging higher education in social change*. Ann Arbor, MI: W. K. Kellogg Foundation.

Barber, B. (1998). Neither leaders nor followers: Citizenship under strong democracy. In *A passion for democracy: American essays*, 95–110. Princeton, NJ: Princeton University Press.

Bass, B. M., and R. E. Riggio. (2006). *Transformational leadership*. 2nd. ed. Mahwah, NJ: Lawrence Erlbaum Associates.

Boyte, H. (2004). *Everyday politics: Reconnecting citizens and public life*. Philadelphia: University of Pennsylvania Press.

Boyte, H. (2008). Against the current: Developing the civic agency of students. *Change 40* (3). Retrieved on July 31, 2010, at http://www.changemag.org/Archives/Back%20Issues/May-June%202008/full-against-the-current.html.

Burns, J. M. (1978). *Leadership*. New York: Harper and Row.

Campus Compact. (2007). Service statistics: Highlights and trends of Campus Compact's annual membership survey. Retrieved on May 31, 2010, at http://www.compact.org/wp-content/uploads/about/statistics/2007/service_statistics.pdf.

Center for Information and Research on Civic Learning and Engagement (CIRCLE). (2009). Youth voting. Retrieved on May 31, 2010, at http://www.civicyouth.org/?page_id=241.

Center on Philanthropy at Indiana University. (2008). Generational differences in charitable giving and in motivations for giving. Retrieved on May 31, 2010, at http://www.campbellcompany.com/articles.html.

Eisenhower Leadership Group. (1996). *Democracy at risk*. (Report from The Center for Political Leadership and Participation, University of Maryland, College Park).

Friel, B. (2007). Gen X execs: The next generation of federal executives has begun its ascent. *Government Executive 39*, no. 19: 53–55. Retrieved on August 2, 2010, at http://www.govexec.com/features/1107-01/1107-01admm.htm.

Gibson, C. (2006). *Citizens at the center: A new approach to civic engagement*. Washington, D.C.: Case Foundation.

Gibson, C. (2008). Nonprofits: The DNA of democracy. *Nonprofit Quarterly* (Winter): 27–30.

Goethals, G., and G. Sorenson. (2006). *The quest for a general theory of leadership*. Northampton, MA: Edward Elgar Publishing.

Greenleaf, R. K. (1991). *The servant as leader*. Indianapolis: Robert Greenleaf Center for Servant Leadership.

Harkavy, I. (2004). Service-learning and the development of democratic universities, democratic schools, and democratic good societies in the 21st century. In *New perspectives on service-learning: Research to advance the field*, ed. M. Welch and S. Billig, 3–22.Charlotte, NC: Information Age Publishing.

Heifetz, R. (1994). *Leadership without easy answers*. Cambridge, MA: Harvard University Press.

Higher Education Research Institute. (1996). *A social change model of leadership development*. Los Angeles: University of California at Los Angeles.

Horton, M. (1998). *The long haul: An autobiography*. New York: Teacher's College Press.

Kelly, A., and H. Lena. (2006). Providence College: The community assistant model. In *Students as colleagues*, ed. E. Zlotkowski, N. Longo, and J. Williams, 121–33 Providence, RI: Campus Compact.

Komives, S., N. Lucas, and T. MacMahon. (2007). *Exploring leadership: For college students who want to make a difference*. San Francisco: Jossey-Bass.

Leighninger, M. (2006). *The next form of democracy: How expert rule is giving way to shared governance and why politics will never be the same*. Nashville, TN: Vanderbilt University Press.

Leighninger, M. (2009). Democracy, growing up: The shifts that reshaped local politics and foreshadowed the 2008 presidential election. Occasional paper series, no. 5. New York: Public Agenda. Retrieved on May 31, 2010, at http://www.publicagenda.org/files/pdf/PA_CAPE_Paper5_Democracy_Mech2.pdf.

Longo, N. and M. S. Shaffer. (2009). Leadership education and the revitalization of public life. In *Civic engagement and higher education: Concepts and practices*, ed. B. Jacoby and Associates, 154–73. San Francisco: Jossey-Bass.

Mathews, D. (1996). Why we need to change our concept of community leadership. *Community Education Journal* (Fall /Winter): 9–18.

Mobilize.org. (October 2007). Youth leaders unveil the "Democracy 2.0 declaration." Retrieved on May 31, 2010, at http://www.mobilize.org/index.php?tray=content&tid=top409&cid=359.

Parks, S. D. (2005). *Leadership can be taught.* San Francisco: Jossey-Bass.

Peter D. Hart Research Associates. (1998). *New leadership for a new century: Key findings from a study on youth leadership and community service.* Washington, D.C.: Peter D. Hart Research Associates.

Preskill, S. and S. Brookfield. (2008). *Learning as a way of leading: Lessons for the struggle for social justice.* San Francisco: Jossey-Bass.

Roberts, D. (2007). *Deeper learning in leadership: Helping college students find the potential within.* San Francisco: Jossey-Bass.

Small Group, A. (2007). *Civic engagement and the restoration of community: Changing the nature of the conversation.* Cincinnati: Peter Block. Retrieved on May 19, 2010, at http://www.asmallgroup.net/pages/images/pages/CES_jan2007.pdf.

Spears, L., ed. (1998). *Insights on leadership: Service, stewardship, spirit, and servant-leadership.* New York: Wiley and Sons.

Tapscott, D. (2009). *Grown up digital: How the net generation is changing your world.* New York: McGraw-Hill.

Yankelovich, D. (1991). *Coming to public judgment: Making democracy work in a complex world.* Syracuse, NY: Syracuse University Press.

Zlotkowski, E., N. Longo, and J. Williams, eds. (2006). *Students as colleagues: Expanding the circle of service-learning leadership.* Providence, RI: Campus Compact.

||||||||||||||||||||||||||

1

||||||||||||||||||||||||||

Courage for the Tough Questions
Leadership and Adaptive Learning

I have been teaching for years, but every time I walk into a seminar room for the first class of the semester I take a deep breath and make a silent wish. May I have the energy and wisdom to be as present as possible to whatever unfolds with these students. Our work together might not be easy, but I know it will be rewarding. I offer this comment to them as we walk through the syllabus. Looking at their friendly, open, inquisitive faces, I can see they have some sense of what our leadership program is about. They make their course choices carefully, and I know they polled previous students before enrolling. I can see they are intrigued, but I can also see they have no real idea of what they are getting themselves into.

What I am about to ask my students to do, both in the classroom and in their community-based research projects around the world during the summer, is to have a live encounter with the messy business of questioning. It will not be the kind of academic questioning they are so good at, where they believe that there is reasonably solid ground, and that they have their bearings—more or less—from many years of getting it right. Rather, this is a kind of questioning that comes from direct engagement with the complexities and difficulties of the world, driven mainly by curiosity and a humble admission of not knowing where the answers may lie, yet guided by a readiness to enter the fray and a strong commitment to exploring the possibilities that present themselves. The year ahead will prime the pump so they can *begin* experimenting with this kind of questioning. My hope is that something inside them will start to shift and turn. I want them to grow more and more comfortable practicing an agile, provocative, improvisational form of questioning that could become part of their everyday lives as well as their professional skill set.

The leadership approach students will investigate this year involves learning to do "a deep read" of context, and exploring the art of raising difficult questions in such a way that others become engaged. In theory this sort of questioning sounds easy. In practice it is anything but. To learn it requires seriousness of purpose matched with a light touch. It requires fierce inquisitiveness and respect for people's blind spots. It requires a mature discipline of self-reflection. And it requires—let's face it—an interest in the well-being of others and a creative, gut sense of how things could be better.

This kind of questioning is a demanding pursuit. It has everything to do with leadership, but at the start of the semester that connection is far from evident to the students. At this moment our entry point is simply trust that some kind of worthwhile learning experience may be in store for us.

I know that the territory ahead—for the students and for me—will be full of ups and downs, twists and turns. The students' experiences in the classroom and in the community are going to stretch them in unexpected ways, and at times this may cause them discomfort. These are students who have gotten where they are today because of their superb capacity for meeting and surpassing crystal clear, high expectations, not because of their skill at dealing with the unexpected.

"Please, just show me the bar. Where exactly are you setting it?" What we call the "exactly" question is emblazoned on their brains. And my work is to help these high-achieving eighteen-, nineteen-, and twenty-year-olds rethink their ideas about the world and their place in it, so that they become increasingly comfortable with chaos and complexity. The world they will inherit has no solid ground. On some level they must know this, but they have not yet had enough life experience to make this truth unavoidably clear. Yet they and I both know that one day they will be running our institutions and trying their best to make sense of the mess.

On this first day of class, when I ask what everyone thinks leadership means, most students believe the primary role of a leader is obvious: set expectations, establish goals, deliver the goods. Do they see themselves as leaders? Well, yes, they think they do. They state this in a low-key way, yet you can see the confidence behind their declarations. They have been told they were leaders since they were in middle school, or even earlier. They have held plenty of leadership positions. And they already have ambitious leadership plans for the future.

"Okay, terrific, but have you ever actually *exercised leadership*?" I ask them.

"What exactly does that mean?" they ask.

"Yes, what does it mean?" I ask. "What do you think the *activity* of leadership looks like? What does it consist of? How would you describe *the work of leadership*? Can you see it? What does it do?" Long pause. This is where the students get stumped, so this is where I start to get their full attention.

Adaptive Leadership

Leadership programs for undergraduates have proliferated in recent years. Typically they are connected to student affairs programming or based in business schools. Civic engagement programs have also proliferated. What is still fairly unusual is for cocurricular civic engagement activities and academic leadership programs to dovetail. These two approaches have been intertwined in the Hart Leadership Program at Duke University since the program's formation. As the first endowed leadership program for undergraduates in the country, Hart Leadership began offering classes in 1987, and from the start we had the advantage of anchoring our curriculum in the field of public policy studies. An emphasis on public problem-solving work and what we call "leadership for public life" has given our students specific, practical contexts for exploring what leadership is, and how it does or does not function in complex institutions. The real-world ambitions of our students, the practitioner profiles of our faculty, and the applied research culture of our home institution, the Sanford School of Public Policy, have helped us avoid the land-of-abstraction, "just follow these steps" syndrome that sometimes drives leadership programming.

We believe that how one defines leadership is important, because it sets up expectations for how we engage in problem analysis and problem-solving work. To us, leadership means mobilizing people to do difficult work in groups, organizations, and large institutions. What kind of difficult work? Addressing the systemic conditions, circumstances, and patterns of behavior that will improve only when we learn to do business in ways that better fit the problematic realities we face. Leadership challenges us to learn our way to more beneficial stages of adaptation. Leadership stirs things up and helps us "learn how to learn" in the midst of chaos and complexity. It involves crossing boundaries and seeing value conflicts as resources in the learning process. It calls for and also develops perseverance and a sense of purpose.

An important element of adaptive leadership is learning to understand how authority functions, and what its relationship is to leadership. If authority is meant to hold things together, to protect the purpose of an enterprise, and to function as a stabilizing influence, leadership is a counterforce that opens things up and destabilizes the status quo. Since the two functions operate in creative tension with each other, our task is to be switched on enough to see the best ways of using each approach when the time comes. For most of my students, a question in their future will be this: can they learn to exercise leadership effectively from a position of authority, to figure out when and how to create useful disturbances when the time comes, if their primary responsibility is to keep things neat and tidy? No one is going to authorize them to exercise leadership. So if they are in charge, will they know when it is time to rock the boat? Will they be able to pace the turbulence as their organization learns its way through to a more productive place? Leadership means becoming skillful at improvisation. It teaches us to become adept at holding a group in a difficult transition. It teaches us how to develop a stomach for conflict, and how to work with strong disagreements skillfully to get at the underlying issues. It teaches us how to become resilient.

Our Approach to Teaching Undergraduates

In our program we specialize in creating what we call "deep dive" learning experiences for students, which integrate immersion experiences in communities with academic study. Through coursework, community-based research, and social entrepreneurship projects, we challenge students to combine action with reflection on what they are learning. We send students around the world to explore how theories interact with life, and we bring them back to campus to deepen their investigations in the classroom.

The messy business of questioning emerges from encounters with real life. Recently, for example, students in our Service Opportunities in Leadership program (SOL) worked to expand educational opportunities for migrant children in Beijing, assess nutrition education programs for homeless children in Arizona, examine the challenges to integration faced by male migrant workers in Korea, foster cross-cultural understanding among middle school students in Brooklyn, and map the treatment-seeking behaviors of malaria patients in India. When students returned to Duke in the fall, they zeroed in on a policy dimension of their summer work that they wanted to study more extensively. They built policy research portfolios about their topics, presented their work to the class for discussion and critique, and analyzed the leadership dimensions of their chosen issues by using the adaptive leadership framework. In the spring the students presented their work publicly at a symposium for undergraduate research.

If there is a recipe to our leadership development approach, it is this: Get out into the community. Take the plunge. Let your passions and interests guide you, even if you are only initially going on instinct. Do this work in connection with a community of learners. Reflect on what you are learning each and every day, and tie your thoughts to a broader intellectual and political context so that you deepen your understanding. Use the tools of research, study, narrative writing, and conversations with your mentors. Test out your questions and insights with others and bring your ideas to larger audiences. And then find creative ways to take action.

What inspires me is that I have seen our students undertake this kind of learning and begin to ask bold questions — questions about current conditions but also questions about the kind of future they want for themselves, others, and the world. In alumni surveys these young people report that their community experiences profoundly shaped their lives. When they have avenues for reflection that include a strong mentoring environment, what they are learning becomes fertile ground to form what educator Sharon Parks describes as the Dream. "The Dream, with a capital D, is something more than night dreams, casual daydreams, pure fantasy, or a fully designed plan. This Dream has the quality of vision. It is an imagined possibility that orients meaning, purpose, and aspiration" (Parks 2000, p. 146).

Tico Almeida, one of the most widely publicized alums of the SOL program, was able as a student to imagine new possibilities based on his experiences in a community. Tico spent the summer of 1997 working as an intern for the Union of Needletrades, Industrial and Textile Employees (UNITE) in New York City. His summer experience deeply affected his view of the world and his own role in it and eventually led to his becoming a founding member of Students Against Sweatshops (SAS).

That summer Tico met men and women from Central America and Asia who worked in the apparel industry for sixty-five or more hours a week with no overtime pay and few breaks. In many cases they were paid less than minimum wage. Few of them could speak English, they were often unaware of their basic labor rights, and they had little sense of what they could do to improve their circumstances. Tico worked with the immigrants in two capacities. Occasionally he documented their working conditions. But for most of the summer, he got to know rank-and-file union workers by teaching them about their rights and instructing them in organizing skills at the Workers' Justice Center run by the union.

When he returned to Duke, Tico immediately began making plans to create Students Against Sweatshops. Tico's leadership style was to bring key people together quietly, to frame issues carefully, and then to tap into the resources of the group to develop realistic approaches to a problem. In no time, SAS began pointing out that Duke needed a stricter code of conduct for the companies that manufactured Duke-licensed apparel and other products. Within seven months of forming the organization, Tico and his friends succeeded in convincing Duke to become the first university in the country to adopt a code of conduct outlining provisions for monitoring the manufacturers of any products licensed with the Duke name.

Students Against Sweatshops could have celebrated its victory and ended its work there, but Tico and the other students had a hunch that it was premature to do so. In 1998 Duke University officials planned to sign a revised code. SAS was concerned that the code did not require the disclosure by manufacturers of their factory locations, so in order to keep up the pressure, the students conducted a well-organized, well-behaved sit-in of the main administrative building at Duke and negotiated with administrators to alter the code. After thirty-one hours of occupying the building, the students got the administrators to agree that the university should require licensees to publicly disclose the locations of their plants.

After the sit-in, a number of student groups followed suit at other universities, including the University of North Carolina at Chapel Hill, and similar agreements were brokered with their administrations. Duke University continued to have the most progressive standards for licensing agreements of any university in the country.

Critical Reflection as the Inner Work of Leadership

Tico is a great example of someone who had a natural instinct for adaptive learning, and who developed his leadership talents by continually reflecting—in the heat of action—on what he was learning. Once he discovered the larger purposes of his work, he never hesitated to take on the tough questions and to engage creatively other key players in the learning process.

The adaptive leadership framework undergirds our work at the Hart Leadership Program. I learned this approach from Ron Heifetz at the Kennedy School of Government at Harvard University, who was one of my professors in graduate school. At the Center for Public Leadership at Harvard, Heifetz teaches mid-career students and structures his courses so that a key context for testing the adaptive framework is case studies of leadership failures in the students' professional experiences. After years of teaching undergraduates at Duke, I have adjusted and molded the adaptive leadership approach to make it my own. Since my students have just started college, their formative leadership experiences are ahead of them. My job is to get them out into the field so that they create a context for exploring these ideas. But they are not exercising leadership yet—far from it. At this point their role is to learn from life in order to learn about life. The purpose of our program is to support their formation. If transformation also occurs—as it did for Tico Almeida, and as it has for many other students through the years—it is a bonus we cannot plan.

My work in SOL focuses on critical reflection, or what I also call "the inner work of leadership," with the primary goal of fostering political engagement among students, but I tell my students that they will eventually have to form their own working definition of leadership. For now, I want them to play with the adaptive leadership framework and to test it out. If it is helpful beyond the program, they can adjust it to their needs and keep experimenting. If it fails to resonate or fit, they should drop it when they finish SOL. Their decision will come by paying attention. The worthiness of any approach must be proven in a tough-minded way by our own experiences—our encounters with real life and real work.

Adaptive problems permeate our world in every direction. They are the issues that are right in front of us, embedded in the fabric of our lives. They demand changes in our own habits and attitudes in order for us to make progress in confronting them. Leadership is what generates adaptive learning, creating momentum for the group to change, which means we ourselves have to change. It is natural to resist the pain. But it is pain that has a purpose and a payoff, and skillful leadership, which can be exercised in a group by different people at different times, helps us hold steady through the rough spots in the transition.

So we begin with a definition of adaptive leadership, and then we move to a framework of analysis that serves as a practical tool for diagnosing problems and planning interventions in groups and organizations. Through case studies in the preparation course, community-based research in the summer, and a policy research project in the capstone seminar, I push my students to test the framework and develop basic proficiency with it.

When we exercise leadership—when we pay attention, learn how to meet people where they are, and help them open their eyes to their shared problems and potential, we build the self-reliance and resilience of a group. This adjustment can be a huge relief. From what I have seen so far, it is usually also just plain hard work. To open things up, we have to wade through chaos and clutter. To create new patterns, we have to break old ones. As policy scholar and dean of New York University's Wagner School Ellen Schall said, when we are working our way into the unknown, into the "indeterminate zones" that lack clear answers, technical expertise by itself will not help us solve our problems. So we might as well learn to love the swamp (Schall 1995).

Adaptive learning comes from insight into how we are in the swamp together. It comes from a willingness to be present to the situation as it is. From there our task is to experiment, assess, and adjust. It is a dynamic, uncertain, and everchanging learning cycle. It may not be easy, but it is creative and full of life, and there is freedom in learning to take this kind of responsibility. The satisfaction comes from locating a robust sense of purpose, one that is guided by a concern for the well-being and the healthy adaptation of the collective.

Through critical reflection, we develop skills for what we call the "inner" and the "outer" work of leadership. Inner work involves understanding oneself in relation to one's context—one's strengths, limitations, sense of purpose, and capacity to handle difficult situations with strategic savvy. Inner work also requires understanding how groups, institutions, and social systems function, and figuring out the best leverage points for intervention. Outer work means taking action. If leadership (outer work) is the art, critical reflection (inner work or adaptive learning) is what helps us get good at it. Throughout the yearlong learning process in Service Opportunities in Leadership, critical reflection is the glue for students, the meaning-making discipline that gives them the opportunity to situate their questions and interests in larger systemic and intellectual contexts. That is the key to their leadership development. All the juicy learning comes from critical reflection. In our program critical reflection is the practice of adaptive learning. And that practice is the focus of my work with these students, because that is what helps us cultivate courage for the tough questions.

On that first day of class I introduce "critical reflection" and "adaptive learn-ing"—terms that must seem bizarre and abstract to the students initially—and then I ask them to forget about the word "leadership" for the time being. Their chance to exercise leadership is going to come down the road. While they are in our program this year, their mission is to have a direct, wholehearted encounter with the complexities and difficulties faced by ordinary people in diverse commu-nities around the world, and to determine how the practice of adaptive learning might apply to their experiences.

Disillusionment and Fruitful Failure:
Reaching the "Okay, Now What Do I Do?" Moment

I remember the phone call from Croatia in the summer of 1998. Matthew Reisman was upset, but he was trying to be calm. "I just met with my supervisor, and she said I've got forty-eight hours to figure out what my project is. If I can't come up with a good way to use my remaining time here, she is going to put me on a plane and send me home. I don't know what to do."

My first thought, although I did not say it, was "Wow, that must be one savvy supervisor." I cannot remember my immediate response, but I am sure that my heart went out to Matt and that I tried to soothe him. I am also sure I must have said something like this: "Okay, Matt, you've been there for almost a month. You can do this. It is time to show us what you've got. Call us in a few days and tell us what you have decided. I believe in you, and I know you can figure this out. Good-bye now, and good luck."

Matt was one of our most talented students, and we had tremendous faith in him. He had invested so much time and energy preparing for this trip that his ex-pectations were bound to be too high for his own good. A sophomore, Matt was assigned to our Refugee Action Project team because of his strong interest in east-ern Europe; his knowledge of the political situation in Croatia, Serbia, and Bosnia; and his maturity for his age. In planning his placement with an international refu-gee resettlement organization in the spring, the staff of the NGO said Matt could assist with a psychosocial healing project for the Serbian ethnic minorities who were returning to their homes in Croatia.

Once he got to Croatia, however, Matt quickly realized his internship plans were not going to be a realistic fit with the day-to-day realities confronting his host organization. The staff was stretched to the limit trying to deal with the in-flux of returning refugees. They appreciated Matt's earnest overtures of help, but because he was neither a professional psychologist nor a professional researcher, they were not sure where he would be useful, and they did not have time to help him find a more suitable niche.

Matt had to see if he could create a new role for himself on his own. If he was successful, he could stay for the summer. If he could not come up with a useful role, he and the staff would shake hands and part ways. The staff had work to do.

So what happened? Matt revisited his experience when he gave a talk at the twentieth anniversary celebration of the Hart Leadership Program. "That internship was my turning point lesson in failure and resilience," he said. Matt explained: "Croatia is where I learned lessons in leadership that have stuck with me ever since and have influenced everything I have done academically and professionally. Those lessons are to be humble, to embrace uncertainty, and to be resilient. The theme of my internship was falling flat on my face. It was the hardest experience of my life up to that point.

"It was only after I got to Croatia that I realized I didn't know the first thing about psychosocial healing. After a couple of weeks I had to think: 'What do I have to offer these people? I don't know what they have been through. What am I doing here?' I didn't complain, and I tried to be as useful as I could. But it must have shown, how miserable I was."

It was around that time when Matt's supervisor gave him the forty-eight-hour ultimatum. Matt said he spent one full, agonizing day in his apartment just staring at the walls, thinking.

> After I got over the shock of hearing this, I said, "Okay, what am I going to do? What do I know? Well, I know how to ask questions, and I know how to listen, and I know how to write a little bit. So maybe I'll try to listen to what these people want from us." I wrote out a plan to do a needs assessment among the refugees who had come back, to find out what inspired them to come back. What things were they afraid of? What kind of help would they want from a program such as this one?
>
> With my boss we assembled a team, visited a dozen villages, and talked to over seventy-five refugees in three weeks. And I made a report, and hopefully it helped move the program forward.
>
> It was humbling. Like most folks who come to Duke, we arrive here after having achieved a lot already, or at least we feel we have. And then we realize we don't know as much as we thought, and we have to accept that.
>
> That felt like a dark moment. But facing that moment, embracing it, was a tremendous source of creativity. And it is only sometimes, in those moments when I have my back up against the wall, saying, "What do I do next?" that the really creative solutions come. I learned to be resilient. Because these situations have come up in my life time and again when I have had to ask, "What do I do now?" If I don't run, but I stand and face it, often great things follow.

Great things did in fact follow Matt when he finished his project in Croatia. First he returned to campus and began telling others about his summer challenges and his insight into combining research with service. By that time our program had had many years of experience helping students design service-learning projects with community partners around the world, but Matt's project was our first research service-learning (RSL) internship.

The next summer Matt joined the leadership program again as an intern. This time he wanted to explore refugee issues from a local perspective, so we sent him to work on a microlending program at a community-development bank in Charlotte, North Carolina. There he designed another ambitious research project, a survey of the small business technical assistance needs of nine refugee communities in Charlotte. Working with a team of translators, Matt quickly discovered the linchpin people in each community. He set up meetings with them to fine-tune the survey and to ask their feedback on the project design. He collected his data, analyzed it, synthesized it, and presented a report to his host organization, other refugee assistance groups in the area, and funders. Matt did such a stellar job with his community-based research project that we have featured it in our training materials ever since.

During his senior year at Duke, Matt became research service-learning coordinator for Hart Leadership, where he continued to create training materials and present workshops to other students about how to design community-based research projects. That was ten years ago. Since then several hundred Hart Leadership students have followed in Matt's footsteps and completed community-based research projects around the world. Their work has spanned four continents and thirty-five countries.

Courage for the tough questions starts by bringing awareness to our own purposes and roles. In our program we think of the adaptive learning process as having three developmental stages that include personal, interpersonal, and public leadership dimensions. The entry point is to ask honest questions of ourselves. Our ability to respond emerges when we open our eyes to the circumstances we find ourselves in. Even though it might not have been particularly pleasant, Matt Reisman's first savvy decision was to bring his full attention to his predicament. He met it exactly as it was, and only then did he begin to see imaginative yet realistic options for turning the situation around.

Each year when our writing coach David Guy trains students to write the personal narrative essays they will submit throughout the summer, he tells them they are bound to face disillusionment in the field, and that no matter how it might feel at the time, it will not be a bad thing. "You have an idea of the way things are going to be, but when you get to your placements, it will be another way altogether. If you have an illusion, it is good to lose it," he tells the students. "Because that is the place where a more authentic relationship with your community, your colleagues, and your own creative powers can begin."

Throughout the preparation course in the spring, I remind everyone that the most intensive and effective learning from their summer experiences will come from confronting realities that turn out to be very different from what they expected. Thus, all the community-based research assignments and critical reflection assignments in the SOL program are designed to hold the students in these "disillusionment dynamics" and so-called failures. And every summer, with every student, something *always* comes up that is the zinger challenge. It is never, ever, what the student thinks it is going to be. It is always a surprise.

Matt's story is one dramatic example, but often the disillusionment-rebound dynamic is more subtle, yet nonetheless has a powerful impact on a student's formation. Such was the case with another SOL intern a few years ago named Priscilla Baek.

Priscilla's disillusionment experiences in the summer blindsided her at first. A merit scholar at Duke whose Korean family had immigrated to the United States when she was a child, Priscilla planned to conduct her community-based research project in a place she knew quite well, where she spoke the language and had lots of family and friends: Seoul, South Korea. For her service internship she worked as an English teacher at two Christian educational institutes that helped youth who had defected from North Korea to resettle in South Korea. She also designed a study of how her host organization could shape its curriculum and train teachers to teach South Korean culture and English to students as quickly and efficiently as possible. In addition to doing the tutoring and the research project, Priscilla's strong hope was that she could create a forum among North Korean activists to share ideas about how best to utilize resources for resettlement. She was excited about all her projects, and at the start of the summer she seemed to be happily heading in several directions at once.

Through Priscilla's tutoring responsibilities, a policy issue quickly emerged that captured her imagination. In providing remedial education to youth defectors, she realized that they faced enormously difficult educational, lifestyle, and employment obstacles in their new lives. South Korea's official policy was to accept and welcome defectors. The reality was that integration into society was a long, hard, and complicated road, compounded by the mixed feelings many South Koreans had about North Korean refugees. Priscilla was surprised to learn that this was so, and she often felt unequal to the task of helping the young adults she tutored.

Priscilla's supervisor at the educational institute was an intriguing older woman named Miss Park, who was a quiet, powerful mentor to her throughout the summer. Priscilla often wrote about Miss Park in her reports from the field—the weekly narrative assignments we call "Letters Home."

Two weeks into her internship, Priscilla sent her first Letter Home, about the problems she faced in her placement. She described one day in particular that she felt was a disaster. She had arrived at her tutoring session late, sweaty, and out of breath. She felt unprepared to begin her lessons.

"Will it be okay to ask how adjusting to life in South Korea after being in North Korea is to the students?" I had asked politely in my awkward Korean. Miss Park, who was normally bubbly and agreeable, frowned very subtly, trying to be just as polite as I had been. She replied in a hesitant voice, "These kids don't want to be interrogated or reminded of their pasts. If you ask and they respond, go ahead, but I don't suggest you probe." I understood the sensitivity of the topic and decided not to push my limits any further. According to Miss Park, there had been multiple Americans in the past who had come to the school just to research North Koreans like lab rats. "I just don't want that to happen again," she said as I nodded in understanding. "You have to first learn how to serve. Then to wait. Only after you have completed both steps can you begin to develop a relationship with these kids and understand what their lives are truly like."

After the exchange with Miss Park that day, when Priscilla was with the students, she did not know what to say. So she said nothing. When the tutoring session ended, she thought she had spoken and taught poorly: "Later, Miss Park approached me and asked how my first class with the two young men went. I told her it was amusing, interesting, fun, but perhaps not very informative. She smiled and patted me on the back. 'Sometimes showing our failures and mistakes is the only way to open a jaded person's heart,' she said. 'Preparing material to teach someone is easy. Preparing your heart to love someone is one of the most difficult things you could do.'"

Priscilla continued in her Letter Home: "I was at a loss for words. Words, although we depend on them so much, never fail to fail us. What we really want to say sometimes is best expressed in silence and awe."

When she returned to Duke in the fall, Priscilla completed an extensive policy research portfolio, "From Loss to Adjustment: Assisting North Korean Defectors' Transition to the South Korean Educational System." She decided she wanted to return to South Korea after graduation to try to help youth defectors enter the South Korean university system. She got a grant from Davis Projects for Peace to implement a project called, "Beyond the Border: Reconciling Relations Among College-Aged South Koreans and Defectors." The summer after graduation, she returned to Seoul to launch the project with two students from Duke and a growing network of friends and colleagues in Korea.

When describing her work, Priscilla said that what drove her was a huge goal, but one that she knew was too big for her own tiny project: the successful integration of defector college students into South Korean society. She hoped her project could take a modest step toward realizing that goal. She started with one university, with the objective of raising retention rates for North Korean college students. Her longer-term goal was to create a community environment—a common space—where sustainable relationships among students of diverse backgrounds could be fostered, and where North and South Korean students could talk with each other and develop a language of mutual understanding that could be helpful in future conflicts. Priscilla Baek's disillusionment experiences had pointed the way for her to discover a much deeper purpose for her work.

What Is Our Role? Curriculum Design for a Robust Understanding
of Complex Problems

Students participating in Service Opportunities in Leadership have completed a wide variety of projects since the program's genesis. They have taught writing to township youth in South Africa, conducted oral history interviews with campesinos in rural Honduras, worked with young mothers in transitional housing in Chicago, created an HIV/AIDS resource library at a Namibian university, helped Asian immigrants gain access to funding from a microlending program in New Mexico, and researched relationships between students and service staff at Duke.

The community-based research project is important, but we see it as just the start. Our view of leadership development is a long one. We are interested in what kinds of citizens our students will be twenty years down the road. Our program is known for being academically demanding, students seem carefully to self-select before they apply, and we draw a highly competitive pool of applicants every year. But the program is not for everyone. Mostly by word of mouth among students and with little advertising, from the beginning the program has tended to attract a certain kind of student: for the most part, mature and motivated to be challenged in new ways. From reading the students' narrative essays each summer I can see they are searching; many of them articulate a wish for a deeper purpose and calling. Yes, they are conscious of the need to build their résumés, but they seem to be looking for a stronger commitment. What also comes across is a yearning for community.

We offer undergraduates two tracks that use distinct but complementary frameworks for community-based projects: research service-learning and social entrepreneurship. They share a common goal of helping students develop problem-analysis and problem-solving skills, and a rich understanding of the demands and rewards of public leadership. While the social entrepreneurship track introduces students to the principles of entrepreneurial leadership and social innovation, and students learn about the role of entrepreneurship in business and public life, the research service-learning track we have developed over the past decade is more closely aligned with adaptive leadership.

We use the research service-learning (RSL) pedagogy in three component programs run by Hart Leadership: Research Service-Learning Pathway, available to public policy majors; Service Opportunities in Leadership, available to all undergraduate majors; and a postbaccalaureate program called Hart Fellows, available to recent Duke graduates. Research service-learning is a great vehicle into complexity. It combines inquiry with service in order to address community needs, and students have to learn how to collaborate with local organizations to conduct community-based research (CBR). Hundreds of students have completed research service-learning projects through a gateway course or capstone course during the school year, a community-based research project in the summer, or a more extensive research project for a community partner during a yearlong fellowship. Each of our RSL programs combines research with critical reflection, mentoring, and "going public" presentations of students' work.

For example, a policy analysis class explored food security issues in Durham. Students worked with a food gleaning program, a meal delivery service, and a food bank. After the harvest, students collected the extra sweet potatoes in local fields. They then helped their host organization develop a plan to incentivize farmers to donate excess crops through a state tax benefit. Other students engaged in regular meal delivery and helped their host organization develop a strategy for volunteer sustainability. The group working with the food bank helped launch a food stamp prescreening process at local food distribution centers. Students produced final memos outlining political strategies to address specific organizational needs of their community partners.

Because students commit to being part of Service Opportunities in Leadership for a year, they are able to participate in an extensive process of critical reflection and a lengthy exploration of the adaptive leadership framework. We began integrating research service-learning with the adaptive leadership approach after Matt Reisman returned from Croatia and had his adaptive-learning epiphany.

To help prepare students for their community-based research projects, the SOL preparation course includes research methods training modules taught by tenure-track faculty in the Sanford School. SOL students complete rigorous writing assignments throughout the summer, in the form of Letters Home, research reports, and reflective essays about what they are learning along the way.

We designed our menu of RSL offerings to give students diverse avenues for participation. We see RSL as a continuum from gateway courses where students are introduced to community-based research, to the intensive, yearlong commitment of the SOL program, to the postgraduate, international projects of the Hart Fellows. The sequence provides increasing intellectual complexity at each step, presenting progressively more demanding challenges to students in the development of adaptive leadership skills.

Context and Relationships Are Everything: Challenging Students to
Shape the Investigation

Courage for the tough questions means courage for complexity. The art is to figure out how to wade through the wilderness to locate what is essential and integrative within it. We want our students to grasp the reflective practice of adaptive learning so that they become great swamp learners down the road. While they are in our program, though, we think of them as leaders in training. We want them to tone down the type A, "I'll fix it right away" impulses that have been ingrained in them, and instead learn to pause and be more fully present to the relationships and complicated realities they are facing in the field. In order for them to learn to look and listen in new ways, they have to loosen up, let go, and build relationships in the community. We call this learning to be a border crosser. One of the books I use in the SOL preparation course is a small, beautifully written series of essays by the Polish writer Ryszard Kapuscinski called *The Other*. This author remarks, "When I stop to think about the journeys I have been making around the world for a very long time now, sometimes I feel that the most worrying problems did not involve borders and frontiers, practical life difficulties and threats, so much as a frequently recurring uncertainty about the form, quality and course of an encounter with Others, with the other people whom I would come across somewhere along the way, because I knew a lot, sometimes everything, would depend on it" (Kapuscinski 2008, p. 79).

The SOL experience provides students multiple creative and confounding encounters with cultures and communities that are not their own. The commitment to collaboratively design a community-based research project is never easy, so it becomes a focal point for the students' learning. The short-term benefits of the CBR project are that students deliver tangible research products for their community organizations. The students themselves learn a tool of leadership analysis that is practical and portable, with broad applications.

The field-based projects allow students to see the human face of social and political issues. With relationships with specific people in the community as the starting point, students can then explore the complicated systemic issues—the larger contexts—from which the social issues emerged. In an alumni survey we conducted not long ago, one former student wrote about this process: "I became more convinced each day that contact with the poor and learning from the 'other,' who is so different yet so much the same as oneself, is perhaps one of the most vital parts of education. It was an extremely formative experience at a crucial time—just when we are trying to decide how to use our energies to do something good."

In response to the question, "What did you value most from your leadership development experience?" another former student said, "It was the relationships I made with the people in my host organization and the way it shaped how I think of my own path, and my own way of interacting in this world. It is a sense of duty. It is not some intangible need to 'give back.' It is the faces and stories of people whom I know quite well and who compel me to live a life that recognizes something wider than the bubble in which it is so easy to live."

Starting with the human context allows us to move to an analysis of the systemic issues, which nearly always come down to questions of policy, politics, and leadership. The natural progression of questions moves from "who" to "what" to "why," and then to "how." And when we get to the "how" questions, we start to see that policy design presents its own intricate set of questions about values, politics, power, and purpose—layers and layers of complexity.

Skillful public leadership calls for diagnosing multifaceted problems, designing strategic interventions, and continually planning next steps. The work necessitates a kind of reflection in action—making sense of the mess—that builds the group's problem-solving ability or "adaptive capacity." This is what we mean by learning to love the swamp.

We structured SOL in sequences to include learning objectives for the personal, interpersonal, and public leadership dimensions of the leadership development process. Writing assignments at each stage allow students to practice adaptive learning skills. These assignments are the Letter Home, the Point-of-View Essay, and the Policy Research Portfolio, which includes a policy memo and a leadership analysis paper.

Each of the stages requires that students deal with people whose perspectives are different from their own. The objective of the personal dimension is that students develop a reflective discipline in the midst of the pressures and competing demands of their summer projects. The reflective discipline could start with something as simple as a brief journal entry each day. Throughout the summer students submit the Letters Home to key program staff, faculty, and their writing coach. And each week the writing coach then sends a detailed letter back to the students. Occasionally the writing coach's comments are about the mechanics of the writing, but most of the time they are direct responses to the content of the letters. The students often respond to these comments, and then a lively conversation develops between students and mentors. The primary purpose of the Letter Home is to give students a safe place to puzzle and question, so shapes can begin to emerge from the fog. It is a place to explore and to vent, and also a place to locate purpose and resolve.

In the interpersonal dimension, the question is how to zero in on what is essential, but not to lose sight of complexity. What is your own point of view about the

TABLE 1.1

Developmental Sequence for Adaptive Learning Assignments

Developmental Stage	Assignment	Learning Objective
Personal dimension	letter home	develop a reflective stance
Interpersonal dimension	point-of-view essay	locate what is essential in complex readings and case studies, develop a distinct voice, learn how to engage others in discussion and debate
Public leadership dimension	policy memo and leadership analysis paper (Policy Research Portfolio)	develop problem framing, problem analysis, and policy design skills

books and articles and divergent viewpoints you are studying? How do you want to engage others in dialogue and debate about these topics? The Point-of-View Essay helps students collect their thoughts so that they learn how to facilitate a spirited discussion in class. We call the facilitation itself "holding a group." First one has to have a compelling analysis of the reading. But then one needs to listen to the range of perspectives in the group, decide how to launch a robust discussion, and actively move it in the direction of clarity and coherence. Students quickly learn that this practice is not as easy as it sounds.

The public leadership dimension is where students apply the analytical tools of the adaptive leadership framework. In the final sections of their Policy Research Portfolios they draft a policy memo about their social issue. They then write a leadership analysis paper that applies four questions to the policy topic:

1. What is the adaptive challenge?
2. How would you call attention to the key issues?
3. What is your strategy for holding the group (organization or institution) in the learning process?
4. How would you give the work back to people? Who needs to own this work in order for the systemic or adaptive change to be successful?

SOL students work with faculty mentors, but they must shape their community-based research projects from start to finish. Added to the mix is the challenge of designing the project collaboratively with the community partner.

We have seen again and again that something important begins to change when a student's primary goal is to try to do something of value for a community. A good research service-learning experience means confronting complications and obstacles. Designing the research question and research methods is an iterative process that requires flexibility, resourcefulness, and a great deal of patience. And what matters most throughout the learning process is the student's relationship with the community. For years we have been working with a gifted organizer and trainer named Gerald Taylor, who is on the national staff of the Industrial Areas Foundation. Gerald's training in the SOL preparation class always provokes students to see their relationships as the center of their work. "What are your relationships teaching you?" he asks. "Relationships are everything. Don't ever get trapped in an issue and forget about the relationship," he adds. He continues: "Do not go into these places ignorant! Understand what you need to learn, and learn it as quickly as possible, to be useful to people. You have to respect the people you are going to work with. You will never change anything if you are not in relationship with people. As you begin and every step along the way, ask yourself if you can be useful in helping people think something through. Can you ask good questions? If you can, maybe you will be able to help, but you have to learn to do it in the right way. Your first and foremost goal *always* is to listen. Listen to the stories. What do you see as the spirit of the place?"

Toward a More Nuanced View of Adaptive Learning: Questions, Insights, and More Questions

They are the best, the crème de la crème of Duke. Academically, the seniors who apply to our Hart Fellows program are stellar. It is a highly competitive program, we can be very selective, and the intellectual talents of the applicants are a given. Most of the applicants speak several languages and have a number of advanced skills. Many of them come to us with sophisticated research experience and extensive service backgrounds. Many also have scientific, artistic, business, or political accomplishments that are impressive.

These are young adults who are on the fast track to professional achievement, every single one of them. They are headed to the top medical schools, law schools, or private sector firms. They are already hugely successful in the terms of the world we are part of, this competitive, performance-driven world of a top university. Most of them have their choice of next steps when they graduate. But there is something they are hungry for. They are hungry for a richer, deeper, more authentic set of experiences. They are hungry for a deeper understanding of themselves, and they want to take this year "off" because they see it as a precious opportunity they otherwise might not have. The applicants themselves tell us this again and again. They yearn to live in a developing country and to be in a situation where they will be profoundly challenged. And they want the structure, mentoring resources, and research support the program provides.

And we see them as the next generation of promising leaders in our country and in the world. Since their academic abilities are a given, we are looking for qualities of character when we choose the fellows, because we want to know if their hunger is serious and penetrating. If they just want an adventure they should join another program. But if they really are ready to take some risks—if they have what it takes to go through a tough process of formation and perhaps transformation—we need to know. Because this is going to be a formative year when they will discover a much more nuanced understanding of how the world works, how their own minds work, and who they are. And it will take lots of gumption on their part because they really do not know what is going to happen.

These are young people who are used to controlling things, and this is a program that says, "You are going to have a very tight structure as a Hart Fellow, and you have got to do this, this, and this, but yet, guess what? Actually you will have little or no control, not because of us, but because of life." Gasp! So if there is a secret, it is just that. The program has such a tight structure because the entire experience is really about encountering chaos. And as the fellows settle into their host communities, they start to see that there are problems upon problems upon problems, as far as the eye can see, and beyond that, too. Who will have the right answers? If the golden repository of right answers is not to be found anywhere, then what? This is about meeting complexity and chaos head-on, with no clear guideposts.

The fellows will have job titles and scope of work, and they will work with many amazing, good-hearted, generous, hopeful, and even heroic people in the field. But they will also see corruption and self-centeredness and apathy and destructive behaviors in their communities. They will face their share of disillusionment. And throughout the year the fellows will craft Letters Home and try to make sense of life.

When they realize they do not know anything, when all the academic learning in the world will not do them any good because the human problems they are witnessing are beyond any of that, they just have to give up and be present to the situation as it is. That is what Hart Fellow Jay Lee saw several years ago when he wrote his last Letter Home, just as he was leaving an orphanage for children with HIV in Bangalore, India:

I'm not quite sure what to make of the past ten months as I close off this chapter of my life. I'm a little more conflicted than I had expected. I thought that those internal battles I was having with myself would end after awhile, as the bigger obstacles of life revealed themselves to me, but I am finding more and more that the battles that happen inside are 99 percent of what happens outside. All those ideas about courage, strength, bravery, virtue, principle, and any other adjective meant to describe a great human being are all descriptions of things that happen inside a person. Everything else is just epilogue.

A part of me has been lost, just as another part of me has grown. I can't pinpoint what it is, but something about the world is decidedly less romantic, while the ability to be astounded by the complexity and the immensity of the world has increased. A dollar a day actually means something to me now, and the difficulty of a single man I know struggling by with $60,000 in the U.S. is a little mind-boggling. I really do not know what life will be like after this.

Sometimes I feel as if the whole fellowship was an absolute and utter failure. I didn't pass on anything but my love, which I will soon take away in some form. And sometimes I feel as if the whole fellowship was a success. I have confirmed that I am indeed a very adaptable person, that I have strength within me that I wasn't sure existed.

I learned to love people much different from me, so that if I had seen myself from a year earlier I would have shaken my head in exasperation. I've discovered that self-doubt is the biggest battle I will be facing for the next several years, and I've begun taking steps to fight it. I've spent hours with brilliant and compassionate people furiously trying to synthesize some way to do things, to solve these problems. I've seen the best and the worst of leaders hard at work, learning piece by piece what leadership means. I've grown in many ways, from confirming the unpredictability of life to witnessing the absurdity of death. I've seen the world for its goodness, and I've seen the world for its evil, and I've seen the world for its brutal indifference. I've seen how much difference a single person can make while suffocating under the difficulty of trying to dent a single problem like AIDS.

And I still don't feel I know anything, let alone myself. It's always a little disappointing to continually reaffirm that the more you learn, the less you understand, but at least I'm more prepared for the next onslaught of life.

There are many things I've picked up in my time here, so I've put together a quick list, another bunch of clichés and contradictions unsolved and unintelligible. . . . I've learned how easy it is to forget that a person has HIV. I've learned that loving someone is one of the most difficult things to do. I've learned that life doesn't need a future to live. I've learned that hope can lie in the beauty of the present, not just in the future. I've learned that life doesn't always have time. I've learned that life doesn't always need time. I've learned that HIV is just a virus. I've learned that HIV is not just a virus. I've learned how precious life can be. I've learned that there are some things I will never understand. I've learned that there are some things I will have to accept.

REFERENCES

Kapuscinski, R. 2008. *The other.* New York: Verso.

Parks, S. 2000. *Big questions, worthy dreams: Mentoring young adults in their search for meaning, purpose and faith.* San Francisco: Jossey-Bass.

Schall, E. 1995. Learning to love the swamp. *Journal of Policy Analysis and Management* 14 (2): 202–20.

Edward Zlotkowski,
Katelyn Horowitz,
and Sarah Benson

2

The Potential of Service-Learning Student Leadership

It is the contention of the editors of this book that there exists an unfortunate, unnecessary, and ultimately dysfunctional gap between the civic engagement movement and programs aimed at developing student leadership. They write that, although civic engagement has become part of higher education, colleges and universities have not considered how civic engagement might help to promote and redefine leadership in young people. The editors also note that most programs to foster civic engagement in the young remain separate from programs to support youth leadership, at the levels both of theory and of practice.

Furthermore, they contend, the growing strength of the civic engagement movement itself reflects the emergence of a far more civically oriented generation than we have seen in many years. And this resurgence of civic interest, sufficiently strong to lead Robert Putnam, author of *Bowling Alone: The Collapse and Revival of American Community* (2000) to speak of the possibility of a "new Greatest Generation" (2008), points not only to a new sense of personal responsibility for enhancing the common good but also to a new, far less individualistic understanding of leadership than that implied by many traditional leadership programs.

Although it is still too early to tell just how committed to the common good the current generation will in fact turn out to be, there is already considerable evidence to suggest that the editors' emphasis on "cultural transformation," that is, on substantive changes in how people work, think, and relate to each other, has considerable validity. Two books in particular deserve to be mentioned in this context: *A New Engagement? Political Participation, Civic Life, and the Changing American Citizen* (2006), by Cliff Zukin, Scott Keeter, Molly Andolina, Krista Jenkins, and Michael X. Delli Carpini; and The Good Citizen: How a Younger Generation Is Reshaping American Politics (2008), by Russell Dalton.

What lends these works special relevance and special importance is their vigorous challenge to the still-prevalent stereotype of youth civic indifference. This they do in two ways. First, they complicate the meaning of "engagement" by including in the concept a broader range of activities than has often been acknowledged. Zukin and his coauthors, for example, distinguish between political and civic engagement in a way that not only makes them complementary but also recognizes the importance of each. In their view, neither form of engagement is sufficient by itself to maintain a healthy democracy. Furthermore, they stress that the line between the two is far less distinct than many suppose. Indeed, this is one of the key conclusions they draw from their research: "First, the line between civic and political engagement is blurry at best, with as many as half of those engaged in civic activities seeing or treating their actions as political. Second, this line is also a porous one, with many of the citizens we have characterized as civic specialists also expressing their public voice in other arguably political, if not always or obviously electoral or government-focused ways" (Zukin et al. 2006, p. 199).

Thus, they caution us against dismissing as an obviously inadequate substitute for traditional political activity the various forms of local, hands-on engagement that many young people tend to favor. Civic, as distinguished from political, activity has considerable value. And while it may not be sufficient by itself to keep democracy healthy, neither is traditional political activity by itself. When students at a Wingspread conference in 2001 insisted that their community-based activities were an "alternative politics" rather than an "alternative to politics," they were making much the same point: "Many of us at Wingspread perceive service as alternative politics, as a method of pursuing change in a democratic society. We want to address immediate problems in our communities as a way to begin. Building relationships with others through service is often preparatory to building a movement, as we learn skills that can help us take on the roles of community organizers" (The New Student Politics 2002, p. 2).

Zukin and his associates lend even greater credibility to the students' position when at another point they note that, besides the intersecting spheres of civic and political engagement, one must also recognize two other kinds of engaged activity: "One is *public voice*, the ways citizens give expression to their views on public issues. Included here are activities such as signing petitions, engaging in e-mail campaigns, starting or contributing to political blogs, or writing letters to the editor. Contacting public officials . . . may be the most direct type of expression of public voice. . . . The fourth type of activity is *cognitive engagement*, that is, paying attention to politics and public affairs. Cognitive engagement includes such activities as following the news in newspapers, talking about politics with friends and family, or simply being interested in public affairs" (Zukin et al. 2006, p. 54). In short, while we should not underestimate the significance of young people's increased participation in the electoral process in 2006 and 2008, our assessment of their participation in public life should not rest solely on their involvement in that process. If Zukin and his coauthors are correct, we need to draw upon a much wider range of indicators in trying to assess young people's—as well as other Americans'—level of public engagement.

The second way in which recent research should lead us to reassess our assumptions about youth engagement is best captured by the distinction Russell Dalton makes between two kinds of citizenship. Acknowledging the work of Zukin and his colleagues, Dalton draws upon his own research to identify two very different approaches to citizenship or participation in public life. He calls these approaches "citizen duty" and "engaged citizenship" (Dalton 2008, pp. 27–28). Explicitly and forcefully rejecting "[a]ssertions about the decline in citizenship norms among younger Americans" (p. 39), Dalton notes that the "generations are changing in the types of citizenship norms they stress" (p. 39): "These two dimensions of citizenship are not contradictory . . . but they reflect different emphases in the role of a democratic citizen. Both clusters involve a norm of participation, although in different styles of political action. Both define citizenship as a mixture of responsibilities and rights, but different responsibilities and different rights" (p. 28).

This shift in understanding as to what it means to be a "citizen" and what it means to be engaged in public life has important corollaries in other areas of activity. In their preface, the editors of the present volume refer to new technologies that have transformed how we communicate, learn, and work. The fact that information is now more readily accessible allows for more voices to be included in what were once considered expert domains. Other scholars have also called attention to this shift away from a closed domain of expert knowledge to an understanding of knowledge as something generated in concert by all relevant stakeholders (Van de Ven 2007; Dzur 2008). However, specifically with regard to today's youth, Tim Clydesdale captures it in an especially useful way when he writes

> Today's students know full well that authorities can be found for every position and any knowledge claim, and consequently the students are dubious (privately, that is) about anything we claim to be true or important.
>
> Contrast that with 50 years ago, when students would arrive in awe of the institution and its faculty, content to receive their education via lecture and happy to let the faculty decide what was worth knowing. Even 25 years ago, that pattern still held among most students. But it holds no more. While students often report satisfaction with their institution and its faculty, after interviewing some 400 students on 34 campuses nationwide, I found few in awe of their institutions or faculty, many averse to lectures, and most ambivalent about anyone's knowledge claims other than their own. (2009, p. 1)

Clydesdale goes on to draw from this development important implications vis-à-vis teaching and learning. We must become, he warns, much more willing to take seriously our students' independence, their willingness and ability—however flawed—to make judgments for themselves. For the fact of the matter is that they will do so regardless of our own attitude toward those judgments: "We need to begin by respecting our students (and the wider public) not just as persons but as the arbiters of knowledge that they have become. Specifically, we must respect students as thinkers." This requires, among other things, "meeting students where they are, so that they trust us to develop their intellectual skills and expand their knowledge base; balancing our elitist values with democratic and more widely achievable goals; and, perhaps hardest of all, lowering the lofty opinion we hold of ourselves and accepting the public obligation that our privileged position entails" (Clydesdale 2009, p. 2).

It was a related recognition of the importance of accepting today's students as in some sense active partners rather than passive recipients that led to the creation and publication of *Students as Colleagues: Expanding the Circle of Service-Learning Leadership* (2006), edited by one of the authors of this chapter, Edward Zlotkowski; one of the editors of this book, Nicholas Longo; and a student at Princeton, James Williams. As we maintained in the introduction to that volume, "service-learning's academic and social impact [would], in fact, not be achieved until the circle of service-learning leadership [was] further extended to include students themselves" (Zlotkowski 2006, p. 2).

That contention was based on several arguments. Students had already played an important role in launching the civic engagement movement during the 1980s, and they bring to civic engagement a distinctive kind of energy and vision. Furthermore, the operational complexity of service-learning, especially when widely utilized at a university or college, places a practical burden on all involved. Bringing qualified students into leadership positions can give students a unique personal and professional development opportunity. But perhaps the most important argument of all is that service-learning's very *raison d'être* demands student leadership. With regard to this final argument, we pointed out that at the 2001 Wingspread conference students had expressed their frustration at being "treated like 'fine china' brought out to impress trustees and honored guests" (Zlotkowski 2006, p. 6). Student voice was not sought or taken seriously.

This is the same situation Benjamin Barber points to in *An Aristocracy of Everyone: The Politics of Education and the Future of America*, where he notes that "students seem more powerless than ever, being offered endless freedom to say no, to indulge their own opinions and needs and desires, but given little real responsibility and no genuine power at all" (Barber 1992, p. 231). To address this problem, Barber suggests we make more extensive use of "education-based community service" — more frequently known as academic service-learning. However, since *An Aristocracy of Everyone* was first published in 1992, our understanding of service-learning, as well as the profile of our students, has changed considerably, and it no longer seems sufficient simply to call for more extensive student participation in service-learning, as important as that is. What is needed now is a recognition that the future of civic engagement as both an educational and a civic movement may well depend upon our willingness to work *with* our students to help them develop new leadership skills in and through the one area that matters most, namely, the academic curriculum.

In researching student leadership programs that address the curricular as well as the cocurricular dimension of the student experience, the editors of *Students as Colleagues* identified four primary areas in which student civic leadership has been developed. These can be understood as a set of increasingly demanding intellectual responsibilities, as a figure created by James Williams illustrates (see fig. 2.1).

It is very important to note that the increasing levels of "intellectual engagement" do not necessarily correspond to either an increasing level of leadership ability or an increasing level of importance vis-à-vis a specific service-learning program. The first level — students as staff — can encompass a full set of very demanding operational competencies, competencies usually thought of as belonging to paid professionals. Similarly, the fourth level — students as engaged scholars — may have relatively little impact on the successful functioning of a campuswide program, since such scholarship may require relatively little program-based collaboration. Furthermore, all four levels are necessary if an institutionalized service-learning effort is to achieve its full potential. Operational responsibilities — including the selection and training of new student leaders, the establishment and maintenance of effective reciprocal partnerships, and strategic decisions about future program developments — *complement* responsibilities centered on helping service-learning participants unpack and process the multiple levels of meaning latent in community-based experiences. Similarly, faculty-student partnerships may include operational and reflection-intensive responsibilities, but may also include feedback on course design and community-based assignments, as well as assistance with student preparation and student assessment. And all of these student leadership opportunities exist independently of any engaged research that students produce as a result of the partnerships a program encompasses or helps to initiate.

In short, student leadership represents a multidimensional set of opportunities, all of which have the potential to turn students from "fine china," in the words of the Wingspread participants, or from individuals with an "endless freedom to say no . . . but . . . little real responsibility and no genuine power at all," in the words of Benjamin Barber, into a force for more substantive academic and

Student Roles in Service-Learning:
A Pyramid of Engagement

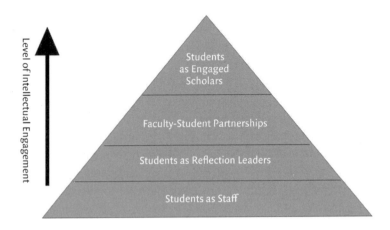

FIGURE 2.1

civic engagement, into harbingers of a more participatory, inclusive democracy. For this to happen, however, service-learning programs around the country must adjust their thinking to accommodate a stakeholder model based on four rather than three key constituencies (see fig. 2.2).

The interests, assets, and needs of faculty, community partners, and the institution itself are, of course, all central to the design of any substantive program, but so are those of students, not just as good foot soldiers in a plan designed by others, but as leaders in their own right. This is the real thrust of a four-quadrant model. However, what we have mostly seen until now is a focus on the faculty, institution, and, to a lesser extent, community-partner quadrants, almost to the exclusion of student-based initiatives. To be sure, students almost always figure as the objects—or perhaps as the measures—of initiatives planned by others. Still, they rarely figure as the coauthors of serious initiatives. Indeed, the reluctance to recognize student agency and student competence in programs outside the domain of student affairs has been profound.

To a considerable degree, this is understandable. Although the contemporary civic engagement movement owes much to student leaders of the 1980s, the legitimization of community-based work within the academic establishment has been a central concern of service-learning proponents for almost two decades. Less pronounced but also reliably present has been a concern for the quality of

The Four Quadrants of Service-Learning Program Design

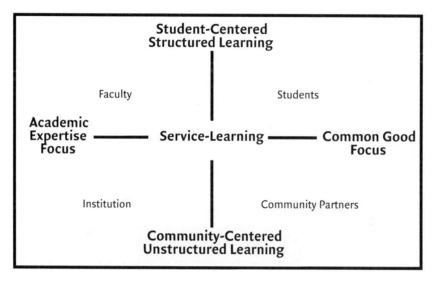

FIGURE 2.2

academy-community partnerships. In fact, debates about the relative importance of substantive student learning and measurable community impact have punctuated the movement for years. (See, for example, Ira Harkavy, "Service-Learning, Academically Based Community Service, and the Historic Mission of the American Urban Research University" [2000].) In comparison, the issue of student leadership has seemed to be at best a matter of secondary importance. However, if the cultural changes referred to at the beginning of this chapter and the unease some have expressed about an apparent stalling of the civic engagement movement (Saltmarsh and Hartley 2009) are any indication, the time may now be ripe to begin paying much more significant attention to this "secondary" issue.

In the sections that follow, we present two different perspectives on what student leadership can mean to a mature service-learning program. First, two of the authors, Katelyn Horowitz and Sarah Benson, explore some of the ways in which Bentley University's service-learning program, the Bentley Service-Learning Center (BSLC), has fostered the development of values described in A Social Change Model of Leadership Development (1996). Then the third author, Edward Zlotkowski, examines some of the problems that may arise when student leadership is not sufficiently integrated into an otherwise mature service-learning program. The chapter concludes with some observations on the implications of these two case studies.

Leadership Development at the Bentley Service-Learning Center

As third-year undergraduate students actively involved in the Bentley Service-Learning Center, we (Katelyn Horowitz and Sarah Benson) have been able to see personal growth from participation in service-learning initiatives firsthand. Indeed, all seven of the values identified in *A Social Change Model of Leadership Development*—consciousness of self, congruence, commitment, collaboration, common purpose, controversy with civility, and citizenship—seem to be present in much of the Center's programming, to no small extent because the BSLC is very much a student-led operation. Hence, we also include here a brief description of one of the key components of our student-focused approach: the Bentley service scholarship program. By deliberately recruiting students with a demonstrated commitment not just to community service but also to student leadership, we have been able to develop layers of student opportunity and student responsibility not found in many other programs.

To understand how the BSLC works, one has to understand its structure. The hierarchy of our student leadership positions calls not only for increasing responsibility but also for a more inclusive commitment to the values or strengths described in the social change model. For example, responsibility for the program as a whole rests with the BSLC's Student Program Coordinators, one of whose most important jobs is to ensure that there is sufficient *congruence* among the Center's initiatives and that everyone is moving forward with a sense of common purpose. Working with the Center's professional staff, the two students chosen annually for this position not only must make important decisions on behalf of the Center as a whole but also must work to motivate their peers and remind them of the organization's core mission. This task is complicated by the intrinsic conflict between keeping everybody on the same page and allowing room for differences among dozens of individual programs. Since the diversity among the Center's programs is considerable and some programs do not relate to others in any obvious way, the coordinators often try to promote the development of a central theme, thereby giving their peers ample opportunity to make connections between their own work and that of others. One theme that recently emerged was "Service-Learning as a Business," which allowed everyone to emphasize the clear and effective use of resources. This theme worked especially well because Bentley itself is a business-focused university, and students were therefore able to bring insights that they had gained in their classes to bear on BSLC initiatives. In this way, each individual program remained distinctive, while at the same time reflecting a shared vision.

Those who guide individual programs are called Project Managers; there are over seventy of them. Together they constitute the very core of the service-learning operation and exemplify how this program is truly student-led. Each Project Manager is responsible for guiding the students participating in his or her respective project, as well as all the logistics associated with that project: coordinating the schedules of students and community partners, organizing transportation, and dealing promptly with any issues that arise. Their responsibilities also include facilitating reflection, running orientation sessions, and monitoring student attendance and performance. Furthermore, Project Managers serve as liaisons between students, their professors, and community partners. Thus, one key to success in this position is an ability to open and maintain effective lines of communication.

As programs have grown, they have sometimes needed more than one person to manage them. Some of the larger programs contain up to five Project Managers who work together to coordinate planning, implementation, and quality control. Controversy and differences of opinion are inevitable in any such situation, and thus it is essential that Project Managers learn to handle *controversy with civility*, which is another of the social change values.

Training is essential to developing this strength. At the start of each semester, Project Managers come together to prepare for what is to come. One of the topics consistently stressed is learning to communicate effectively. In workshops developed on the theme "service-learning as a business," communication was framed to include an understanding of what is involved in being a responsible professional and how one might use negotiation strategies.

In addition to the general training sessions they must attend, Project Managers are expected to arrange meetings within their functional groups to coordinate ideas and perspectives. Through negotiation, active listening, and open debate, they explore complex strategies for problem solving and working through differences. Because of this emphasis on process, a problem often leads not just to a resolution but also to an arrangement clearly superior to that which existed before the problem arose.

This organized sharing of ideas and insights has contributed considerably to the growth and development of BSLC programs. It has also led to the creation of a new position: that of Project Coordinator. As we have already noted, when similar projects are linked, their managers are expected to work together and to discuss related needs, issues, resources, and strategies. The English Language Learners (ELL) program is a case in point. There are four school-based sites for this program, each with its own Project Manager. For although the work at these sites is very similar, it would be extremely difficult for one manager to coordinate all of it. This is because each site has a different curriculum, location, schedule, and group of teachers. Indeed, because each site has its own complex of characteristics requiring attention, even finding sufficient time for the managers to remain in contact is no easy undertaking. It was out of situations such as this one that there developed the position of Project Coordinator, which allows a single individual to ensure that all relevant parties receive the same information, are fully aware of shared plans and deadlines, and have opportunities to communicate.

Sarah Benson, one of the authors of this chapter, took on this position for the relatively new People-to-People program. The People-to-People program began when three organizations in Waltham, Massachusetts, where Bentley is located, began to work together. The organizations started to share ideas because there was an inherent overlap in their missions: each individual program focuses on people in the community who have mental disabilities. However, despite this shared focus, the structures of the three organizations are extremely different and require individual attention. Therefore the Center assigned a Project Coordinator to do what the three individual Project Managers, even working together, would have had difficulty doing. Sarah was able to oversee all aspects of each unit, collect feedback and updates from each unit in turn, and identify the ways in which the three units could most effectively communicate. Promoting *collaboration* lies at the heart of the Project Coordinator's work.

Much of what we have discussed thus far involves what one might call "operational clarity." But the social change model of leadership clearly envisions more than just effective organization. The remaining four values — *common purpose, commitment, citizenship, and consciousness of self* — point in a more internal direction, and thus reveal themselves in more indirect ways. Take, for example, the role student leaders play in working with courses that have a mandatory service-learning component, what the BSLC calls "embedded courses." Clearly all such courses provide a framework or establish a *common purpose* that helps define their community-based work. This shared purpose is typically established by the professor's curriculum and is explicitly spelled out in the course syllabus. However, faculty-defined requirements are not the only way to go about developing a sense of common purpose, nor are they necessarily the best way. As *A Social Change Model of Leadership Development* points out, a sense of common purpose can also emerge from or be explicitly formulated by a group or class as a whole.

Reflection is one such way in which a sense of common purpose can be identified and developed, and although reflection may not translate directly into leadership skills, it can set the stage for the emergence of such skills. When reflection helps clarify a common purpose grounded in service-learning activities, what had been merely an academic project can turn into a personally transformative experience. Thus, by facilitating reflection, a Project Manager or other experienced service-learning student can play a key role in helping other students discover their own drive to contribute to the common good. At Bentley, all faculty teaching embedded courses have the right to request a student service assistant, and such assistants are prepared to play a wide variety of roles, from helping the instructor choose among available community partners, to facilitating logistical arrangements, to monitoring student-partner interactions. Furthermore, by participating in small-group discussions and leading reflection sessions focused on common student concerns, beliefs, and assumptions, an experienced peer leader can facilitate certain kinds of learning that are not easily facilitated by more formal, faculty-led discussions. Such student-to-student exchanges can also have a profound effect on student *commitment*, yet another of the social change values.

Commitment implies two kinds of investment: one of time and the other of personal energy. If a community-based project includes a time requirement, a Project Manager can track and record student compliance fairly easily, and a student who meets that requirement will in almost every instance be assessed more positively than a student who does not. However, there is no simple formula for weighing personal investment as a factor in grading. Is it sufficient for students to do exactly what is assigned, or can they also be required to respond to the spirit as well as the letter of a project? Many times we have seen even those students who are passionate about a particular issue fail to maintain their enthusiasm on-site. This may be due to any one of a number of reasons — from being uncomfortable working with a particular partner to being inadequately prepared for the specific work at hand.

However, as we have noted, a good Project Manager can sometimes succeed in boosting commitment when faculty cannot. When a teacher at an elementary school became frustrated because the college students she was working with were sending her their lesson plans too late for her to integrate them into other activities, the students' professor issued several warnings, all to no avail. Then his student assistant called for a special reflection session on understanding partner needs. In it she managed to get the students to appreciate the vast difference between their own sense of "enough time" and that of their partner. She did this by informally working through the ways in which most students — herself included — tended to approach assignments, in contrast to the kinds of time constraints elementary schoolteachers face. Peer identification and personal experience managed to accomplish what faculty threats could not, and the problem was quickly corrected.

The final two social change values, *citizenship* and *consciousness of self*, are so fundamental that they thread their way through almost every BSLC activity. *Citizenship* centers on the recognition that one belongs to multiple communities — large, small, on- and off-campus — and has a responsibility to contribute to all of them. This idea was recently addressed at a meeting of the BSLC's Reflection Committee, a small group of service-learning scholars committed to exploring the role of reflection. This question was posed: what is your duty to the communities you are a part of?

We know that many students are uncomfortable with the idea that working for the common good may be a duty more than a matter of individual choice. We also know that many students define themselves solely in terms of their family and friends. Thus, one of our key tasks is to help students see things from other perspectives. A frequently used reflection activity deals with assumptions. Students are given a photograph of some people. They do not know where the photo comes from—even those leading the exercise may be unsure of its origin. Beginning with this blank slate, students are challenged to tell the story of the people in the picture: Where are they? How did they get there? What is their socioeconomic class? What is important to them? What allows an observer to make assumptions about them? How trustworthy are those assumptions? What are their consequences? Through exercises such as this one, service-learning challenges our preconceptions and gives us the tools we need to adjust them. If citizenship is about being an active member of one's communities, one must learn to recognize the assumptions that get in the way of identifying with people who at first seem very different.

Ironically, this reaching outward also involves a reaching inward. As one becomes more aware of one's role in society, one also begins to develop a more complex self-awareness, an awareness not only of one's self as it currently is but also of one's potential to become a leader. This is not surprising, since the more social issues to which one is exposed, the more likely one will find something of special importance and real personal resonance. When one of the authors, Katelyn Horowitz, came into the Bentley Service-Learning Center as a first-year student, she was asked what programs she wished to work with. Since she didn't know what she was most interested in, she agreed to work with a program tutoring elementary school students in English as a second language. She enjoyed the people she worked with, but, because the program was very structured, she found there was little room for innovation. Since she recognized in herself a desire to help create service structures rather than simply implement them, she transitioned into a new role working with faculty members. After working with several different professors, she discovered that she especially liked working with older, more mature students, which allowed her to spend less time addressing minor logistical and operational problems and more time identifying ways to make a project more substantive and effective. In other words, *consciousness of self* involves more than just being able to say who one is; it also involves an awareness of those situations in which one works best.

One of the most creative and, from a community standpoint, effective projects developed by a Bentley service leader draws upon a related set of ideas. *2+2=5: The Power of Teamwork* involves a curriculum of game-based activities that places elementary school students in situations designed to help them identify and reconcile conflicting points of view. Each week focuses on a specific theme—for example, communication, diversity, conflict, team roles, emotions—and, as the semester progresses, the children become more and more skilled at working together in a way that taps their individual strengths. Consciousness of self through consciousness of what a situation demands leads to tremendous personal growth. Both the children and the BSLC student facilitators themselves learn to substitute flexibility and dialogue for attachment to a single "right" answer.

Thus, all seven of the values identified in the social change model of leadership development find an important place in the BSLC and help make it what it is. However, there is at least one other factor that contributes significantly to the success of this student-led program: the mechanism used to identify potential student leaders.

Given the attention the BSLC pays to structure, it should not be surprising that much of its work is organized into committees. The students who make up these committees are often the most proactive in the Center. However, most of these committee members have something else in common: they are service scholarship students. That means they receive a stipend in exchange for their contributions to the Center. These contributions include, in addition to active involvement in general, a community service requirement of twelve hours per week, responsibility for developing or significantly expanding a service program by the end of their sophomore year, and completion of a service-learning internship during their junior year.

Most scholarship students are chosen even before they arrive at Bentley. The program was created some twenty years ago to ensure that the BSLC would always have a core of students with a primary allegiance to making it work effectively. Thus, in some ways, the service scholarships resemble athletic scholarships, building on and around individuals who have already demonstrated special interests and skills. Scholarship students are not simply students who have done a lot of community service, they are students who have shown leadership potential in and through their service activities, students who can identify community opportunities and needs, take the initiative, and motivate others to get involved. They are, in other words, prime candidates to develop the seven values or strengths identified in the social change model.

Every year, the BSLC pulls together a team of students to sort through the applications of all incoming students who are potentially candidates for a service-based award. This Scholarship Selection Committee includes representatives of each academic class. There are no formal guidelines to determine who participates on the committee, but many people find the experience rewarding enough to volunteer more than once. Each member of the selection committee is given copies of roughly sixty applications to read carefully and rank on a scale of one to ten for the following characteristics: leadership, teamwork, initiative, and the ability to reflect. The depth and breadth of each applicant's involvement in service projects is also carefully weighed.

After telephone interviews with roughly the top twenty applicants, about eight students are offered this scholarship. After accepting the award, each new scholarship student is given a mentor to aid in the transition to college life in general and to the work of the Center in particular. The mentor-mentee relationship is especially important in helping new students meet the challenge of handling the same responsibilities as their upperclassmen counterparts, including compiling performance evaluations of students involved in the Center's many service programs. Not surprisingly, these early relationships often extend well beyond the first year, as the word *mentor* is replaced by the word *friend*.

From the very beginning, the scholarship program facilitates leadership growth by removing the option of students' staying in their comfort zone. It is, for example, not easy for a first-year student to explain to a senior that he or she will be monitoring the senior's service work and will be reporting to the senior's professor! However, this fast start comes in handy when the first-year student faces the responsibility of creating or significantly expanding a community-based initiative by the end of the sophomore year. For some students, this project follows naturally from activities in which they are already involved. It allows them either to replicate an especially successful initiative, thereby increasing its community impact, or to make significant improvements to an existing program. Continuity has long been a strength of the BSLC, and students are as eager to sustain and improve programs as to start new ones.

Nevertheless, some students do choose to launch new initiatives. This requires, first of all, earning the community's trust, since many potential partners are understandably skeptical that young students will be able to follow through in a way that justifies their own investment of time and energy. In this regard, the fact that most Bentley students are business majors may enhance their credibility, since so much of their education focuses on organizational effectiveness and developing real-world skills. Certainly the students themselves are aware of both the risks and the potential benefits of starting a new program. Few of their non-BSLC peers are able to state on their résumés that as sophomores they designed and implemented a program serving both the off-campus community and their fellow students!

The final requirement for maintaining a service scholarship, namely, participation in a for-credit, nonprofit internship during the junior year, creates a bridge between the scholarship student's community-based work and the curriculum. Like the requirements for the sophomore project, the requirements for the internship are left deliberately broad to allow students to pursue activities in which they have a special interest. Thus, one of us, Katelyn Horowitz, developed a financial literacy program for a homeless shelter to complement her work in accountancy, while the other, Sarah Benson, brought her growing marketing skills to an organization that works with disabled individuals.

The service scholarship program not only serves the needs of the BSLC and its community partners but also provides powerful opportunities to develop the seven values or strengths discussed earlier. We are extremely proud of the fact that this program, like so much else at the BSLC, sustains itself largely thanks to the dedication of our student leaders. That in itself is testimony to the strengths they have developed.

Student Leadership in a Research-Intensive Institutional Setting

We now move from looking at student leadership through the eyes of students in a business-oriented academic culture to considering a very different kind of institutional culture. During the past year, one of the authors, Edward Zlotkowski, was invited to visit a research-intensive university with a well-developed, widely respected service-learning program. For several years the institution has followed a deliberate, focused strategy in growing its program, paying particular attention to questions of faculty understanding, competence, and ownership. Workshops for faculty are plentiful and well promoted; the administration has made a substantial financial commitment to the program and has also given it significant moral and cultural support. Responding to the very real needs of the surrounding community, the university has made academy-community partnerships an active part of its mission and identity. In short, if one were to use as one's guide the service-learning program design matrix introduced earlier in this chapter, one would have to conclude that the faculty, institution, and community partners' quadrants have received the kind of attention they deserve.

The student quadrant, however, is another matter. Students have, of course, figured centrally in the thinking of all the other constituencies; indeed, the program has recently developed an initiative that trains students to assist faculty in implementing service-learning courses. Here too there would seem to be little cause for criticism. And yet students in the assistantship initiative reported they were not satisfied. Although they had been included, they did not feel they had been consulted. Some of them complained that the faculty they were assisting regarded them as little more than gofers. They had no substantive academic or intellectual responsibilities. They had no opportunity to help shape or process their fellow students' community-based work. They were not asked for input or feedback based on their own service experiences. In short, they had not been given any opportunity to *lead*.

Even less satisfied, and far more vocal, were students who had assumed major service or community-related leadership responsibilities in organizations and projects outside academic service-learning. Some of these students had also been trained to assist faculty, but they had found this opportunity so limiting that they decided instead to commit themselves to projects and partnerships outside the curriculum, where they could play a more substantive, shaping role and could allow both their accumulated expertise and their deep commitment freer rein.

Given the fact that this latter group included some of the most experienced and thoughtfully engaged students on campus, their comments seemed to me especially valuable. They had no desire to criticize the flagship service-learning program simply out of pique or envy, but they were deeply frustrated by what they saw as counterproductive procedures and damaging blind spots. Since they themselves spent considerable time at community sites and came in constant contact with students working on course-based projects, they knew what was going on there better than most faculty members. They noted, for example, that for too many of their peers, service assignments remained just that—assignments. Indeed, in some cases, peer attitudes could best be described as negative, and stereotypes seemed only to have grown stronger. Some peers were so vocal about their discontent that they injudiciously said things on-site that could be hurtful to community members. If the first rule of community-based work is "do no harm," the very rationale for the program was in trouble.

Negative student attitudes are not, of course, unusual, especially when an assignment is mandatory and requires some extra effort. However, information such as that shared by these student leaders must be quickly channeled to the appropriate individuals in a service-learning program. In this case, that wasn't happening because these extracurricular leaders, despite their experience and commitment, did not see any way to participate in the faculty-focused curricular program. There was no student-based advisory committee and no role for students on any training or review committee. Although the student leaders, familiar with faculty practices thanks to their own earlier experiences, had many ideas about how improved student preparation and reflection could begin to address the relevant problems, they had no idea if their observations and suggestions would even be welcome. Their sense was that the program placed such a strong emphasis on academic legitimacy that the importance of other dimensions of the work was simply underappreciated. They themselves identified very strongly with the community and were afraid that, at least in some instances, the community functioned more as a faculty opportunity than as a faculty partner. Reciprocity might be touted as a core program principle, but in practice that principle did not always prevail.

And yet there was no good reason why the student leaders could not have served as more of a program resource. The service-learning initiative did represent a genuinely good-faith effort to implement the scholarship of engagement. Faculty took their work seriously, and the community wanted to partner with them. On many levels and in many ways the institution itself had recognized the importance of academy-community partnerships. It had invested in the program and had even taken some risks in embracing it as thoroughly as it had. The trouble was not a moral or a civic failing but a design flaw. The value that student leaders could add to the program had yet to be fully recognized. Training students to assist faculty in their service-learning courses was certainly a step in the right direction, but it did not represent the kind of genuine respect—or power-sharing—that was ultimately needed.

Thus, in an unintended way, the engaged students at this institution could be said to function a little like the "fine china" (*The New Student Politics* 2001, p. 11) the Wingspread students complained about. It was also clear that, like their Wingspread peers, they were, to all intents and purposes, "organizationally illiterate"—"unaware of how to participate in the [formal] college community" and "lack[ing] access to the institutional system" (p. 11). The Wingspread students speculated that such illiteracy might even be by design, "just so that students will not try to 'reform' the system" (p. 12). But even if this was not the case, the results were similar: despite the students' eagerness to help reform—or at least improve—their school's service-learning program, they felt stymied by what they experienced as a closed feedback loop. In the end, this arrangement served no one well, not even the faculty whose needs it prioritized.

Like other forms of the scholarship of engagement, service-learning challenges widely accepted perspectives and procedures. This is well recognized within the civic engagement movement, but it is also acknowledged in the academy in general, insofar as many traditionalists see community-based work not as a form of excellence but as an alternative to excellence. Ironically, something similar plays out when it comes to creating synergy between academic and student affairs. However often individuals in both divisions lament their lack of collaboration, most faculty remain convinced that what happens in student affairs is ultimately of secondary importance, while those on the student affairs side zealously guard their prerogatives from academic encroachment, sometimes to the point of withholding from academic service-learning programs their assistance and expertise. Thus, the concept of students as colleagues runs up against still another institutional barrier. It is easier for both sides if students simply focus their energy and creativity on traditional, student-run programs, leaving faculty free to shape credit-bearing programs as they see fit, with no outside interference.

At the beginning of this chapter we looked at evolving cultural expectations. The insistence, overt or covert, on keeping faculty and student affairs in separate, airtight compartments would seem to resist this evolution. According to the received wisdom, students should be encouraged to take the initiative, but not in areas related to the curriculum. Faculty should see their students holistically but need not respect their potential to contribute to the design of their educational experiences. Separate and, at best, theoretically equal would seem to be the name of the game.

But elsewhere much traditional thinking has already been called into question. We no longer accept without question what our doctors prescribe. We no longer believe priests, ministers, and rabbis necessarily know best. We actively second-guess our government's decisions. Indeed, we have, to return to Russell Dalton's useful formulation (2008), ceased to believe it is our job to be "dutiful" citizens and have embraced instead the necessity of engaging personally, objecting directly, withholding both credence and assent. And as our most distinctive philosopher John Dewey pointed out over a century ago, there is a significant relationship between what happens in education and what happens in society in general. Hence, "whenever we have in mind the discussion of a new movement in education, it is especially necessary to take the broader, or social, view. Otherwise changes in the school institution and tradition will be looked at as the arbitrary inventions of particular teachers, at the worst transitory fads, and at the best merely improvements in certain details—and this is the plane on which it is too customary to consider school changes" (1899/1964, p. 296).

Although Dewey thought of education as leading the way, the interrelationship between educational and social change can also work in the opposite direction, with education the beneficiary of social innovation. In other words, we do not *need* to regard the notion of students as colleagues as radical—despite the reluctance of the academy to change. Faculty serve their own interests at least as much as their students' when they recognize they are no longer the sole arbiters of what is important. As one of Tim Clydesdale's students put it: "'It is imperative that someone studying this generation realize that we have the world at our fingertips—and the world has been at our fingertips for our entire lives. I think this access to information seriously undermines this generation's view of authority, especially traditional scholastic authority'" (Clydesdale 2009, p. 1).

Giving more students a substantive opportunity to develop knowledge and practices that matter, by allowing them to work *with* faculty rather than simply *for* faculty, is a no-brainer. Not only does it speak to the more direct, less hierarchical approach to civic engagement documented by Zukin and his coauthors (2006) and by Dalton (2008), it also reflects more accurately the democratic core of service-learning as a philosophy of education. As Jennifer Bunn, Mei Elansary, and Cory Bowman write in their chapter in *Students as Colleagues* (2006): "On a more theoretical level, service-learning is a pedagogy that emphasizes democratic development . . . and thus is a natural fit with a course that employs a democratic learning process from course creation through implementation. The goals of both service-learning and democratic development are met to a greater extent when the two are employed together in the same course than when employed individually" (pp. 199–200). If a new culture of engagement is emerging not just in higher education but in American society as a whole, it will not only make possible but will actually require a new, more robust, more substantive understanding of the possibilities of student leadership.

REFERENCES

Barber, B. R. (1992). An aristocracy of everyone: The politics of education and the future of America. New York: Ballantine Books.

Bunn, J., M. Elansary, and C. Bowman. (2006). Penn's West Philadelphia partnerships: Developing students as catalysts and colleagues. In Students as colleagues: Expanding the circle of service-learning leadership, ed. E. Zlotkowski, N. V. Longo, and J. R. Williams, 193–205. Providence, RI: Campus Compact.

Clydesdale, T. (2009). Wake up and smell the new epistemology. Chronicle of Higher Education (January 23): B7.

Dalton, R. J. (2008). The good citizen: How a younger generation is reshaping American politics. Rev. ed. Washington, D.C.: CQ Press.

Dewey, J. (1899/1964). The school and society. In John Dewey on education: Selected writings, ed. R. D. Archambault, 295–310. Chicago: University of Chicago Press.

Dzur, A. W. (2008). Democratic professionalism: Citizen participation and the reconstruction of professional ethics, identity, and practice. University Park: Pennsylvania State University Press.

Harkavy, I. (2000). Service-learning, academically based community service, and the historic mission of the American urban research university. In Connecting past and present: Concepts and models for service-learning in history, ed. I. Harkavy and B. M. Donovan, 27–41. Washington, D.C.: American Association for Higher Education.

The new student politics. (2001). Providence, RI: Campus Compact.

Putnam, R. D. (2000). Bowling alone: The collapse and revival of American community. New York: Simon and Schuster.

———. (2008). The rebirth of American civic life. Boston Globe, March 2. http://www.boston.com/bostonglobe/editorial_opinion/oped/articles/2008/03/02/therebirth_of_american_civic_life/.

Saltmarsh, J., and M. Hartley. (Forthcoming). Democratic civic engagement. In Higher education and democracy: The future of engagement, ed. J. Saltmarsh and M. Hartley. Philadelphia, PA: Temple University Press.

A social change model of leadership development: Guidebook. Version III. (1996). Los Angeles: Higher Education Research Institute, UCLA.

Van de Ven, A. H. (2007). Engaged scholarship: A guide for organizational and social research. Oxford: Oxford University Press.

Zlotkowski, E., N. V. Longo, and J. R. Williams, eds. (2006). *Students as colleagues: Expanding the circle of service-learning leadership*. Providence, RI: Campus Compact.

Zukin, C., S. Keeter, M. Andolina, K. Jenkins, and M. X. Delli Carpini. (2006). *A new engagement? Political participation, civic life, and the changing American citizen*. London: Oxford University Press.

II Leadership and Civic Engagement in Context, Then and Now

3

The Civic Engagement Movement and the Democratization of the Academy

The past two and a half decades have seen the emergence of myriad efforts aimed at reclaiming the civic purposes of American colleges and universities (Harkavy and Hartley 2008; Hartley and Hollander 2005). The sheer scope of these efforts—championed by dozens of associations and through the establishment of many new networks—has led some observers to liken them to a movement (Hollander and Hartley 2000; Kezar, Chambers, and Burkhardt 2005). Like a social movement, the civic engagement movement has relied on the talents and energies of many committed people to fulfill its aims. Of particular relevance to this volume is the integral role that students have played by supporting the growth and institutionalization of civic engagement efforts at colleges and universities across this country. For example, students played a key and often leading role in developing community service programs in the 1980s on hundreds of campuses. Service-learning initiatives throughout the 1990s could not have grown as dramatically without the enthusiastic involvement and support of students.

In this chapter we argue that, for the movement to fulfill its original purpose of strengthening communities and democracy, additional approaches need to be available for students to play a leadership role and optimally benefit from civic engagement activities. These approaches need to be part of the core work of the academy (learning and developing new knowledge to improve society) and challenge traditional norms about students as passive learners, the community as a laboratory and passive recipient of assistance, and the faculty member as expert.

The entire civic engagement movement grew out of widespread discontent with the status quo, including the then-dominant role of the academy in society. In the early years, the range of factors contributing to this sense of collective unease included a faltering economy and the prevalence of societal critiques about the fragmentation of American society (Putnam 1995). Critics often directed invective against higher education (A. Bloom 1987; Smith 1990; Sykes 1989). Even friendly critics voiced concerns. In an interview in 1986, Ernest Boyer, then the President of the Carnegie Foundation for the Advancement of Teaching, summarized the prevailing mood on campuses that he had visited when researching his book on the undergraduate experience (Boyer 1987): "We didn't find dramatic examples of failure; rather, we found a loss of vision, of vitality, a sense of marking time" (Marchese 1986, p. 10).

This discontent set the stage for a dramatic and important shift in the predominant practices of the academy. Active pedagogies that linked community-based activities with disciplinary learning (service-learning) began to gain ground, along with conceptions of scholarship that were contextually driven and involved collaboration with university colleagues and with members of the community. Such efforts have changed the academy for the better. They have democratized it.

To appreciate the magnitude of the shift, it is instructive to recall the nature of the discourse two decades ago. In 1986, for example, more than one hundred college and university presidents met to establish a new association. Originally called the Coalition of College Presidents for Civic Responsibility, the group's name soon changed to Campus Compact. A comment from one president at that meeting, which was recorded and transcribed, is particularly illustrative: "I'd like to ask a question—and this is probably dangerous—how many in the room either give or think it would be alright to give some form of academic credit for service? [Some hands go up.] How many would be opposed? [Some hands go up.] And the rest are just in the middle waiting for leadership. It looks like a real minority" (Coalition of College Presidents for Civic Responsibility 1986).

In 1991, the first survey of Campus Compact members (at that time there were 235) found that only 16 percent of their students were involved in service efforts of any kind—volunteer or curricular; only 15 percent of Compact institutions had or were considering establishing (which means they did not yet have) offices to support this work; 59 percent of the presidents characterized the extent of their faculty's involvement in this work as "little" or "not at all." By contrast, the most recent survey of Campus Compact members in 2007 (approximately 1,100 members) found:

- A third of all students participate in service and service-learning courses annually

- Eighty percent of member institutions have an office or center coordinating service-learning and/or civic engagement efforts

- Thirty-four percent of institutions take activities such as service-learning and engaged scholarship into account in promotion and tenure decisions for faculty

- Ninety percent of these institutions' strategic plans specifically mention instilling in students a sense of responsibility to their community as an important student outcome

One would be hard pressed to point to another higher educational reform movement that has had that kind of sweeping impact in so relatively brief a time.

A central concern of this movement has been to cultivate the civic agency of students. Not only have students frequently played a key role in promoting civic engagement on their campuses, the democratic ideals of this movement have opened up new opportunities for students to take on leadership roles: as colearners, coresearchers, and coleaders of their institutions. That said, though important and promising practices have emerged, the truly engaged, democratic university has not yet been fully realized in American higher education.

One promising strategy is Problem-Solving Learning (PSL). PSL entails bringing faculty, students, and community members together to grapple with complex, real-world problems. Creating sustainable, safe, healthy communities that promote human dignity and offer individuals, in the fullest sense, the inalienable rights of liberty and the pursuit of happiness cannot be achieved through expert advice or technical fixes. To significantly reduce barriers to this goal such as poverty or inadequate schooling requires not only theoretical knowledge but also contextual knowledge—an understanding of what is happening on the ground. It also requires an ability to collaborate and the imagination to devise strategies for meaningful change. For us, PSL is an approach to leadership education that cultivates a sense of civic agency among students and faculty, as well as members of the community. It is leadership education predicated on the idea that solving complex, real-world problems requires individuals to work and learn together in order to make meaningful change.

In the remainder of this chapter, we briefly chronicle the civic engagement movement and note some of the key ways that students have contributed to the movement. We then discuss some of the challenges of creating institutions of higher learning that practice and advance democracy. Finally, we discuss several promising practices, including PSL, and offer suggestions as to how the movement can better realize the goal of creating the democratic, engaged, civic university.

The Civic Legacy of American Higher Education

To understand the reemergence of civic engagement and why the perception of its decline in the early 1980s spurred such a widespread response, it is helpful to recall that America's colleges and universities were established to serve society.

The earliest colleges were founded to educate successive generations for civic and religious leadership. For example, Benjamin Franklin founded the University of Pennsylvania because he believed that "the great aim and end of all learning" is to help students develop "an inclination joined with the ability to serve Mankind, one's Country, Friends and Family." Variations on Franklin's mission, usually with a religious, as opposed to a secular, orientation, are evident in the founding documents of hundreds of colleges established in the aftermath of the American Revolution (Rudolph 1962). A similar civic impulse led to the creation of the public land grant colleges and universities in the nineteenth century. In 1873, for example, the trustees of the Ohio Agricultural and Mechanical College (now Ohio State) said that they intended to educate students not just as "farmers or mechanics, but as [individuals], fitted by education and attainments for the greater usefulness and higher duties of citizenship" (Pollard 1953, p. 18). However, during the twentieth century, competing commitments began to displace such educational and civic ideals. Formational education—the desire to shape the moral and civic lives of students—began to recede. The ethos of "value freedom," taken from the model of the German research university, heavily influenced academic norms and led to a de-emphasis of higher education's role in shaping students' values (Reuben 1996). As historians Lee Benson and Ira Harkavy explain: "[although] 'value-free' advocates did not completely dominate American universities during the 1914–1989 period . . . they were numerous enough to strongly reinforce traditional academic opposition to real-world problem-solving activity, and they significantly helped bring about the rapid civic disengagement of American universities" (Benson and Harkavy 2002, p. 13). By 1980, many leaders in higher education felt that the historic civic purposes of colleges and universities had been significantly eroded and were even in danger of being lost.

The Emergence of the Civic Engagement Movement

The current civic engagement movement emerged at a time of intense self-reflection within the academy. The early 1980s were characterized by a faltering economy, which fueled anxiety at colleges and universities about the necessity of widespread retrenchment. Some experts predicted that as many as a third of all colleges would merge or close (Keller 1983). This crisis helped spur the management revolution in higher education. Calls for greater efficiency, the conception of "students-as-customers," and a market mentality began to prevail (Bloom, Hartley, and Rosovsky 2006). A number of institutions pursued market-driven strategies that resulted in a deviation from their historic missions. For example, a significant proportion of institutions that provided or sought to provide a liberal arts education began to develop new professional programs and majors in an effort to appeal to prospective "customers" interested primarily in job preparation (Breneman 1994; Brint 2002; Hartley 2002). Such shifts produced dissonance and questioning on many campuses as to whether higher education should exist primarily to prepare students for jobs or for a broader civic purpose.

Alongside the unease brought about by a hostile economic environment, larger social critiques developed, including Christopher Lasch's claim of a rising "culture of narcissism" (Lasch 1978) and social critic Tom Wolfe's declaring that the 1980s were "the Me Decade." In a more scholarly vein, sociologist Robert Bellah and his colleagues, writing in the bestselling *Habits of the Heart*, argued that although individualism was a distinguishing characteristic of American social thought and behavior, it had now "grown cancerous" (Bellah, Madsen, Sullivan, Swidler, and Tipton 1985).

There also were concerns about political disengagement and disaffection. By almost any measure—knowledge of political processes, awareness of current events, participation in activities of voluntary associations, trust in government—civic capacity was diminishing to an alarming degree (Putnam 1995). On campuses, the highly visible political activism of the 1960s had seemingly vanished. Calls began for educational institutions to address the situation. For example, the Association of American Colleges (later renamed the Association of American Colleges and Universities) published a special issue of *Liberal Education* in 1982 on the role of colleges and universities in American democracy (Cawallader 1982). The sum total of all these concerns—about the academy and the larger society—created an environment that seemed to demand a response.

Under close scrutiny, the charge that college students were wholly apathetic proves problematic and simplistic. As noted above, American society as a whole was experiencing a decline or at least a shift in traditional civil and civic activities (Putnam 1995). Also, college students in the 1980s focused their attention on societal issues in ways that were quite distinct from (and less obvious than) those of their 1960s counterparts.

The experience of Wayne Meisel, who cofounded the Campus Outreach Opportunity League (COOL), an organization supporting student-led community engagement efforts on college campuses, sheds some light on that shift in student engagement. Meisel was a recent graduate of Harvard who on January 6, 1981, began a "Walk for Action" that took him on foot to sixty-seven colleges and universities in the Northeast. With a letter of introduction from Derek Bok, Harvard's president, Meisel met with administrators and student leaders at these institutions. His aim was simple: to see what was occurring and to encourage more student involvement and leadership in community-based activities. Drawing a parallel with the economic concept of structural unemployment—intentional slack in employment rates—Meisel argued that students were plagued by "structural apathy." They weren't indifferent; rather, their institutions were not organized or structured to provide meaningful community engagement opportunities. "[Students] find themselves in a society which unknowingly and unintentionally fails to inspire, tap, and channel their resources" (Meisel 1984, p. 6). Meisel characterized the majority of service efforts as small and fragmented, consisting of student service clubs and the periodic volunteer or philanthropic activities of fraternities and sororities. Meisel wanted to integrate the piecemeal efforts and broaden the appeal of community service by drawing to it students from a wide variety of backgrounds and interests who could assume leadership of their own important projects.

The walk ended in Washington, D.C., on May 29, 1984. An exhausted Meisel initially felt that the effort had been a failure. His effort had resulted in very little press coverage (though that would come later). However, the walk accomplished several important things: First, the experience positioned Meisel to speak authoritatively about the state of community service on nearly seventy campuses in the Northeast. Second, Meisel realized that few of the people engaged in community-based work had any idea of what was happening on other campuses; no network existed to allow for mutual support and to highlight collectively the activities happening on these campuses. (Within a few years, COOL would be supporting student-led efforts on more than 400 campuses.) Third, his experience provided a compelling counternarrative to the notion of student apathy and self-centeredness. Student inaction was not caused by an absence of moral resolve, but rather by a failure to provide venues through which students might meaningfully engage in civic work. The potential for student leadership was great, if students could be given the support and resources to pursue and broaden their community involvement.

Shortly after Meisel's odyssey ended, Frank Newman, director of the Education Commission of the States, wrote an influential book, *Higher Education and the American Resurgence* (1985). In it he outlined the significant challenges facing American higher education. A central theme of the book was civic disengagement. Newman argued: "If there is a crisis in education in the United States today, it is less that test scores have declined than it is that we have failed to provide the education for citizenship that is still the most significant responsibility of the nation's schools and colleges" (Newman 1985, p. 31). It was a message echoed by the American Political Science Association's Task Force on Civic Education for the 21st Century: "We take as axiomatic that current levels of political knowledge, political engagement, and political enthusiasm are so low as to threaten the vitality and stability of democratic politics in the United States" (American Political Science Association Task Force on Civic Education in the 21st Century 1998, p. 636). Among the hundreds of thousands of college freshmen surveyed by the Higher Education Research Institute at UCLA, the percentage who agreed that it is "important for me to keep up to date with political affairs" sharply declined from 58 percent in 1966 to 26 percent by 1998 (Sax, Astin, Korn, and Mahoney 1999). The question that concerned Newman and others was how best to recapture the historic imperative of cultivating an enlightened citizenry.

From Volunteerism to Service-Learning

Newman's report caught the attention of the presidents of Brown, Georgetown, and Stanford Universities. They too were concerned about the failure of colleges and universities to instill in students a sense of social and civic responsibility. In 1986 these individuals founded Campus Compact, a presidential organization aimed at helping students express "civic responsibility." It was an organization whose time had clearly come. Within one year the network had 113 members, and less than a decade later its membership had swelled to 520.

At the group's first meeting in 1986 Newman argued: "There is a need for community service to become more widespread and the idea of civic responsibility to be widespread—there needs to be in the country a sort of clear statement of that to students." Though some of the presidential members bemoaned student apathy, Newman and others pointed to efforts on their campuses and Meisel's walk as evidence of a nascent desire on the part of some students to become more meaningfully engaged. Very quickly the group decided to focus its attention on promoting community service, which members of the organization often referred to as "public service."

Two things are notable about these early efforts to advance civic engagement. First, the discourse at the time framed the role of students as recipients of support and guidance rather than as leaders and agents of change. Second, there was a conscious effort to avoid the appearance of supporting overt political activism. In fact, student activism remained very much alive on many campuses (though certainly less visible than during the 1960s) (Rhoads 1998). In the 1980s, such efforts included students' encouraging their institutions to divest themselves of stock in companies doing business with the apartheid-backed regime in South Africa. In the 1990s, they included the queer student movement, multicultural movements, and the Free Burma Coalition (Rhodes 2009). However, these activities remained separate from institutionally sanctioned civic engagement efforts. In part this was because, at the time, politics had come to be viewed with suspicion. As Robert Bellah and his colleagues put it: "For a good number of those we talked to, politics connotes something morally unsavory, as though voluntary involvement were commendable and fulfilling up to the point at which it enters the realm of office holding, campaigning, and organized negotiating. Their judgments of public involvement and responsibility turn negative when they extend beyond the bounds of their local concerns" (Bellah et al. 1985, p. 199). Campus Compact understandably also cast its work as nonpartisan. In the 1980s, one of the main goals of the group was to advance state and federal legislation supporting community service among college students. Both Republicans and Democrats supported such legislation. (Indeed a bipartisan coalition in the Senate and House was required for the legislation to pass).

Although a nonpartisan approach made good sense and helped the movement to grow, the narrow focus on volunteerism and community service had significant drawbacks. Early on some members of Campus Compact argued for efforts to move beyond volunteerism to linking service with the academic core. They were, in effect, arguing for a move from community service to credit-bearing service-learning. This agenda was contested (as the divided straw vote of Campus Compact members in our introductory section underscores). Many member presidents raised concerns about the propriety and rigor of allowing students to engage with community members without the firm guiding hand of a faculty member. Nevertheless, advocates of connecting service with academic study made their case with increasing effect.

The first Campus Compact newsletter, published in April 1987, reported on a session organized by Campus Compact at the American Association for Higher Education (AAHE) conference, at which Tim Stanton from Stanford spoke of the negative impacts of volunteering with inadequate preparation, including "drawing unwarranted conclusions from the experience" and "a general decline in commitment that developed into cynicism" (Campus Compact 1987). He argued that curricular efforts could significantly improve the learning from these experiences. Soon thereafter, Campus Compact sponsored a seminal study that Stanton led and whose findings were conveyed in "Integrating Public Service with Academic Study: The Faculty Role, A report of Campus Compact." Published in 1990, the report noted the various ways in which service was being linked to the curriculum. It also pointed to the important work at hand: "There appears to be developing, at least among Campus Compact institutions, a growing sense that the faculty role in the public service initiative is critical to its success. However, much work remains to be done to address structural issues such as rewards and incentives for faculty involvement or the intellectual questions related to problem-oriented inquiry and knowledge development. . . . With few exceptions, Campus Compact institutions have yet to involve faculty on a broad scale in ensuring that students both serve well and learn effectively from the experience" (Stanton 1990, p. 21).

A range of groups soon began to address these important issues. In 1990, the National Society of Internships and Experiential Education (NSIEE) published *Combining Service and Learning: A Resource Book for Community and Public Service*, edited by Jane Kendall. The book offered readings that pragmatically explained how service might be incorporated into the curriculum and why such work was consonant with academic work. It also reflected the consensus that had emerged among practitioners of service-learning (which is what the pedagogy came to be called), as codified in the "Principles of Best Practices for Combining Service and Learning in 1989." Some of these shared principles were:

- Service-learning is a legitimate pedagogical strategy and is as effective as traditional methods (such as lectures) for imparting knowledge and promoting learning

- Service-learning enables students to grapple with complex, messy, real-world problems; it shifts the emphasis of service from personal charitable acts (community service) to efforts aimed at understanding root causes of social problems

- Service-learning helps people learn to engage in collective problem solving, in which problem definition and development of solutions occur as joint acts rather than as expressions of technocratic expertise; therefore, projects must be developed through the formation of reciprocal and committed university-community partnerships

Clearly implied in the emergent consensus about these activities are the highly democratic underpinnings of the work. Service-learning is not merely another learning strategy, for it has an expressly civic intent. It is collaborative and collective work that addresses pressing problems by understanding the complex contextual environments in which they occur. Service-learning also explodes the notion of students as empty vessels that need to be filled with knowledge, or where deposits of information need to be placed (Freire 1970). It turns passive learners into active civic agents.

In addition to a proliferation of how-to materials, various initiatives aimed at promoting institutional change were launched. In 1991, Campus Compact created the Integrating Service with Academic Study (ISAS) initiative, which was funded by the Ford Foundation. Over the next three summers, ISAS worked with teams from more than sixty institutions, helping them integrate service-learning into their curricula. The initiative also funded 130 service-learning workshops nationwide and developed a host of written materials and sample syllabi from a wide range of disciplines. Perhaps service-learning was most significantly advanced by the creation of the Corporation for National and Community Service in 1993. Learn and Serve America, the service-learning and higher education component of the corporation, became one of the most important funding sources for "enhanc[ing] students' civic skills through service-learning." A 1999 RAND report indicates that: "LSAHE awarded approximately $10 million in direct grants to about 100 higher education institutions and community organizations for each of the three years from Fiscal Year 1995 through Fiscal Year 1997. Through subgranting, these funds reached close to 500 higher education institutions — nearly one of every eight colleges and universities nationwide" (Gray et al. 1999).

These funds were an extremely important lever for securing the support of senior administrators for community and civic engagement initiatives on many campuses. The growth of service-learning as a pedagogy is reflected in part in Campus Compact's rising membership, from 305 in 1992 (the year before the corporation was established) to 650 in 1999, since service-learning was the principal thrust of the organization's work during the 1990s.

Democratizing Scholarship

Other changes were stirring in the academy as well. Specifically, there were efforts aimed at reconceptualizing the core work of faculty. In 1990, Ernest Boyer offered a broader conception of faculty work in *Scholarship Reconsidered*, one of the most influential higher education texts of the twentieth century (Braxton, Luckey, and Holland 2002). According to Boyer's close collaborator, Eugene Rice, the book "reframed the issues so that we could get beyond the old teaching-versus-research debate, rise above the theory/practice hierarchy plaguing the discussion of scholarship, and begin to think in new ways about the alignment of faculty priorities and institutional mission" (Rice 2005, p. 17).

Boyer's ideas were significantly advanced by the Carnegie Foundation for the Advancement of Teaching's partnership with the American Association for Higher Education (AAHE), and by the launching in 1991 of an annual Forum on Faculty Roles and Rewards, which drew thousands of administrators and faculty from across the country to rethink faculty roles (Miller 2005) and to reconsider which practices ought to count as scholarly activities and products. Such efforts had considerable effects over time. One idea that achieved particular salience was the need to move beyond a model that excessively privileged expert knowledge and that recognized only disciplinary venues (peer-reviewed journals) as arbiters of what constituted a scholarly product. Faculty members increasingly worked in concert with community partners. New methodologies, such as participatory action research, gained ground and established their legitimacy as useful means of generating new knowledge.

Institutional structures, such as centers aimed at promoting university-community partnerships, developed to encourage such reciprocal arrangements (Harkavy and Wiewel 1995). These activities resulted in significant shifts in institutional behavior. In one recent survey of 729 chief academic officers (provosts and vice presidents for academic affairs), two thirds (68 percent) said that their institutions had developed policies or engaged in efforts to encourage and reward a broader definition of scholarship (O'Meara and Rice 2005). The general direction of these changes was toward teaching, research, and learning that was more democratic.

It is important to underscore the role that students played as partners in advancing these various efforts. Without the passionate interest of many students in becoming involved in their communities, institutional initiatives would have lacked a vital energy necessary for growth and success. A significant motivation for faculty involvement in service-learning (especially important because community-based teaching and learning take far more preparation time than conventional, lecture-based teaching) has been the enthusiastic response of students to this pedagogy. As one early study found, a major reason why faculty chose to teach service-learning courses was that those courses "[improve] student satisfaction with education" (Hammond 1994). Given the limited resources of professional staff that institutions generally contribute to promoting community-based activities, students have played a key role by serving as point persons for various university-community partnerships.

A Higher, Democratic Aim

As we have written about elsewhere, a significant limiting factor for civic engagement efforts on campuses has been what we call "disciplinary ethnocentrism, tribalism, and guildism" (Benson, Harkavy, and Hartley 2005). Colleges and universities are bound by powerful norms as to what sorts of activities are appropriate expressions of scholarship. In an effort to produce "new" scholarship, disciplinary specialists find themselves mining ever more obscure and esoteric veins of knowledge. The question, of course, is whether scholarship of this sort is primarily what the world needs. A report that elegantly employs disciplinary expertise to analyze a situation in the community often falls under the rubric of "service" when faculty productivity is being evaluated. Peer-reviewed articles in top-tier journals remain the coin of the realm at the majority of institutions. Happily, there are efforts being made in some disciplines to counter this trend. (The work of Michael Burroway and others in advancing the concept of "public sociology" is illustrative.) These efforts attempt to return the disciplines to their initial purpose of producing knowledge to improve human life, thereby rejecting the current solipsistic approach of knowledge of the discipline, by the discipline, and for the discipline.

In more recent years that movement has broadened its efforts and sought to advance a larger agenda aimed at strengthening democracy. Such a goal cannot be achieved without the full partnership of students. On hundreds of campuses across thirty states, students were leaders in the "Raise Your Voice" campaign, an effort sponsored by Campus Compact and the Pew Charitable Trusts (Cone, Kiesa, and Longo 2006). Students engaged in a range of activities such as asset-mapping on their campuses and in their communities, organizing public dialogues on a host of societal and community issues, including literacy, hunger, child care, and the war in Iraq.

When the efforts of the academy shift away from a disciplinary emphasis toward one that seeks to grapple with pressing and significant real-world problems, new and powerful possibilities for learning and change emerge. Our own experience at the University of Pennsylvania (Penn) offers one example in which the leadership of students redirected the attention of a number of individuals toward something of great importance to West Philadelphia, the community in which the university is located. In the spring and summer of 2002, a group of undergraduates at the university, who were participating in an academically based community service seminar offered by one of us (Ira Harkavy), decided to focus their research and service on one of the most important issues identified by members of the West Philadelphia community—the issue of health. The students' work with the community ultimately led them to propose establishing a center focused on health promotion and disease prevention at a public school in West Philadelphia, the Sayre Middle School. The public school is in many respects the ideal location for health-care programs, as well as other programs that serve the neighborhood: it is not only where children learn but also where community residents gather and participate in a variety of activities.

From their research, the students learned that community-oriented projects of this sort often founder because of their inability to secure stable resources. They postulated that a powerful way of accomplishing their goal would be to devise meaningful ways to integrate issues of health into the curricula at schools at Penn and at the Sayre School itself. They argued that the health promotion and disease prevention center at the school could serve as a learning venue for medical, dental, nursing, arts and sciences, social work, education, design, and business students. Their proposal proved to be so compelling that it led to the development of a school-based Community Health Promotion and Disease Prevention Center at Sayre Middle School. The center was formally launched in January of 2003. It functions as the central component of a university-assisted community school designed both to advance student learning and democratic development and to help strengthen families and institutions within the community. Penn faculty and students in medicine, nursing, dentistry, social work, arts and sciences, and design, as well as, to a lesser extent, other schools, now work at Sayre, which became a high school in 2007, through new and existing courses, internships, and research projects. Health promotion and service activities are also integrated into the Sayre students' curriculum. In effect, Sayre students serve as agents of health-care change in the Sayre neighborhood (Benson, Harkavy, and Puckett 2007). (It is worth noting that one of the undergraduates who developed the Sayre project, Mei Elansary, received the 2003 Howard R. Swearer Humanitarian Award, given by Campus Compact to students for outstanding public service.)

This example of student leadership underscores how working to solve real-world problems can serve as the organizing principle of university-community partnerships. This approach, Problem-Solving Learning (PSL), is conceptually close to Problem-Based Learning (PBL), which has been employed in professional schools for three decades, having originated at the medical school at Canada's McMaster University. But Problem-Solving Learning is different in that the focus is on *solving* a pressing problem in the real world. It invites people with various kinds of knowledge and expertise (disciplinary and practical), including faculty, students, and community members, to work together on societally significant issues, such as poverty, inadequate healthcare, substandard housing, and hunger, as those issues are manifested locally. Such an approach, which is embedded in many service-learning courses at Penn, derives from John Dewey's theory of learning, summarized in the following quotation: "Thinking begins in . . . a forked road situation, a situation which is ambiguous, which presents a dilemma, which poses alternatives" (Dewey 1910/1990, p. 11). In our judgment, focusing on the local manifestations of important real-world community problems is the best way to apply Dewey's proposition in practice.

Academically based community service courses (the term used at Penn to describe problem-solving service-learning) do more than provide hands-on experience for students and an opportunity for them to apply disciplinary knowledge, though they certainly do provide those benefits. These courses enable all of the partners—community members, faculty, staff, students, and children—to participate actively in solving real-world problems in all their social, cultural, and political complexity. Problem-solving learning encourages participants to respond to problems democratically, since the ideas, insights, and knowledge of academics, students (at all levels of schooling), teachers, and community members are needed if genuine solutions are to be found and implemented.

In spite of what we judge to be its obvious benefits, problem-solving learning is not widely practiced. Among other things, it is difficult to change longstanding, if dysfunctional, approaches, which Benjamin Franklin critically characterized in 1789 as "ancient Customs and Habitudes" (Best 1962, p. 173). To reduce obstacles to change and to stimulate discussion and debate, we propose that higher education institutions take the following step to advance problem-solving learning and the education of students for democratic, collaborative leadership: *act locally and democratically*. This proposal is derived from one of John Dewey's most significant propositions: "Democracy must begin at home, and its home is the neighborly community" (Dewey 1927/1954, p. 213). Democracy, Dewey emphasized, has to be built on face-to-face interactions in which human beings work together cooperatively to solve the ongoing problems of life. In effect, we are updating Dewey and advocating this proposition: democracy must begin at home, and its home is the engaged, neighborly college or university and its local community partner.

We have found the benefits of a local focus for college and university civic engagement programs to be manifold. Ongoing, continuous interaction is facilitated by working in an easily accessible local setting. Relationships of trust, so essential for effective partnerships and effective learning, are also built through day-to-day work on problems and issues of mutual concern. In addition, the local community also provides a convenient setting in which service-learning courses, Problem Solving Learning courses, and community-based research courses in different disciplines can work together to solve a complex problem and produce substantive results. Work in a college or university's local community, by facilitating interaction across schools and disciplines, can create interdisciplinary learning opportunities. And finally, the local community is a democratic, real-world learning site in which community members, faculty members, and students can pragmatically determine whether their work is making a real difference, whether both the neighborhood and the institution are better off as a result of common efforts.

The above recommendation provides a strategy for putting into practice the primary argument of this chapter: democratic, problem-solving service-learning, focused on specific, universal problems that are manifested in a university's locality, is a promising approach for developing effective civic leadership and for realizing the democratic purposes of the civic engagement movement. PSL underscores the idea that solving important problems requires democratic collaboration. And, as we see it, collaborative, democratic leadership is the kind of leadership needed to create a better society and world.

REFERENCES

American Political Science Association Task Force on Civic Education in the 21st Century. (1998). Expanded articulation statement. PS: Political Science and Politics 31 (September): 636–37.

Bellah, R. N., R. Madsen, W. M. Sullivan, A. Swidler, and S. M. Tipton. (1985). Habits of the heart. Berkeley: University of California Press.

Benson, L., and I. Harkavy. (October 6–7, 2002). Truly engaged and truly democratic cosmopolitan civic universities, community schools, and development of the democratic good of society in the 21st century. Paper presented at the Seminar on the Research University as Local Citizen, University of California, San Diego.

Benson, L., I. Harkavy, and M. Hartley. (2005). Integrating a commitment to the public good into the institutional fabric. In *Higher education for the public good: Emerging voices from a national movement*, ed. A. J. Kezar, T. Chambers, and J. Burkhardt, 185–216. San Francisco: Jossey-Bass.

Benson, L., I. Harkavy, and J. Puckett. (2007). *Dewey's dream: Universities and democracies in an age of education reform*. Philadelphia: Temple University Press.

Best, J. H. (1962). *Benjamin Franklin on education*. New York: Teachers College, Columbia University.

Bloom, A. (1987). *The closing of the American mind*. New York: Simon and Schuster.

Bloom, D., M. Hartley, and H. Rosovsky. (2006). Beyond private gain: The public benefits of higher education. In *International handbook of higher education*, ed. P. G. Altbach and J. Forrest, 293–308. The Netherlands: Springer.

Boyer, E. (1987). *College: The undergraduate experience in America*. New York: HarperCollins.

———. (1990). *Scholarship reconsidered*. Princeton, NJ: Carnegie Foundation for the Advancement of Teaching.

Braxton, J., W. Luckey, and P. Holland. (2002). *Institutionalizing a broader view of scholarship through Boyer's four domains*. Vol. 29. San Francisco: Jossey-Bass.

Breneman, D. W. (1994). *Liberal arts colleges: Thriving, surviving, or endangered?* Washington, D.C.: Brookings Institution.

Brint, S. (2002). The rise of the "practical arts." In *The future of the city of intellect*, ed. S. Brint, 231–59. Stanford, CA: Stanford University Press.

Campus Compact. (1987). Campus Compact at AAHE: Linking service with learning. *Campus Compact Newsletter* 1, no. 1 (April). Brown University, Providence, RI.

Cawallader, M. L. (1982). A manifesto: The case for an academic counterrevolution. *Liberal Education* 68: 403–20.

Coalition of College Presidents for Civic Responsibility. (1986). *Coalition of College Presidents for Civic Responsibility, Georgetown University, Washington, D.C. January 16, 1986.*

Cone, R. E., A. Kiesa, and N. V. Longo, eds. (2006). *Raise your voice: A student guide to making positive social change*. Boston: Campus Compact.

Dewey, J. (1910/1990). *How we think*. Boston: Heath.

———. (1927/1954). *The public and its problems*. Denver: Alan Swallow.

Freire, P. (1970). *Pedagogy of the oppressed*. New York: Herder and Herder.

Gray, M. J., E. H. Ondaatje, S. Geshwind, R. Fricker, C. Goldman, T. Kaganoff, et al. (1999). *Combining service and learning in higher education: Evaluation of the Learn and Serve America Higher Education Program*. Santa Monica, CA: RAND Education.

Hammond, C. (1994). Integrating service and academic study: Faculty motivation and satisfaction in Michigan higher education. *Michigan Journal of Community Service Learning* 1 (1): 21–28.

Harkavy, I., and M. Hartley. (2008). Pursuing Franklin's democratic vision for higher education. *Peer Review* 10 (23): 13–17.

Harkavy, I., and W. Wiewel. (1995). Overview: University-community partnerships: Current state and future issues. *Metropolitan University* 6 (3): 7–14.

Hartley, M. (2002). *A call to purpose: Mission-centered change at three liberal arts colleges*. New York: Routledge Falmer.

Hartley, M., and E. Hollander. (2005). The elusive ideal: Civic learning and higher education. In *Institutions of democracy: The public schools*, ed. S. Fuhrman and M. Lazerson, 252–76. Oxford: Oxford University Press.

Hollander, E., and M. Hartley. (2000). Civic renewal in higher education: The state of the movement and the need for a national network. In *Civic responsibility and higher education*, ed. T. Ehrlich, 345–66. Phoenix, AZ: Orynx Press.

Keller, G. (1983). *Academic strategy: The management revolution in higher education*. Baltimore: Johns Hopkins University Press.

Kendall, J. C., and Associates, ed. (1990). *Combining service and learning: A resource book for community and public service*. Raleigh, NC: National Society for Experiential Education.

Kezar, A. J., T. Chambers, and J. Burkhardt, eds. (2005). *Higher education for the public good: Emerging voices from a national movement*. San Francisco: Jossey-Bass.

Lasch, C. (1978). *The culture of narcissism*. New York: W. W. Norton.

Marchese, T. J. (1986). College: Raising a new vision. *Change* 18 (6): 10–17.

Meisel, W. (1984). Walk for action [Pamphlet]. Cambridge, MA.

Miller, M. A. (2005). AAHE's legacy. *Change* 37 (5): 8–13.

Newman, F. (1985). *Higher education and the American resurgence*. Princeton, NJ: Carnegie Foundation for the Advancement of Teaching.

O'Meara, K., and R. E. Rice, eds. (2005). *Faculty priorities reconsidered*. San Francisco: Jossey-Bass.

Pollard, J. E. (1952). *History of the Ohio State University: The story of its first seventy-five years*. Columbus: Ohio State University Press.

Putnam, R. D. (1995). Bowling alone. *Journal of Democracy* 6 (1): 65–78.

Reuben, J. (1996). *The making of the modern university: Intellectual transformation and the marginalization of morality*. Chicago: University of Chicago Press.

Rhoads, R. A. (1998). *Freedom's web*. Baltimore: Johns Hopkins University Press.

Rhodes, R. (2009). Learning from students as agents of social change: Toward an emancipatory vision of the university. *Journal of Change Management* 9 (3): 309–22.

Rice, R. E. (2005). Scholarship reconsidered: History and context. In *Faculty priorities reconsidered: Rewarding multiple forms of scholarship*, ed. K. O'Meara and R. E. Rice, 17–31. San Francisco: Jossey-Bass.

Rudolph, F. (1962). *The American college and university: A history*. New York: Alfred A. Knopf.

Sax, L. J., A. Astin, W. S. Korn, and K. M. Mahoney. (1999). *The American freshman: National norms for fall 1999*. Los Angeles: Higher Education Research Institute.

Smith, P. (1990). *Killing the spirit: Higher education in America*. New York: Viking Press.

Stanton, T. K. (1990). Integrating public service with academic study: The faculty role. A report of Campus Compact.

Sykes, C. J. (1989). *ProfScam*. New York: St. Martin's Press.

Kathleen Knight Abowitz, Stephanie Raill
Jayanandhan, and Sarah Woiteshek

Public and Community-Based Leadership Education

> By "public leadership," we mean the acts, great and small, of individuals and groups as they tackle challenges facing a community or society.
>
> (Gergen n.d.)

> At their best, community leaders create the social space in which citizens can recognize their own interests, assess the community's needs and opportunities, share their beliefs and ideas, and create a pathway to put shared beliefs into action in pursuing the good. This understanding of leadership signals a "Copernican turn" from leadership revolving around the superiority of leaders to leadership revolving around the authoritative action of followers—in the exercise of their freedom and power.
>
> (Schweigert 2007, p. 327)

Leadership studies and leadership education, fields of research and practice in higher education since the mid-twentieth century, have recently evolved to encompass more collaborative, adaptive, and relational leadership practices. This evolution is a movement away from a singular focus on trait-based and position-based theories of leadership, following Burns's call (1978) for more compelling, creative, moral, and intellectual foundations for leadership theory and practice. Since that time, we have seen the proliferation of inclusive and process-oriented leadership models—what has been called the postindustrial paradigm—with an increasing emphasis on social responsibility and integrity, as a trend shaping leadership education programs in U.S. colleges and universities (Faris and Outcalt 2001). Many of these new models insist that leadership is a process of fostering change to transform society, to "empower change agents" to "work for the betterment of others" (Understanding the social change model of leadership development, para. 1). The emergence of these models has been well documented and signals a promising shift in the overall directions of leadership theory and practice in this new millennium. A similar yet distinct trend attempts to renew an old tradition within leadership studies, the study of public leadership, and explicitly to resituate it in relation to the contemporary challenges and contexts of the cities, towns, communities, and regions in which institutions of higher education are located. Public leadership, widely associated with the work of elected officials, is a term that includes thousands of others serving in civic capacities: appointees, community activists, educators, nonprofit officials, and others whose work affects our civil society and wider social life.

While these broad shifts are promising, we believe that the specific context of educating for and enacting leadership in the public sphere necessitates a particular approach to leadership education and understanding of the leader's role. In this chapter, we call this specific approach *public and community-based leadership*. We provide definitional statements and a rationale for this approach and then outline practical suggestions for enacting public and community-based leadership education in higher education.

We begin with a definition of leadership and an analysis of its key concepts. *Leadership, practiced in and for public life, is comprised of the actions of citizens who convene, deliberate, inquire, collaborate, and act with the intent to improve life for fellow citizens in their communities and the larger society.* In describing this model of leadership, we use three key terms: public, community, and of course, leadership itself. We begin our analysis with perhaps the most common but least understood of these three concepts.

Public refers to the ideal of shared, diverse, and "universally accessible dimensions of collective life, as well as those things which have a general impact upon the interests of all; the realm of interdependence" (Cooper 2001, p. 55). The public is a more defined and specific site than the social, a term often found in the new leadership education literature and that often includes social change as a central value. While *social* signals the characteristics of living, coexisting organisms as they interact and share common systems and meanings, *public* refers to a specific political ideal commonly espoused in democratic nation-states. It is a notion reaching back thousands of years to the early Greek city-states in the earliest documented forms of democratic governance. The public is a "pluralist, heterogeneous social space of many different interests, viewpoints, and community histories," where the aim is "common action on public problems" (Boyte 1993, p. 766). The public is the realm of political activities, large and small, formal and informal, a space where people come together to do the difficult work of solving collective problems in the face of competing interests and multiple viewpoints. Public work requires "acknowledging differences in interest and power and working alongside people with whom we might disagree deeply about moral issues. It means recognizing that no one perspective or interest usually suffices for adequate resolution of public problems" (Boyte 1993, p. 764).

Public is not a term that narrowly refers to government agencies. Nor are public leaders only those who are elected or appointed to work as public officials, though this is the meaning that has had the greatest influence in the field of public leadership studies, which is dominated by political scientists and historians. The study of public leadership in leadership research has mostly comprised the "great man" tradition of leadership theory, the study of those who have occupied high political office or who have been authoritative and positional political leaders in history. As Kellerman and Webster point out, the actual theory and practice of public leadership is far broader and more diffuse than the scholarly literature suggests, and "there is a great deal of work on public leadership that does not so self-describe" (2001, p. 511). Still, this body of work is relatively sparse in comparison to writing on other approaches to leadership. This trend can be explained, in part, by the erosion of general interest in public life and a decline in its perceived value, which has been well documented by historians, social scientists, and philosophers alike. The concept of public itself is becoming more vague and meaningless to new generations of youth and adults in the United States (Putnam 1995; Cohen 2003; Galston 2004; Hannay 2005). One way to counter this erosion of public meanings and shared public life is to reclaim and broaden leadership education programs so that they are inclusive of a clearly public orientation (see Longo and Shaffer 2009). The conception of leadership we offer here tries to do just that.

Joined to the emphasis on public leadership is a focus on community. While public is a term emphasizing difference and heterogeneity in an inclusive and broad sphere, community refers to the common values, interests, and concerns that are built in the social and cultural contexts of neighborhoods, towns, villages, and regions. Community refers to both the commonalities found and created in these contexts among groups of people, and the communication that helps construct and maintain the relational ties that bind these groups. The public is a network of many diverse communities interconnected in limitless formations.

Community-based leadership has an intended double meaning here. It refers to leadership education situated within real places and cultural contexts, in the regions in which colleges and universities are located, as well as to the vehicle through which the learning of leadership itself occurs. In the first meaning, leadership is learned within and through the practice of leadership as experienced in collaboration with local communities. Students learn leadership through work with community citizen-leaders, who serve as both collaborators and role models for leadership work (Couto 1992). As Rossing notes, learning leadership in communities entails the critical task of building relationships and constructing shared purposes: "In the new forms of community that must form the essential building blocks of effective future public and organizational life, the practice of leadership must change. Gardner emphasizes the importance of widespread participation in defining and pursuing shared purposes. 'Leaders must devolve initiative and responsibility widely throughout the system,' (1989, p. 79). Rost (1993) defines this new form of leadership. 'Leadership is an influence relationship among leaders and their collaborators who intend real changes that reflect their mutual purposes.'" (Rossing 1998, p. 99)

But community-based leadership education also refers to the pedagogy and curricular design of such leadership programs. Community-based leadership learning is ideally situated in learning communities where students, faculty, staff, and community partners all play key roles in, and assume responsibility for, teaching, learning, acting, reflecting, and evaluating leadership work and learning outcomes. Again, Rossing explains: "Powerful new approaches to community leadership development, in the short term, can be based on establishing situated, yet temporary, action-focused learning communities that consciously practice and test new modes of shared leadership, collaboration and community building, and that support learners in applying their new learning in their action-based home or organizational communities" (Rossing 1998, p. 72).

A recent analysis of undergraduate leadership programs backs up Rossing's assertion. Eich found three general attributes common to high-quality undergraduate leadership programs: "(a) participants engaged in building and sustaining a learning community, (b) student-centered experiential learning experiences; and (c) research-grounded continuous program development" (2008, p. 176). Community is a central concept for the new leadership paradigms emerging today, and learning within and about community contexts is a central element of the public and community-based leadership model we are discussing here.

Finally but most critically, the term *leadership* must be clarified. Multiple and sometimes conflicting meanings of this term can be found in academic and popular literature. The definition we offer here, which draws from the discourses of public participation and community-based learning discussed above, focuses on the qualities and skills necessary for mobilizing citizens to tackle shared problems in the public sphere. *Leadership, practiced in and for public life, is comprised of the actions of citizens who convene, deliberate, inquire, collaborate, and act with the intent to improve life for fellow citizens in their communities and the larger society.* This definition has several important elements:

1. It identifies leadership as a practice with a specific moral purpose.
2. It is action-centered rather than person-centered

3. It involves a definable and flexible set of skills and capacities—all of which can be learned—thus emphasizing the belief that, as the saying goes, "great leaders are made, not born" (From Cohen 1998, in Goldsmith 2008, para. 1).

Although often described as a special human gift or capacity possessed by some individuals and not others, leadership is a practice, following Heifetz's notion (1994) of leadership as activity. A practice is a socially established, cooperative human activity that aims at human improvement, has normative standards that govern its activity, and adapts to local contexts and innovations over time. Like playing soccer, building furniture, or baking bread, leadership is a practice. As a practice, it has a commonly recognizable set of activities associated with it; when called *leadership*, these activities are aimed at improving our lives in some way (even when leaders are terribly wrong about what they think might improve our lives). Like soccer players, leaders must adapt their practices of leading to local conditions: players will consider field conditions and their opponents' strengths and weaknesses before establishing a game plan. Players in a rural village in India may play soccer using different techniques and approaches from those of players in Edinburgh or Brooklyn. Leadership practices must be similarly adaptable to contexts and conditions, though based on a set of skills and knowledge that are learned through both formal and informal programs and experiences. The soccer player has a knowledge of her craft; her practice is based on that knowledge, as well as her ability to adapt the practice as need demands.

The definition of leadership as a practice and activity helps us avoid the tendency, so prevalent in the leadership studies literature and popular culture depictions, to think of leadership capacity or talent as residing magically in individuals. The trait-based approach in leadership studies has represented a longstanding effort within the field to "reduce the ideal leader to his or her essence—the quintessential characteristics or competencies or behaviours of the leader" (Grint 2004, p. 19). Leaders are indeed people, but not isolated individuals operating as heroic loners, particularly in the public realm. Rather than focusing on the magical traits of leaders, our definition of leadership focuses on the knowledge, values, and skills leaders must learn in order to help solve problems in public and community life. Leadership, in its essential form, is the simple act of convening people and framing conversations that enable participants to become responsible and committed to shared action. "This conception of leadership is a shift from the dominant conventional belief system that the task of leadership is to set a vision, enroll others in it, and hold people accountable through measurements and reward" (A Small Group 2007, p. 10).

Education focused on public and community-based leadership requires initiating young adults into the specific knowledge, values, and skills that are necessary for this particular type and domain of leadership work. Leadership education that is specifically focused on the public and local or regional communities is particularly apt for higher education institutions today, as colleges and universities respond to the clarion call to rediscover and rededicate themselves to the public good (Glenn 2009; Kezar, Chambers, and Burkhardt 2005). As a recent report by the National Center for Public Policy and Higher Education noted, "The challenge for the years ahead is to achieve a public agenda in an era of diminished public purposes" (2008, p. 3).

Why Is Public and Community-Based Leadership Education an Important Focus for U.S. Higher Education Today?

The weakening of the public sphere has been well described by scholarly and popular commentators. Most famously, Putnam's "Bowling Alone" thesis (1995) linked diminishing social networks and ties with a decreased willingness and sense of obligation to participate in public life and decision-making forums. Independently wealthy people dominate the ranks of elected officials, and the influence of well-funded interest groups and corporate lobbyists is publicly acknowledged. In the current context of economic crisis, rates of public engagement in civic life have declined (National Conference on Citizenship 2009).

The picture of civic life in the United States is, of course, complex, and there are some recent signs that citizens may be reengaging with public and community life. The 2008 Civic Health Report shows that, while most Americans polled did not envision themselves participating in the political process beyond election day, a vast majority support publicly oriented policies such as national service and public deliberation initiatives; the 2009 report showed continued support for such initiatives (National Conference on Citizenship 2008, 2009). The 2009 renaming of the White House's Liaison Office as the Office of Public Engagement, done in consultation with numerous community groups and organizations that facilitate and promote public dialogue, indicates recognition of the value of public participation by citizens and holders of public office. Still, indicators of participation in both governance and community life continue to trail those of previous generations. And in many cases, the demographics of those active in public life are not representative of who is in the electorate, as elected and appointed officials tend to be far less racially and ethnically diverse, and far more wealthy, than the citizens they represent.

Concerns about the decline in social capital and public participation have helped push colleges and universities to place renewed focus on their civic mission and responsibilities. The continuing growth in the membership of Campus

Compact, which is committed to advancing the public purposes of higher education, is one sign of this affirmation (Campus Compact 2008). Another is rates of civic engagement among youth. Young people, particularly those with college experience, participate in community service in high numbers.

These trends in higher education are encouraging signs, yet they are largely disconnected from the dominant practices in leadership education programs in higher education today. These trends, moreover, are not leading to strong improvement in learning outcomes related to public and community-based leadership capacities. Findings from the College Senior Survey in 2007 reveal that just 27.6 percent of the 26,710 students taking the survey self-reported that, compared with when they first began college, they were stronger or much stronger in their "understanding of the problems facing your community" and 26.6 percent of respondents self-reported that they had improved in the "ability to get along with people of different races/cultures" (Spinosa, Sharkness, Pryor, and Liu 2008, p. 16).

There is a large gap in understanding and practice between the service and community engagement efforts of colleges and universities, and the discourses of public participation and leadership education. As noted above, current scholarship in leadership studies frames leadership as collaborative, adaptive, and relational. Too many university leadership education and leadership development programs, however, continue to shape leadership education around positional leadership roles (for example, offering leadership development opportunities targeted to organization leaders or student government participants). Too many programs espouse vision-driven orientations to leadership, according to which leadership means developing an individual vision for "change" and enlisting followers to realize that vision. (For example, the popular LeaderShape workshop is based on this model.) Such approaches to leadership education emphasize "selected qualities in exceptional individuals" and locate the work of leadership in individual leaders' efforts (Schweigert 2007, p. 327). Students are socialized into the expectations of positional leadership roles through the emphasis placed on organizational titles and the division between officers and members of a student organization. Students thus come to expect that their postcollege leadership work will follow these same patterns, yet this may not be the case with leadership in public life, which can be characterized by fluidity, deliberation, conflict, and the shared shaping of aims and vision, as well as informal leadership roles and capacities.

Leadership programs such as LeaderShape win accolades, are often popular among students, and are seen as a valuable part of college life. But they generally fail to link leadership with an understanding of public life and commitments, the contexts and demands of public settings and real communities. Such leadership programs do not go far enough in educating students for public problem solving and for their future roles as leaders in public settings: in neighborhoods, civic associations, or government positions. In addition, those types of leadership education increasingly fail to meet the leadership needs of the private sphere, as it too moves toward collaborative workplace structures and a greater orientation toward teamwork. But in the public sphere, collaboratively developing and realizing goals is not optional—it is a moral obligation. Schweigert describes this distinction in leadership education as a move away from a focus on individual leaders and toward understanding "the qualities of social settings that facilitate information exchange and deliberation on means and ends," to "'draw out' from residents their sense of citizen responsibility and authority to take action on behalf of their communities" (2007, p. 329).

Contemporary college students are lacking important knowledge and skills for engaging in public and community leadership work. We know that students who "have more frequent contact with diverse peers have greater attributional complexity, self-confidence in cultural awareness, development of a pluralistic orientation, a belief that conflict enhances democracy, and tend to vote in federal and state elections" (Hurtado 2003, p. 15). The National Survey of Student Engagement revealed "only 57% of first-year students and half of seniors receive substantial encouragement from their institutions to interact with students of different economic, social, and racial or ethnic backgrounds" (2008, p. 11). There are other indicators that college graduates are ill-prepared for the difficult deliberations of public life with diverse others. The Higher Education Research Institute designed the Multi-Institutional Study of Leadership assessment to collect data on students' leadership outcomes, surveying a total of 49,078 students from fifty-four colleges and universities in 2005. Two of the several "critical values" of leadership they assessed are "controversy with civility," the recognition that differences in viewpoint are inevitable and must be aired openly and civilly, and "change," the belief in the importance of making a better world and a better society for oneself and others, or the belief that individuals, groups, and communities have the ability to work together to make that change (Wagner 2006, pp. 8–10). "Of all the critical values assessed in the survey, students scored lowest on their self-reported abilities with these two critical values" (Dugan and Komives 2006, p. 16). Finally, the Higher Education Research Institute's *American Freshman* study (2009) documented a rising level of political interest among students but found that students consider their political skills quite limited. The 2009 survey included new questions about "skills for a diverse workplace." While first-year college students rate themselves highly in terms of tolerating those with different beliefs and in terms of working cooperatively with a diverse range of people, they rate themselves much lower on the important public skills of openness to having one's own views challenged, and the ability to discuss and negotiate controversial issues. Tellingly, these were framed as "workplace" as opposed to public or civic skills. Sadly, the phrase *public life* would likely be a nonstarter survey question for many college students and nonstudents alike.

Public and community-based leadership education thus fills a void in current efforts in higher education leadership programs. It helps broaden and deepen education for leadership for the communities, regions, and states that have a shared stake in the educational outcomes of colleges and universities. It links the growing trends of college student volunteering and community service to the critical need for publicly oriented, community-based leadership in the United States today. It helps develop more and more skilled leaders for the shared problems of today and tomorrow that face the communities and world in which we live.

How Do We Optimally Enact Public and Community-Based Leadership Education in Today's College and University Settings?

Public and community-based leadership education requires a number of programmatic and content considerations. First, what is the best place within institutions to house or locate such educational programs? Second, what kinds of content knowledge should be given the highest priority in terms of setting the curriculum or desired learning outcomes for students? Third, what sorts of capacities or skill-based abilities are important to learn for public and community-based leadership? And finally, what pedagogies are best suited to engage students with this type of leadership learning and development? We will address each of these questions. While we realize that program development is highly context-dependent, we present some parameters here that are consistent with the view of public and community-based leadership education articulated in this chapter.

Where Do Such Programs "Fit" in Our Institutions?

In higher education, leadership programs for undergraduates have either resided in academic departments or in student affairs units. Academic units related to business, communications, organizational theory, political science, and government are common sites for undergraduate course work in leadership. Student affairs units related to student activities and Greek life are among the most common places in which to find leadership education and training outside the curricular realm. It is rare to find leadership programs that bridge this pervasive divide in higher education, because our colleges and universities still tend to separate student academic and cocurricular realms of learning. Yet to meaningfully educate the whole person for leadership, multiple organizational strengths are necessary. Both academic expertise and student affairs expertise are needed. Leadership education is powerful when it marries the knowledge of the cocurricular and curricular spheres. From student affairs practitioners, knowledge of the whole student and student development theory provides a student-centered view; from faculty, discipline-based content knowledge enables public leaders to prepare for action in a complex society and world. As stated by the editor of *Learning Reconsidered*, "*learning* is a comprehensive, holistic, transformative activity that integrates *academic learning* and *student development*, processes that have often been considered separate, and even independent of each other" (Keeling 2004, p. 2; emphasis in original).

From academic affairs comes the depth of disciplinary content knowledge. Typical leadership education programs utilize some combination of a few disciplines, such as management, organizational theory, or political science. But public and community-based leadership demands that disciplinary and professional knowledge in a wide array of arenas—the humanities, the social sciences, sciences, and the arts—be brought to bear on public problem solving. Students learn to practice public leadership "through a learning process that teaches them how to understand and embed their professional and disciplinary knowledge within a repertoire of civic concepts" (Boyte 1993, p. 764). Programs that link one, or better yet, multiple disciplines in a curriculum oriented toward public leadership help students bring professional knowledge to public settings and deliberations in more effective ways.

From student affairs comes expertise in community engagement practices, student development theory, and leadership development for undergraduate students. Student affairs professionals bring expertise in the cognitive, interpersonal, and moral development of students, along with a more holistic sense of students' learning needs and interests than do most faculty. Student affairs staff also consider building learning communities on campus to be a central part of their professional purpose. As stated earlier, public and community-based leadership education is not just community-based in its orientation toward the communities that surround colleges and universities. It is also based on a philosophy of teaching and learning that is communal. Students learn about community leadership in community with one another, their faculty teachers, and their community mentors and supervisors who serve as role models and coaches for their leadership work.

While institutional arrangements may vary, public and community-based leadership education requires multiple institutional stakeholders, including community partners themselves. Too often, higher education programs design community-based learning with a deficit approach in mind, where university experts (faculty) and experts-in-training (students) work to "fix" deficits in the community. While program structure and design for leadership education, as well as particular critical-learning objectives, are ultimately the responsibility of faculty and staff employed by the university, communities and their leaders must be true partners and collaborators in the work and help shape program design. Both community and university representatives bring their "own experience and expertise to the project," but this kind of reciprocity "requires a substantial change in the prevalent culture of academic institutions" (Lynton, quoted in Saltmarsh, Hartley, and Clayton 2009, p. 9). Too often, higher education engagement with community is framed in such a way as to position colleges and universities as the source of expertise and knowledge to solve community problems. Public and community leadership programs should not seek an expert model in designing community-based learning, but cultivate opportunities for leadership learning in collaborative and problem-oriented work with community leaders and partners. Such a model uses university expertise where possible, but it is primarily oriented toward cultivating shared understanding and knowledge that are the fruit of successful, collaborative problem solving.

On What Types of Content Knowledge Should We Focus in Leadership Education?

"Leadership . . . is different from management and governance" (Safty 2003, p. 84). Most would agree with this statement, yet many leadership studies programs continue to be based on these disciplinary orientations. While the content knowledge for generic kinds of leadership may well be found in the fields related to management and governance, public and community-based leaders will need to rely on far more diverse and interdisciplinary sources of knowledge for their practice. We suggest three sources of knowledge that are of critical importance to public and community-based leadership, and for which we can draw on multiple disciplines: sociocultural, place-based, and political.

Sociocultural leadership has been explained as follows: "Developing community leadership begins with recognizing that both the practice of leadership and the situation in which it occurs need to be understood. We consider leadership as a collective relational phenomenon. This collective relational phenomenon is also 'cultured,' that is, it is a phenomenon that grows out of, and is a product of its setting. It is what we call sociocultural leadership" (Kirk and Shutte 2004, p. 235).

Learning community leadership is facilitated by social and cultural knowledge of the communities, cultures, and regions in which higher education is situated. Such knowledge can be derived from a wealth of disciplines, departments, or sources outside the university itself, including community leaders, elders, and texts. Departments devoted to subjects ranging from anthropology, history, and environmental studies to geography and education might provide students with the kinds of sociocultural knowledge that will enable them better to understand the communities and regions in which they will learn and practice leadership. An American studies curriculum on globalization gives students at Miami University a theoretical set of lenses through which to examine local challenges in the region, including immigration, local food movements, and urban decay in deindustrializing America. These examinations lead to informed, collaborative action with community partners on behalf of local efforts to address such issues (Longo and Shaffer 2008).

Public and community-based learning is not abstract; it must be tied to a place or places that are concrete, meaningful, and fraught with the realities and contradictions of genuine communities (Longo and Raill Jayanandhan 2008). Place-based leadership learning not only helps students situate their leadership practices in a real setting, on projects that potentially contribute to public problem solving that is local and regional, but also helps students learn how to learn about place. In a very mobile time of their lives, during which young people are typically moving from one geographical area to another, this learning how to learn about the places in which they reside is tremendously important for cultivating the local social and cultural knowledge in which community problems are situated. Capacities for discovering and tapping into local networks, politics, and organizations that are engaged in public problem solving constitute transportable skills that are useful for future community leaders to learn.

A third important but often ignored knowledge base necessary for public and community-based leadership is that of political engagement and power relations. Kirk and Shutte describe this in their discussion of community-based leadership, a practice that "should not be a picture of a group of people working harmoniously with their shared values and beliefs, in joint endeavour, with unity of purpose. This romantic and sentimental hue with its unitary perspective, that was part of the Human Relations thinking in the 1950s about organization, depended on a 'well knit group.' The reality of people working in teams from the same or from different organizations is the existence of differing political agendas and unequal power distribution. This places a greater value on the rigour of collaboration through plurality. It requires in our view a more robust view of leadership able to engage with the hard realities (not just the sound bytes) of concepts like inclusivity, collaboration and diversity" (2004, p. 237).

Boyte echoes this view, describing the civic challenge before us not as one of graduating more experts at governance or management, nor as one of helping students learn how to build perfect moral and political consensus on public problems. Rather, our work should be to enable students to "cultivate the public leadership skills that allow people to work productively with others, whether or not they like or agree with each other" (1993, p. 764). Such skills are based on knowledge of the formal and informal politics that are at the heart of public life. Learning about the exercise of power in civic and public life and in political institutions and structures, and about the ways in which distinct political interests can deliberate and attempt to reach achievable, acceptable solutions for all parties involved, is a critical knowledge base for public leadership work.

Social and cultural knowledge of communities, the sense of local and regional place, and the knowledge of political engagement can all be learned through various disciplines or majors, but they can also be learned in the community itself. But without the capacities to think about the social, cultural, place-based, and political aspects of public leadership, our future leaders will be operating from the leadership playbook without understanding the real, concrete practices of leadership in diverse communities and public settings.

What Sorts of Capacities Are Important for Public and Community-Based Leaders to Learn?

Leadership is ultimately defined by action. The practice of public and community-based leadership is based on eight distinct but overlapping abilities that should form the skill content of educational efforts:

- *Convening*: the ability to bring multiple interests to the (metaphorical) table for collaboration, deliberation, and exchange. This is one of the most basic but most challenging tasks of leadership work. "We might say that leadership is the capacity to invite, name the debate, and design gatherings" (A Small Group 2007, p. 10). How does a leader get the right set of diverse community citizens to the table to work on common problems? How do we create real and virtual spaces for busy citizens to come together?

- *Inquiry*: the ability to ask good questions, seek reliable information through trustworthy sources, and seek multiple perspectives and a diversity of community citizens' input, for knowledge forms the foundation of community-based leadership. Community-based research skills and resources enable students to conduct various kinds of inquiry to understand the communities and public problems of their locality or region.

- *Collaboration*: the ability to work with diverse others in ways that utilize the strengths and voices of all for the benefit of everyone. Collaboration with diverse individuals and coalitions is necessary in all types of leadership, from public to community to business contexts. Collaborating with diverse others involves a set of interpersonal skills including listening, dialogue, identifying mutual concerns, compromising, and the willingness to share resources and "turf."

- *Naming and framing*: the ability to help a group of people name and frame the issues and problems that they face together. The way we name and frame public problems has enormous consequences for whether we can successfully tackle these challenges; problems that are not named and framed in ways that resonate with community members' experiences will not elicit the kinds of input and involvement that public problem solving requires in our communities. In her study of students involved in a "political civic leadership development" opportunity, Janc draws a clear connection between students' civic leadership development and their ability to understand and frame complex problems: "Students as civic leaders recognize a particular set of issues on their campuses that need to be addressed via policy recommendations, forums, or public testimonies, and educate themselves through the Board and respective campuses on the complexities of these concerns" (n.d., p. 12).

- *Deliberating*: the ability to find and use one's political voice to seek with other citizens the solutions to complex problems facing our communities. Public deliberation models vary, but they have in common the assumption that diverse citizens, representing multiple and often conflicting interests, must come together to weigh competing values and try to arrive at reasonable solutions acceptable to all. Deliberation abilities are related to some of the key communication skills necessary for collaboration that were described above, including listening, speaking clearly, and building consensus.

- *Conflict management*: the ability to use conflict to seek creative and productive outcomes of human difference and controversy, which are unavoidable aspects of public and community existence. Collaboration and deliberation will yield conflicts of various kinds; public leaders must be able skillfully to harness these differences.

- *Action with integrity*: the ability to take action on behalf of finding or enacting solutions to public problems. Integrity in public leadership involves qualities of transparency, honesty, and responsibility to others. Leadership practice in public arenas, in concert with community citizens, is a powerful learning application with regard to real-world ethical questions that naturally arise in such work. Recent calls for ethical leadership from public and private arenas alike point to the urgency of helping students learn how to grapple intelligently with such questions.

- *Reflection*: the ability to take stock of one's own actions and contexts in order to understand, assess, evaluate, and become more responsive and effective in leadership work. Alma Blount, Director of Duke's Hart Leadership Program, explains that "critical reflection is not about distancing yourself from experience, but rather about cultivating an attentive awareness of your current circumstances. It is an approach for being more grounded in the here and now and has strong utilitarian functions as a diagnostic and intervention tool for problem-solving work in organizations, institutions, and social systems" (2006, p. 272).

What Pedagogies Are Best Suited to Public and Community-Based Education?

Eich's study of effective undergraduate leadership programs highlights the importance of three program attributes that were common to all the programs surveyed: "(a) participants engaged in building and sustaining a learning community; (b) student-centered experiential learning experiences; and (c) research-grounded continuous program development" (2008, p. 176). These findings underscore the need for community structures to support student learning, the central role of experience and reflection, and the need for assessment practices that help ensure that the curriculum continues to respond to student and community needs.

Schweigert puts it a different way; he states that learning about community-based leadership "can be summarized in three basic dynamics: belonging, paying attention, and practicing" (2007, p. 329). The power of belonging to a group of student peers, faculty and staff educators, and community collaborators and mentors makes leadership learning meaningful and creates a natural setting in which to teach concepts and skills of integrity (responsibility to others), collaboration, deliberation, inquiry, and conflict management. "Paying attention" for Schweigert signals the power of observation and experimentation for leadership learning; our pedagogy should put students where they can focus their attention on leadership in action in public and community settings. "Practice" refers to the experience of leadership work itself. Whether it is through collaborative projects based on community problems or service-learning placements where individual students work with organizational partners on community and public problems, students must be able to engage their whole bodies and selves in the work, and then be led to reflect on the meaning of that practice to gain better, more complex conceptions of public and community-based leadership. As Schweigert reminds us, "Learning is not simply internalizing knowledge; it is 'increasing participation in a community of practice [that] concerns the whole person acting in the world' (Lave & Wenger 1991: 49). What must be learned is not merely 'content' or 'subject matter' but identity, a provisional new self" (2007, pp. 333–34).

Forming a "new self" that is capable of taking on leadership work that addresses the toughest problems of our communities and public life requires a holistic pedagogy, one that addresses the whole self that learns — its cognitive, affective, and social dimensions. Practical experience in real settings, where students are mentored and guided by community leaders, has been shown to be a most effective form of leadership learning (Longo and Shaffer 2008; Vogt 2007).

Practical learning about leadership, with and in communities, will also enable students to understand and find ways of working through the messiness of public work and life. One leadership educator calls this aspect of leadership development "learning to love the swamp." Many programs in leadership development emphasize the "high ground" of leadership theory and development, but the practice of public and community-based leadership is fraught with "swamp problems." As Blount argues, "effective public leadership means learning to manage in the 'indeterminate zones' where no clear formulas exist for how to approach, much less solve, swamp problems. A different kind of experiential learning is required that incorporates both high ground and swamp learning. Problem-solving work must incorporate diverse—even competing—perspectives, encourage improvisation, and reinforce the group's purpose as literally to learn its way through the problem. If public leaders must master both high ground and swamp approaches, mastery means developing an instinctive understanding of when and how to use each approach in the most strategically effective manner for addressing the policy problem at hand" (2006, p. 274).

Unlike some types of educational programs or curricula in higher education in which pedagogy is driven by tidy learning objectives and a teacher-centered classroom, public and community-based leadership education is messy. This is partly because public work is messy, as Blount argues, but also because community partnerships, student engagement, and experiential education are all pedagogical strategies that dislodge the professor as the "sage on the stage." Helping faculty to engage in these partnerships with community and students, and enabling intersections of high ground classroom learning with lessons from the swamps of public life and experience, are necessary to move this agenda forward. Encouraging faculty to learn to work in partnership with student affairs staff is a required part of this work as well. The community-building and reflective aspects of this work, so critical to this kind of leadership learning, call upon the expertise of student affairs practitioners. In addition, student affairs staff can often help facilitate and enable the community partnerships and logistical details that are so central to this type of leadership education.

Leadership, practiced in and for public life, is comprised of the actions of citizens who convene, deliberate, inquire, collaborate, and act with the intent to improve life for fellow citizens in their communities and the larger society. In defining and describing this notion of leadership as a grounding framework for leadership education, we join a growing group of educators, citizens, and activists who seek to combine leadership education with the broader movements to reenergize public life (Kezar 2005).

Students utilize higher education primarily as an avenue for delving more deeply into a discipline or a professional field with the hope of becoming a "productive" member of society, which often implies a successfully employed person. Our challenge within higher education is to create opportunities for students to meet a dual outcome of developing healthy and consistent behaviors as both wage earners and productive community citizens.

Students are faced with multiple expectations from family, friends, and society regarding their roles as college graduates. Many students in college today work to check off experiences, in order to build a résumé, to obtain a job, to become a particular leader or a particular rising star of a profession. While this notion of productivity is tied to building a foundation of experience to highlight leadership skills that have been acquired, many students are not given the space and opportunity to understand the deeper responsibility of those skills in relationship to their local communities and local public issues.

Building the collegiate educational experience around the public leadership framework and philosophy begins the effort to join the dual expectations of becoming a "productive member of society" and taking a role more deeply embedded in civic life. This obligation is based on a philosophy of contribution to the local and global communities to which college graduates are and will be affiliated. Connecting the dual aspects of a "productive" life, then, does not require a binary of individual gain versus community gain. A prolonged community-based experience that builds the public leadership capacities described in this chapter strives to reconcile these roles of self and public, worker and citizen, taxpayer and community leader.

Although the nature of public work is messy, it pushes students toward the reality of the necessary struggles and complicating factors that contribute to public work. Placing the disciplinary studies of academia within our public leadership framework challenges students to apply their discipline- or profession-based education. It enables them to apply their education in a way that honors the expertise of the community, negotiates the practical and philosophical differences of lived experiences, and often provides them with alternatives to classroom learning. Students consistently struggle to make sense of the gap between the classroom and applications to real public work, and they seek support from others who are familiar with the struggle of public work. It is important that educators allow students to work through the ambiguity and that they support students as they make meaning of their experience and their role in public work.

The practice and pedagogy of public leadership are not opposed to our mission within higher education. Indeed, these educational efforts push higher education institutions to claim and fulfill their public missions. We advocate an educational agenda that can produce a new cohort of leaders for tomorrow's public problems.

But unlike most existing approaches to leadership today, this is an agenda directly aimed at helping to educate leaders for the public sphere of our existence. That is a realm whose future health and well-being cannot be taken for granted.

REFERENCES

Blount, A. G. (2006). Critical reflection for public life: How reflective practice helps students become politically engaged. *Journal of Political Science Education* 2 (December): 271–83.

Boyte, H. (1993). Civic education as public leadership development. *PS: Political Science and Politics* 26 (4): 763–69.

Burns, J. M. (1978). *Leadership.* New York: HarperCollins.

Campus Compact. (2008). 2007 service statistics: Highlights and trends of Campus Compact's Annual Membership Survey. Providence, RI: Campus Compact.

Cariño, L. V. (2001). Private action for public good? The public role of voluntary sector organizations. *Public Organization Review: A Global Journal* 1: 55–74.

Cohen, L. (2003). *A consumers' republic: The politics of mass consumption in postwar America.* New York: Alfred A. Knopf.

Cohen, W. (1998). Great leaders are made, not born. *Network World* (December 21).

Cooper, T. (1991). *An ethic of citizenship for public administration.* Englewood Cliffs, NJ: Prentice Hall.

Couto, R. (1992). Defining a citizen leader. In *Public leadership education: The role of citizen leadership,* ed. S. Morse, 3–9. Dayton, OH: The Kettering Foundation. Available from: http://www.eric.ed.gov/ERICWebPortal/contentdelivery/servlet/ERICServlet?accno=ED368596.

Dugan, J. P., and S. R. Komives. (2006). Select descriptive findings from the multi-institutional study of leadership. *Concepts and Connections* 15 (1): 16–18.

Eich, D. (2008). A grounded theory of high-quality leadership programs: Perspectives from student leadership development programs in higher education. *Journal of Leadership and Organizational Studies* 15 (2): 176–87.

Faris, S. K., and C. L. Outcalt. (2001). The emergence of inclusive, process-oriented leadership. In *Developing non-hierarchical leadership on campus: Case studies and best practices in higher education,* ed. C. L. Outcalt, S. K. Faris, and K. N. McMahon, 9–18. Westport, CT: Greenwood Press.

Galston, W. A. (2004). Civic education and political participation. *PS: Political Science and Politics* 37: 263–66.

Gardner, J. (1989). Building community. *Kettering Review* (Fall): 73–81.

Gergen, D. (n.d.). Welcome from director David Gergen. Retrieved March 7, 2009, from Center for Public Leadership, John F. Kennedy School of Government, Harvard University. Available from: http://content.ksg.harvard.edu/leadership/index.php?Itemid=4&id=2&option=com_content&task=view.

Glenn, D. (April 17, 2009). After the crash, scholars say, higher education must refocus on its public mission. *Chronicle of Higher Education* 55 (32): A10. Available from: http://chronicle.com/daily/2009/04/15232n.htm.

Goldsmith, M. (January 14, 2008). Great leaders are made, not born. *Harvard Business*

Publishing. Retrieved from: http://blogs.harvardbusiness.org/goldsmith/2008/01/great_leaders_are_made_not_bor.html.

Grint, K. (2005). *Leadership: Limits and possibilities.* London: Palgrave.

Hannay, A. (2005). *On the public.* New York: Routledge.

Heifetz, R. (1994). *Leadership without easy answers.* Cambridge, MA: Belknap Press of Harvard University Press.

Higher Education Research Institute. (2009). *Political engagement among college freshmen hits 40-year high.* Los Angeles: University of California, Los Angeles, Graduate School of Education and Information Studies. Available from: http://www.gseis.ucla.edu/heri/pr-display.php?prQry=28.

Hurtado, S. (2003). Preparing college students for a diverse democracy. Final Report to the U.S. Department of Education, OERI, Field Initiated Studies Program. Ann Arbor, MI: Center for the Study of Higher and Postsecondary Education. Available from: http://www.umich.edu/~divdemo/presentations.htm.

Janc, H. (n.d.). A case study: Student political civic leadership development in a higher education coordinating board. *Journal of College and Character.* Available from: http://journals.naspa.org/cgi/viewcontent.cgi?article=1399&context=jcc.

Keeling, R., ed. (2004). *Learning reconsidered: A campus-wide focus on the student experience.* Washington, D.C.: National Association of Student Personnel Administrators and the American College Student Personnel Association. Available from: http://www.myacpa.org.

Kellerman, B., and S. W. Webster. (2001). The recent literature on public leadership: Reviewed and considered. *Leadership Quarterly* 12: 485–514.

Kezar, A. J., T. C. Chambers, and J. C. Burkhardt, eds. (2005). *Higher education for the public good: Emerging voices from a national movement.* San Francisco: Jossey-Bass.

Kirk, P., and A. M. Shutte. (2004). Community leadership development. *Community Development Journal* 39 (3): 234–51.

Lave, J., and E. Wagner. (1991). *Situated learning.* Cambridge: Cambridge University Press.

Longo, N. V., and S. Raill Jayanandhan. (2008). Report on public and community leadership. Oxford, OH: Wilks Leadership Institute. Available from: http://community.muohio.edu/wilks/research/kettering.

Longo, N. V., and M. S. Shaffer. (2009). Leadership education and the revitalization of public life. In *Civic engagement in higher education: Concepts and practices,* ed. B. Jacoby and Associates, 154–73. San Francisco: Jossey-Bass.

National Center for Public Policy and Higher Education. (2008). Engaging higher education in societal challenges of the 21st century. A report from the National Center for Public Policy and Higher Education, San Jose, CA. Retrieved May 20, 2009, from http://www.highereducation.org/reports/wegner/index.shtml.

National Conference on Citizenship. (2008). *2008 civic health report: Sustaining civic engagement beyond election day.* Washington, D.C.: National Conference on Citizenship, 2008. Available from: http://www.ncoc.net/index.php?tray=content&tid=top9&cid=92.

National Conference on Citizenship. (2009). *2009 civic health report.* Washington, D.C.: National Conference on Citizenship. Available from: http://www.ncoc.net/index.php?tray=content&tid=top5&cid=2gp54.

National Survey of Student Engagement. (2008). *Promoting engagement for all students: The imperative to look within — 2008 results.* Bloomington: Indiana University. Available from: http://nsse.iub.edu/nsse_2008_Results/.

Putnam, R. (1995). Bowling alone: America's declining social capital. *Journal of Democracy* 6 (1): 65–78.

Rossing, B. E. (1998). Learning laboratories for renewed community leadership: Rationale, programs, and challenges. *Journal of Leadership Studies* 5 (4): 68–81.

Rost, J. C. (1993). Leadership development for the new millennium. *Journal of Leadership Studies* 1 (1): 91–110.

Safty, A. (2003). Moral leadership: Beyond management and governance. *Harvard International Review* (Fall): 84–89.

Saltmarsh, J., M. Hartley, and P. Clayton. (2009). Democratic engagement white paper. Boston: New England Resource Center for Higher Education.

Schweigert, F. J. (2007). Learning to lead: Strengthening the practice of community leadership. *Leadership* 3 (3): 325–42.

Small Group, A. (2007). *Civic engagement and the restoration of community: Changing the nature of the conversation.* Cincinnati: Peter Block. Available from: http://www.asmallgroup.net/pages/content/resources.html.

Spinosa, H., J. Sharkness, J. H. Pryor, and A. Liu. (May 2008). *Findings from the 2007 administration of the college senior survey (CSS): National aggregates.* Los Angeles: Higher Education Research Institute, University of California. Available from: http://www.heri.ucla.edu/publications-brp.php.

Understanding the social change model of leadership development: Blueprint leadership development program. Retrieved on March 10, 2009, from the University of California, Berkeley, at: http://students.berkeley.edu/files/osl/Student_Groups/Understanding%20the%20SCM.pdf.

Vogt, K. (2007). Leadership development at university: Comparing student leaders with different levels of involvement in a leadership education program. Masters of Arts Thesis, Simon Fraser University.

Wagner, W. (2006). The social change model of leadership: A brief overview. *Concepts and Connections* 15 (1): 8–10.

5

No One Leads Alone
Making Leadership a Common Experience

For the past fifteen years, I have taught a course on leadership designed for graduate students aspiring to public service careers. Year after year, I introduce the course by asking the class, "How do you define leadership?" One student responds that a leader is someone in management or the head of an organization, such as a chief executive officer or a four-star general. Someone else suggests that a political leader is someone who holds elected office. And another student says that the real leaders are those people throughout history who have spearheaded social movements or started revolutions for just causes.

Next, I ask the class to do an exercise. I ask them to compile a list of leaders who have contributed to the public good, locally or globally. Mahatma Gandhi, Dr. Martin Luther King Jr., César Chávez, Franklin Roosevelt, Winston Churchill, Mother Teresa, Nelson Mandela, and Colin Powell routinely make the list. Presidents Kennedy and Reagan are frequently named, too. More recently, President Obama, Secretary of State Clinton, and Bill and Melinda Gates have been listed.

And this is where it gets really interesting, every single time. The classroom suddenly gets quiet and the discussion grinds to a halt. The students run out of names. "Oh, come on," I demand. "Surely there are other notable leaders who come to mind. What about the individuals and groups exercising leadership in your own communities across this country—not to mention around the world?" Silence ensues.

What is wrong with this picture? What is wrong is that students, like so many of us, narrowly define leaders as people with titles, positions, and power. Leading can and often does manifest itself in such ways, but the real essence of leadership is something more profound. During our time together, I challenge my students to test their assumptions about leadership: what it is and what it isn't; where it's taking place, and by whom; and, most importantly, to what end. Finally, I urge the students to discover acts of leadership in their everyday lives; to identify and have conversations with people who inspire and intrigue them; and to reflect upon their own capacity for leadership and the talents they bring to bear as private citizens and in their chosen careers, their homes, and their communities.

Happily, by the last day of class, when students are asked to name people whose acts of leadership are contributing to the public good, the list is much longer. It still includes prominent national figures, but it also includes a group of moms who founded a college access program for recent immigrants in their school district; a high school teacher who, with his students, established a technology learning center in a rural community; or a group of college students who, outraged that the maintenance workers on campus had to work two or three jobs to make ends meet, mobilized support for a living wage increase. Each of these leaders saw a need and wanted to address it. Most of all, they understood that their success would be determined more by collective action and less by their individual feats.

What my students have learned about leadership is as simple as it is profound: we all have the capacity to lead. It is how we recognize, develop, and act upon our leadership potential that counts. If I have done my job right, these students leave the class with a new framework with which to view leadership, one that includes the following tenets:

- Leadership for public purpose requires a shared vision of a common good
- Leadership is as much a developed skill as an intrinsic quality
- Leadership is about actions and solutions, not titles or positions
- Leadership demands a conscience and the courage to act on it
- Leadership can come from the most unexpected places

Although few students leave the class knowing exactly when, how, and where they will put their own leadership skills into action, what they have gained from their time in the class is an opportunity to shift their attitudes and aspirations and to see leadership as a collaborative, inclusive, participatory process, in which they all have a role to play. In short, they have learned that each of us can lead and use that leadership to solve public problems.

Leadership Education for Public Purpose

Leadership education for public purpose is not a new idea. The ancient Greeks prepared young people for citizen leadership through an educational system called *paideia*. Much later and closer to home, the Dwight D. Eisenhower Leadership Development Program was established by the United States Congress in the Higher Education Act of 1965 to provide federal support for leadership education in American colleges and universities. In the early 1990s, thirty-eight colleges and universities throughout the country received Eisenhower grants from the U.S. Department of Education (DOE) to develop and implement leadership courses or projects (see Appendix 1).

My involvement in and enthusiasm for leadership education stems from my experience as the director of one such project, CivicQuest, a two-year, joint project between the University of Maryland at College Park and John F. Kennedy High School in Silver Spring, Maryland. Launched in 1994, the project was designed to create and field-test a leadership curriculum model for high school students (Kretman 1996). For me, it is a powerful example of the positive impact that leadership education can have on students and faculty.

When I began directing CivicQuest, we had more questions about leadership than we had answers. Could leadership be taught? Which leadership concepts and competencies should be emphasized? What kind of training do educators need to teach leadership? In our search for answers, we invited leadership scholars from around the country to visit the high school; observe the classes in session; talk to the students, teachers, and parents; and serve as our advisers.

By the project's end, we discovered that by infusing leadership principles and practices into core high school subjects, and by supplementing those subjects with experiential learning activities in the community, the Kennedy High School students were motivated to become more active learners and engaged citizens. We were not alone in our findings. Before the Eisenhower Leadership Development Program was terminated in 1996, Donald Bigelow, its director, assembled the Eisenhower Leadership Group (a group of eight educators, of which I was one) to capture the lessons learned from the thirty-eight projects. We attempted to shed light on the question: what role should educational institutions play in preparing students for the responsibilities of citizenship? Our group interviewed scholars and practitioners recognized for their seminal work in the fields of democratic theory, civic engagement, and education.

The culminating report, *Democracy at Risk: How Schools Can Lead*, called for a twenty-first-century model of leadership that is collaborative, inclusive, participatory, and change-oriented. It also argued that there is no better place to prepare young people for civic engagement than the schools, beginning in kindergarten and continuing through postsecondary education. The report said: "Every democracy requires a large number of citizens willing and able to make a difference. One place we learn to participate is in our schools. Schools powerfully affect how we learn, what we learn, and whether—throughout our lives—we are willing to meet the challenges of civic engagement" (Eisenhower Leadership Group 1996, p. 1).

Those we interviewed were unanimous in their view that higher education institutions needed to be more intentional in providing students with classroom and community opportunities to learn the principles of democracy and the practices of civic engagement. Our survey of the thirty-eight Eisenhower project directors revealed that leadership education:

- Can be introduced at colleges and universities without great difficulty by faculty and administrators
- Does *not* require a large investment of human capital or money
- *Does* require an institutional commitment from the top and faculty willing to get out of their comfort zones and academic silos; to take risks; and to model collaborative, creative, and courageous leadership

In sum, the Eisenhower Leadership Group concluded that "leadership can be learned, and that a collaborative and participatory approach motivates students to be interested in and capable of doing the work of leading social change. . . . In the next millennium it is [leadership education] that will be key to progress—in the workplace as well as the nation at large" (Eisenhower Leadership Group 1996, p. 12).

After the Eisenhower program ended in the mid-1990s, some of the grantee institutions found other champions and funding to sustain their leadership initiatives. But leadership education—especially with the public purpose these schools were trying to advance—did not catch on as much as we had hoped. Concurrently, however, the service-learning movement was gaining momentum on college campuses across the country, due in large part to funding from another federal program, the Corporation for National and Community Service's Learn and Serve America. Service-learning was a key component of the Corporation's strategy to increase citizens' involvement in addressing the needs of the nation's communities through service. What makes service-learning different from other volunteer activities is its intentional combination of community service *with* learning: learning about underlying societal issues, analyzing the government's response to challenges, and exploring alternative and innovative solutions. Service-learning at its best is a natural part of the curriculum that extends into the community and allows students an opportunity to reflect not only on their observations and experiences but also on their own self-development as collaborators, organizers, problem solvers, advocates, innovators, and, in fact, leaders. But, in most instances, leadership learning gets short shrift.

The reality is that service-learning, civic education, and leadership education for public purpose can and should go hand in hand. Yet, although the three share many of the same general pedagogical practices and student learning objectives, their commonalities have not been fully explored, explicitly stated, and intentionally integrated with one another into a solid curriculum. Each requires that a similar set of competencies be mastered by students: critical and creative thinking, decision making and problem solving, oral and written communication, collaboration, conflict resolution, and cross-cultural understanding. In each, academic course work should provide the underpinning for the students' exploration of democratic institutions, values, and efficacy. And in each it is the real-world application that enables students to see themselves as active and engaged citizens and change agents.

The late Ernest Boyer argued that what is needed in higher education is "not just more programs, but a larger purpose, a larger sense of mission, a larger clarity of direction" (Boyer 1994, p. A48). Campuswide, interdisciplinary models that intentionally link leadership development to civic education, students to community, and theory to action have the potential to produce just that.

Infusing Leadership for Public Purpose into the Life of the University

Noting the unprecedented rise in the number of students seeking ways to make a social contribution in recent years, Dr. Dan Porterfield, Georgetown University's vice president for Public Affairs and Strategic Development, has said, "it's a right and smart thing [for a university] to help them become infused with the skills and attitudes to be successful" (D. Porterfield, personal communication, December 12, 2006). Dr. Bernard Cook, assistant dean of Georgetown College, agrees: "We are producing the next generation of leaders, but we are not systematic about doing it. We need to consider ways that we could consciously form their experiences" (B. Cook, personal communication, January 15, 2007).

What does a systematic way of educating leaders look like in practice? How does a university make leadership learning for public purpose part of the mainstream educational experience? Research and experience suggest several key factors that are important in this process:

- A model of leadership education that embraces values of collaboration, inclusiveness, and social change is reflected in the actions of all those involved in the university, from the trustees and the president to the deans and department chairs, and is accessible to all students

- An acknowledgment of the importance of preparing students for leadership for public purpose appears in institutional mission statements

- A commitment of funding and resources exists to design, implement, and sustain effective leadership education over time, because all too often, some of the most promising educational initiatives are cut short due to financial constraints

- Training and professional development activities (for example, symposia, workshops, and stipends for course development) are available to help prepare faculty successfully to integrate leadership theory and competencies into the curricula of their respective disciplines

- A culture of interdisciplinary cross-pollination of ideas and activities is present

- Students are taught how to think across silos and sectors to address public problems

- Academic and experiential learning are combined through internships, community-based research, and service initiatives

- Activities and events that make reference to leadership education opportunities are widely available (for instance, student orientations; course descriptions in college catalogs; internships; community engagement initiatives; and involvement in student organizations that cultivate students as issue advocates, social entrepreneurs, and change agents)

- Alumni are enlisted to serve as mentors and network-builders for students

- Institutions reach out to and engage the communities in which they are located by providing internships, conducting community-based research projects, and offering service initiatives that benefit students and community partners

Walking the Talk at Georgetown University

Since its inception, Georgetown University has integrated civic action into its academic focus. Georgetown's founder, John Carroll, created Georgetown with the goal of "educat[ing] women and men . . . to be responsible and active participants in civic life, and to live generously in service to others" (Georgetown University Office of the President, n.d.). Infusing "leadership learning" for public purpose into curricular and cocurricular activities is a natural extension of Georgetown's mission, and leadership learning is playing out at the university in a variety of traditional and nontraditional ways.

Community-based, experiential learning is one of the main features of Georgetown's Undergraduate Learning Initiative. Adopted in 2007 and endorsed by faculty across departments, the Community-Based Learning Credit attracts students from all four undergraduate schools at Georgetown. "Whether through direct or indirect service, we hope to provide experiential learning opportunities that challenge participants to question more critically, to reflect more deeply, and to act more creatively and collaboratively in meeting the pressing needs of our day," says Georgetown's Center for Social Justice Web site (Georgetown University Center for Social Justice, n.d.).

At Georgetown, community-based learning is specifically defined as "an academic course-based pedagogy that involves student work with disadvantaged and underserved individuals or groups (or organizations working with and for disadvantaged and underserved individual or groups) that is structured to meet community-defined needs" (Georgetown University, 2009). Similarly, community-based research is a collaborative enterprise that creates partnerships between university and community partners, as well as a process that combines classroom learning and skills development with social action to empower community groups to shape their own futures. It emphasizes students' development of knowledge and skills that prepare them to be active creators and effective agents in their civic participation. It is, in other words, leadership education for public purpose by another name.

The following are some examples of community-based leadership education at Georgetown:

- In a justice and peace studies course titled Social Justice Documentary Video, students learn about the relations between documentary media and social change by producing two short documentary films about Washington, D.C., community-based social justice organizations. Working in small groups, students perform archival and original research. They produce, film, and edit the documentary. Not only does this create a unique interdependence rarely experienced in the traditional group project, but students also have an opportunity to explore creative ways to develop critical arguments about history and culture.

- Serving as a yearlong capstone course for a social justice analysis concentration, Project DC: Research Internship on Urban Issues enables students to undertake community-based research while working in partnership with Washington, D.C., community organizations or local government agencies. The research partnership results in a collaboratively developed product for the community organization, a research project report, and a set of resources about the community and the social issues addressed in the project.

- Through grants from the Sunshine Lady Foundation's Learning by Giving Program, and the Eugene and Agnes E. Meyer Foundation, students in a course titled Philanthropy and Social Change award $15,000 to community-based organizations in Washington, D.C. Students are first matched with nonprofit organizations on whose behalf they write a grant proposal for the funding, and then the class is divided into two foundations that review the proposals and eventually determine the grant recipients.

- The International Health Certificate blends the study of public health and health systems management with an emphasis on environment, culture, economics, and politics as key factors in improving the health status of whole populations. Students are required to intern abroad and in Washington, D.C., in clinics providing direct services to vulnerable populations.

While the content of each of these courses is quite different, what they share is their emphasis on applying knowledge to real-world situations to effect social change.

As this chapter has shown, leadership education in a university setting can take many forms, ranging from an experiential sociology course to a master's degree in international diplomacy. In my experience, however, the difference between a good and a great leadership learning experience comes from four essential elements: cross-disciplinary course work, cross-sector solutions, community-based learning, and opportunities to practice and reflect on experience. The universities that incorporate these four elements can make leaps and bounds toward solving the daunting social problems of our day by empowering students to become leaders in their own lives and communities. As arrows shot forth into the future, students can fly farther and lead better when they learn to think across disciplines, when they look for answers across all segments of society, when they experience leadership learning outside of the classroom, when they practice their advocacy and entrepreneurial skills, and when they learn from their successes as well as their failures. By endowing future generations with the skills for leadership, we can grow into a more whole society.

At the end of the semester in one of my leadership classes, a student wrote: "I now understand that public leadership is not just what goes on in the Oval Office or the Senate floor. It is the work that we do together as citizens, every day, to make our communities, our country, and the world a better place."

We in higher education have a responsibility to our students, raised on the ethic of service, to promote a notion of leadership that is not just about position, but about people—people as problem solvers, social innovators, and community builders. A vibrant democracy requires many citizens willing to do the hard work of leading change. There are students sitting in our classrooms who have the untapped potential to unite us and involve us in addressing the nation's challenges, both here and abroad, and to remind us that public service is a noble and worthy calling. We educators have an unparalleled opportunity to unleash their energy and talents and to prepare them for a new kind of leadership.

Speaking at Georgetown University's 2009 Conference on Global Development, Grameen Bank founder and Nobel Prize winner Muhammad Yunus called on universities to take the lead in preparing a new generation to understand how the critical issues of our times—poverty, population, health, conservation, and human rights—are all interconnected and require sustained, comprehensive, cross-sector solutions. No one leads alone; rather, we all have a part to play in leading our community life forward. I believe (to paraphrase the late John W. Gardner) that with some imagination and social inventiveness, higher education institutions have unparalleled opportunities to meet Yunus's challenge and to tap the extraordinary talents of men and women—not just for government, not just for business, and not just for nonprofits, but for all the diverse leadership needs of a dynamic society.

REFERENCES

Boyer, E. L. (1994). Creating the new American college. *Chronicle of Higher Education* (March 9): A48.

Eisenhower Leadership Group. (1996). *Democracy at risk: How schools can lead.* College Park: University of Maryland.

Georgetown University. (2009). Community-based learning courses, definitions, criteria, procedures. Approved by the Provost and Council of Deans of Georgetown University on January 14, 2008, Washington, D.C.

Georgetown University Center for Social Justice. (n.d.). Teaching. Retrieved on May 18, 2010, at http://socialjustice.georgetown.edu/areas/teaching/.

Georgetown University Office of the President. (n.d.). University mission statement. Retrieved on May 18, 2010, at http://president.georgetown.edu/sections/governance/missionstatement/.

Kretman, K., ed. (1996). *Learning leadership: A curriculum guide for a new generation, grades K–12.* College Park, MD: Center for Political Leadership and Participation.

III Practices

Tania Mitchell, Virginia Visconti,
Arthur Keene, and Richard Battistoni

6

Educating for Democratic Leadership at Stanford, UMass, and Providence College

This chapter examines the power of sustained, developmental, cohort-based curricular programs on student leadership through civic engagement. We do this by describing and analyzing three models at three different institutions of higher education. These models have been in existence for at least a decade: Stanford University's Public Service Scholars Program; the Citizen Scholars Program at the University of Massachusetts Amherst; and the Public and Community Service Studies Program at Providence College.

The goal of this book is to introduce a "new leadership" that emphasizes relationship over position and action over attainment. We argue that students' connection to this new leadership is at least in part fostered through civic engagement—specifically, a curricular program that builds civic agency and challenges participants to see themselves as engaged scholars and actors working for a better world. This notion of leadership is centered in community and the common good. Not driven by the idea of being in charge, the new leaders who are targeted through these programs are looking to contribute in meaningful ways. The increasing number of opportunities on college and university campuses for students to participate in service has made them more aware of the issues and concerns facing communities. This growing awareness has, in turn, inspired students to take action. For this generation of students, leadership education prepares them to engage collaboratively in and with communities for positive social change.

We argue that a sustained, developmental, curricular approach to civic engagement, one that attempts to build on the single course, single experience civic or service learning opportunities that shape most students' college years, is better able to engender new civic leaders, because it creates students who invest in community through service, scholarship, and action. In addition to describing each program in some detail, we analyze why these kinds of curricula work to enhance student leadership through civic engagement, as well as the challenges to implementing similar programs on other campuses.

Conceptual Framework: Civic Identity and the New Leadership

Knefelkamp describes the values, skills, and actions of "fully engaged, fully human citizens" who have a more developed civic identity. She says: "They seek knowledge of both historical and contemporary conditions. They apply this knowledge using the skills and competencies they have developed, working independently and interdependently on whatever challenges they face. They approach these challenges with a sense of discernment, responsibility, and justice seeking. They are both idealistic and realistic, patient and persistent, committed to thoughtful engagement and aware that others may engage differently. They see their role in life as contributing to the long-term greater good. And perhaps most importantly, they have the courage to act" (2008, p. 3).

This heightened sense of civic identity, which leads directly to civic action, is key to the new student leadership defined in this volume and elsewhere (see Colby et al. 2007). For students to reach this level of civic leadership requires "opportunities for agency and industry, for social relatedness, and for the development of political-moral understandings" (Kahne and Sporte 2008, p. 742), and sustained, developmental, cohort-based curricular programs provide the environment, structure, and impetus to engender this commitment to engaged citizenship and leadership.

A Sustained, Developmental Approach

One criticism of traditional civic engagement programs has been "that one assignment, one semester, is not enough" to create a sustainable change in either the individual or the community (Bickford and Reynolds 2002, p. 234). A sustained civic engagement program serves to support civic identity and leadership development by creating opportunities over time for students to work on issues and concerns in increasingly complex roles; to invest deeply in an issue, agency, or relationship that creates connection and a sense of belonging; and to create community both on and off campus that builds the critical awareness and skills necessary to take action and mobilize others in meaningful and constructive ways.

Developing a civic identity that results in a commitment to leadership and active citizenship is a process that takes time and requires persistent engagement (Knefelkamp 2008; Youniss et al. 1997; Roholt et al. 2009). The accumulation of experiences through a sustained process of engagement is believed to have a lasting effect on identity (Bronfenbrenner 1993), so the programs reviewed here require one to four years of involvement with increasingly complex tasks and experiences. The sustained, developmental approach honors the environment, relationships, and learning opportunities that influence identity construction (Evans et al. 1998) by providing continuity and repetition while integrating new knowledge, new challenges, and more complexity in ways that foster identity development (Bronfenbrenner 1995; Chickering and Reisser 1993; Renn 2004).

Commitment to Fundamental Values

Values clarification and congruence are tasks fundamental to establishing identity (Chickering and Reisser 1993; Evans et al. 1998) and to moving citizens to action (Knefelkamp 2008; Colby et al. 2007). It is this process that confirms identity, allowing students to develop purpose that can guide their actions in service to others or for the greater good. Developing a commitment to the fundamental values of diversity, social justice, and active citizenship creates the condition whereby citizens act "on a specific issue or condition because it is the right thing to do and not to do so would go against who [they are]" (Roholt et al. 2009, p. 12).

These values guide the programs reviewed in this chapter because they inspire the civic agency and the courage to act that are implicit in this new leadership (Boyte 2008; Knefelkamp 2008; see also Gibson and Longo [Introduction in this volume]). The frameworks that guide these programs are not irrelevant but represent an intentional focus of civic engagement programs committed to greater social change (Bickford and Reynolds 2002; Mitchell 2008). Therefore, the curriculum and civic engagement activities that guide these programs include readings, assignments, and experiences that invoke these values and challenge students in a dynamic between action and reflection to find congruence between their actions and beliefs and to motivate their peers to action toward desired ends.

A Cohort Model

Civic identity can best be described as making sense of how your life should be lived every day in order to contribute optimally to the world around you (Knefelkamp 2008; Roholt et al. 2009). This process of making sense is never isolated. Sensemaking is inherently social, shaped and reshaped by interactions with others and the perspectives and experiences they share (Bronfenbrenner 1993; Weick 1995; Youniss et al. 1997). The cohort model that guides the civic engagement programs presented here establishes a community wherein students develop respect and trust. The relationships central to the new leadership fostered in this cohort experience provide spaces for students to take risks, to succeed, and to fail, in a supportive environment (Roholt et al. 2009). Moreover, the intellectual and ideological diversity encouraged by all three programs featured here ensures spirited debates, but the quality of students' exchanges with one another is largely a function of their commitment to dialogue not as a tool or method but rather as a way of existing in the world. When conceptualized ontologically, dialogue is "based on mutual understanding, respect, a willingness to listen and risk one's opinions and prejudices, a mutual seeking of the correctness of what is said" and defines "a powerful regulative ideal that can orient our practical and political lives" (Bernstein 1983, p. 163).

Student communities are an important influence on identity development (Chickering and Reisser 1993). Participants learn from one another's experiences and perspectives, challenging each other to think differently, to act with more intention, and to question the circumstances that create social problems (Mitchell 2007; Polin and Keene, under review). The cohort experience fosters identity development best when students meet regularly, when membership is diverse, when opportunities exist for collaboration and teamwork, and when the cohort persists long enough to serve as a "reference group" for one another (Chickering and Reisser 1993).

The cohort experience continually reinforces the values fundamental to these programs by providing an internal community to develop and practice the skills that embody commitments to diversity, solidarity, and justice before and after engaging with a community outside the university setting. The safety net created by the cohort experience ensures that participants do not test their ideas alone but act in concert with others who are learning together what it means to be an active and engaged community member. The significance of this for program participants is evident in the recollections of Stanford alumna Susan Bobulsky: "The best part by far was the support network. Writing your thesis without a community to follow your progress and share your frustrations must be miserable. [The program] gave me both the drive to make measurable, steady progress and the opportunity to reflect on my work in a context aside from its academic function" (Goldstein, Marino, and Mathewson 2005, p. 19).

Public Service Scholars Program, Stanford University

Just how do these three programs foster civic leadership development? After describing each in some detail, we analyze the key elements that make them models for creating new student leaders.

On the occasion of its tenth anniversary, Timothy Stanton, the cofounder of the Public Service Scholars Program (PSSP), recalled the impetus for the program's creation: "Public service shouldn't just be something extra you do at Stanford while you're a student. In fact, many students became involved in public service work because they weren't sure why they were here as Stanford students. Or they wanted a 'refuge' from their academic work, which they did not find all that fulfilling or connected to what they cared about most—community service. This was a challenge for us at Haas. We had to help them figure out how to connect their passion for service with their academics, and PSSP helped us do that (Goldstein, Marino, and Mathewson 2005, p. 5).

Toward that end, the Haas Center for Public Service at Stanford established the PSSP in 1994 to provide guidance to undergraduate students eager to integrate their public service commitments with their academic course work and research interests through an honors thesis capstone. (For a discussion of capstone models and best practices related to civic learning outcomes, see Kecskes and Kerrigan 2009.) Each year since its inception, the PSSP has brought together ten to fifteen senior-level students from a wide range of departments and interdisciplinary programs to examine critically what it means to practice academic research as a form of service to communities beyond Stanford University. To date, the PSSP has graduated more than 150 alumni and continues to attract students whose civic values motivate them to pursue an honors thesis with an intentional public purpose.

Students admitted to the PSSP participate concurrently in their departmental honors program and a yearlong, credit-bearing seminar (Urban Studies 198: Senior Research in Public Service) with their PSSP peers. With the assistance of their faculty thesis advisers—and often with input from community partners—students design and implement research studies that meet the standards of academic rigor in their disciplines. The PSSP seminar challenges students to explore how their research may contribute not only to the public good but also to the development of their individual civic identities. Thus, it complements students' disciplinary training and academic learning with civic learning, grounded in a collaborative pedagogy and an appreciation for engaged scholarship as a legitimate form of research that reflects traditionally high standards of quality.

A Sustained, Developmental Approach to Public Service

Among the criteria used to select participants for admission to the PSSP is experience with public and community service, especially in areas relevant to the student's proposed thesis research (Haas Center n.d.). Students' public and community service experiences are as varied as their research projects. They constitute students' personal service histories and provide a backdrop against which students interpret the material presented in the PSSP seminar. The PSSP curriculum is designed to activate prior knowledge gained through these experiences in order to promote students' understanding of the relationship between civic identity, engaged scholarship, and civic engagement.

The yearlong PSSP seminar comprises three quarters of instruction. Each quarter is organized according to one or more of the following themes: researcher positionality and the power and privilege associated with academic research; the practical and political implications of engaged scholarship; the role of the public intellectual; and the conditions that facilitate civic engagement at individual and institutional levels. Readings, oral presentations, and written assignments allow students to explore these themes and synthesize what they learn in the classroom and the field during the course of their research. Although the curricular program is well defined, students shape their participation in the PSSP through individual learning plans. The learning plan is a living document that students create in consultation with their faculty thesis advisers and the PSSP director and that they revisit throughout the year as a tool for reflection and conversation.

As students progress through the program—and their data analyses grow in sophistication—they develop community-based "translations" of their research. For example, students are asked to write an op-ed for publication to raise awareness of the topics they have investigated. As students compose their pieces, they not only enhance their written communication skills but also exercise their civic imaginations by learning how to frame issues for particular audiences. The op-ed represents the convergence of the student's knowledge with a public voice. Students' work has appeared in campus publications and newspapers such as the *Christian Science Monitor*.

Students also make brief, highly condensed presentations of their research findings and recommendations to a mock board that consists of community members, faculty, and university staff. The presentation helps students think strategically about how to communicate their research results to groups of decision makers appropriate to their topic. In order for their recommendations to be actionable and sustainable, students also need to demonstrate that they understand how organizations function and what resources are available to the decision makers they hope to influence. After they conclude their remarks, students field questions from the board members and receive feedback on both the content and style of their presentation. This assignment proves particularly challenging because the presentation format differs significantly from what students are accustomed to in their other courses. In those settings, they are generally given longer periods of time to speak, expected to comply with the conventions of academic discourse, and listened to by classmates and instructors with whom they are familiar. Faculty from the Center on Teaching and Learning facilitate reflection on the experience by videotaping the presentations so that students can later review their performance and improve their oral communication skills.

Throughout the school year, students develop a public service plan that outlines the rationale and means for sharing their research with a particular community or organization. This assignment exemplifies the applied orientation of the PSSP: it requires students to formulate multiple strategies for action, including service, advocacy, and policy change (Musil 2009) and to respond thoughtfully to their explicit and implicit obligations to community partners. As might be expected, students' public service plans vary widely in their scope and feasibility, which are subject to the time constraints under which students conduct their research and complete the writing of their theses. Some public service plans involve the production of policy briefs, Web sites, and educational outreach programs. In many instances, the plans reflect significant input from community members and organization personnel regarding the nature of deliverables and forums for dissemination.

Theresa Zhen's public service plan offers a compelling example. A sociology and economics major, Theresa studied the educational obstacles confronting Asian and Asian-American students who reside in the low-income, first- and second-generation community of Chinatown, San Francisco. Based on her research, Theresa was able to assist her community partner, Community Education Services (CES), in the evaluation of its bilingual college fair, popularly known as Chinatown to Collegetown. She designed a survey instrument and distributed it to parents who attended the fair. CES intends to share the results of Theresa's data analysis with philanthropic foundations and other granting agencies to secure funding for the fair in years to come. Upon graduation, Theresa offered the following advice to future participants in the PSSP: "Never lose sight of what your thesis means to a community. Without the refueling motivation, the writing process may seem sterile and unmoving, without inspiration or anticipation that your thesis will make an impact on this world" (Haas Center, n.d.).

Community Building among Program Participants

Shortly after the academic year begins, students take part in an overnight retreat that becomes the foundational community-building experience for the cohort. During the retreat, students discuss what it means to be a "community" and how they intend to support one another. Their ideas form the basis of a PSSP "covenant" that establishes group norms and expectations for the remainder of their year together. These can be playful as well as serious, as the following examples illustrate: "be flexible and adventurous," "be proactive about looking after each other," and "maintain open communication at all hours." Students continue to cultivate relationships with one another through weekly meetings of the seminar, which typically commence with a check-in period that gives students a chance to discuss obstacles to completing their theses and an opportunity to solve problems collaboratively. Because the seminar is interdisciplinary, students are exposed to new and multiple perspectives on a wide range of topics.

Contributions to the New Leadership

Student leadership development as a prerequisite for civic engagement builds upon the expression of civic creativity and courage. Students who are admitted to the PSSP possess these two qualities in abundance, but they require guidance in how to channel them to the greatest positive effect. This process begins with a collaborative pedagogy that relies upon program participants as coeducators. Students invest in one another's learning through peer-to-peer instruction that enhances their understanding of research as a form of service and deepens their respect for one another's contributions to the seminar's learning environment. It continues with critical examinations of what it means to engage with public issues through research and of how best to leverage university and community knowledge and resources in the pursuit of social justice. Each participant's public service plan represents the culmination of these efforts and embodies a unique expression of civic agency coupled with that of community partners. PSSP participants appreciate the profoundly intersubjective nature of the civic engagement on which our democracy depends.

Citizen Scholars Program, University of Massachusetts Amherst

The Citizen Scholars Program (CSP) is a two-year, scholarship-supported, service-learning-based academic leadership program at the University of Massachusetts (UMass) that aims to produce a new generation of civic leaders who have the knowledge, the skills, and the vision to bring about progressive change in their own communities (see the CSP Web site: http://www.comcol.umass.edu/academics/csl/students/citizenScholars.html; Mitchell 2005). The program was founded twelve years ago by Art Keene and Dave Schimmel in an effort to address some of the frustrations that they were experiencing in their own start-up service-learning courses. Most notably, Keene and Schimmel discovered that their vision of service-learning did not fit neatly into the artificial fourteen-week confines of an academic semester. Just about the time that their students were getting comfortable at their service sites, establishing meaningful relationships, and learning to link book learning to work in the community, the term was over. The abrupt termination of relationships and learning processes proved frustrating for all stakeholders: community partners, their constituents, students, and faculty.

Keene and Schimmel addressed this frustration by combining their two courses into a yearlong experience. After a year, and with the support of the new Commonwealth Honors College, they expanded the program into a full curriculum that included a required four-course sequence, an elective, and a number of cocurricular activities. Admission to the program is competitive and currently limited to students enrolled in the Commonwealth Honors College. Students receive a scholarship of $500 for each semester that they are active in the program and are eligible to compete for up to $2500 in funds to support approved summer internships in nonprofit administration, public policy, or community organizing. Students in the program participate in a minimum of 240 hours of community service, ideally with a single community partner. The program maintains about ten active partnerships that range from those providing direct service (a survival center with a soup kitchen, a multicultural after-school program, a mentoring program) to programs more explicitly aimed at addressing issues of social and economic injustice by promoting structural change (a community-development corporation and an adult literacy program with an explicit citizenship component).

The CSP aims to prepare students for lives of engaged citizenship. The curriculum specifies eighteen detailed learning objectives (see Appendix A at the end of this chapter) that leave students with specific knowledge, skills, and values that promote effective citizenship. The course sequence includes: "The Good Society," which examines visions of the good society, explores issues involved in working toward the common good, and endeavors to liberate the imagination; "Tools for Change," which explores tools for bringing about structural change, including contemplative practices, communication skills, political mobilization, and participatory action research; "Public Policy and Citizen Action," in which students explore how laws and policies are made, meet with legislators, practice lobbying, and undertake a substantial policy research project; "Organizing for Change," in which students work in partnership with a community-based organization to formulate a community-organizing project that will mobilize a constituency to take action to meet a community need; and an elective course in service-learning or in social or political theory. The framework presumes that the work of citizenship begins with having a vision of what is desirable. After liberating the imagination and developing a vision, students are introduced to the tools available to make change happen. In the second year of the program students undertake action projects in policy and organizing that aim to put the concepts of the first year to work.

Community Building and Cohort Learning

In the CSP we endeavor to create a community of scholars, teachers, and learners in which all stakeholders take responsibility for the intellectual and social development of others. Students and faculty spend four semesters working together and in the process form an intimate learning community in which everyone, student and faculty member alike, is both learner and teacher. We do this for a number of reasons:

1. Foremost, we believe that citizenship and community are interdependent. A healthy democratic society requires informed citizens who have the skills and the will to create and sustain vibrant communities. Our experience shows that our students come to us with minimal knowledge of or experience with building or working effectively within a community framework.

Hence, much of what we do in the CSP aims to give students practical experience in this area. Students not only explore how a community works within the context of the communities where they serve but also actively create community within and among their cohorts in the program.

2. We believe that the kinds of knowledge, skills, and attitudes we seek to develop in students (see Appendix A) will be learned more deeply within a learning community in which everyone takes responsibility for their own learning and the learning of others.

3. We believe that the work of civic leadership, community service, and advocacy for social justice is challenging, hard, and developmental and requires considerable self-discovery, as well as the discovery of unfamiliar ways of being in the world. We believe that students can more readily sustain their commitments to this work if they share in mutual support with other students making similar discoveries and commitments. The community that we build gives students a support system to step outside of cultural norms, in addition to a challenging but safe environment in which they can explore difference, take risks, and challenge their own social identities. We have found that our students enter the program craving community and the social solidarity that it brings but have little idea of how to build it or sustain it. This changes profoundly over the course of two years.

4. We believe that the work of civic leadership, community service, and advocacy for social justice will continue to be challenging and hard after students complete the program and move on through their lives, and that they will be better equipped to sustain this work if they have the skills to build supportive networks of like-minded people wherever they are.

5. We believe that having a fundamental understanding of community and how it works better prepares students to work in communities that have been battered, dismantled, or dismembered (Medoff and Sklar 1994) and to understand the challenges faced by leaders who seek to facilitate community revitalization.

Within the CSP, building and teaching about community is an active and conscientious process that includes off-campus retreats, considerable biographical work, team- and trust-building exercises, and setting aside time in and out of classes to connect our lives inside the program with our lives outside it. Asked to reflect on their experience of the program as they prepare to graduate from it, students most frequently point to the importance of their experience of community with other students, staff, and faculty.

These elements of the program are evident in the experiences of students such as Jill Meade. Jill came to the CSP in her sophomore year (2006), after a positive experience in the UMass curricular-alternative spring-break program (Addes and Keene 2004). Jill completed two years of community service with Youth Build of Holyoke, Massachusetts, a community-development program that aims to develop both neighborhoods and human capacities by working with local young people between the ages of eighteen and twenty-four who have dropped out of school and are unemployed. Youth Build teaches these young people skills for the construction trade, employs them in neighborhood development projects, and simultaneously prepares them to complete their GED. Jill worked initially as a GED tutor and later as a teacher. Then, as part of her capstone organizing project, she worked in collaboration with Youth Build and a local museum to pursue a $10,000 grant to engage local youth in researching and preparing an exhibit on Holyoke's Puerto Rican history. The project was successful on many fronts: the grant was obtained, young people were enlisted in writing their community's history, and a successful public exhibit was displayed at the museum. The project was eventually the subject of a documentary film. This engagement in praxis solidified for Jill her own approach to leadership. She notes: "This is where I began to redefine my idea of what it means to be a leader, and also what it means to work as an ally. Through the grant project with YouthBuild, I realized that . . . the project was about the students communicating their history to the public; there's no way I could have done that for them. Through my praxis with CSP while doing this project I learned that I could "serve as a catalyst" like [Saul] Alinsky put it, but could not lead the way. I had to spend time supporting and developing others as leaders, giving them opportunities to make decisions and create the project" (Meade 2009, p. 19).

Throughout her two years at Youth Build, Jill was conscious of her own positionality as a white woman and a privileged college student working in a poor Puerto Rican community. Her sense of leadership evolved within this context as she tried to figure out how to build bridges, craft alliances, and work for justice. In her concluding reflection, she comments: "Overall, the Citizen Scholars Program further expanded my knowledge and understanding of what it means to work in a community that is not my own, and more specifically made me face my privilege head on and learn to work with it, rather than ignore it, to be an ally to those whom I may systematically oppress" (Meade 2009, p. 20).

Jill completed the CSP in her junior year. In her senior year she worked as an intern with the National Movement for Recovered Enterprises in Argentina, an organization that represents workers who have taken over abandoned factories and who run them cooperatively. Such enterprises have been at the forefront of activism against the devastating impacts of neoliberal economic policy in Argentina (Klein 2007) and were featured in Naomi Klein's documentary film The Take.

Jill returned to UMass in her final term to coteach the organizing component of the capstone sequence in the CSP. She remained at UMass for an additional year following graduation, serving as a Massachusetts Campus Compact VISTA volunteer. Her VISTA duties included assisting in the development of collaboration in service-learning across a five-college consortium and once again coteaching the organizing capstone.

Public and Community Service Studies Program, Providence College

Unlike the programs at Stanford University and the University of Massachusetts, Providence College's approach to student leadership through civic engagement is grounded in an academic major and minor in Public and Community Service Studies. (PSP is the shorthand designation given to the program at Providence College.) The PSP program began in 1993, through a generous endowment from Rhode Island philanthropist Alan Shawn Feinstein, who tied his gift to the creation of an undergraduate degree in public service. The major and minor are interdisciplinary in design, and though the academic curriculum was originally developed by faculty from different disciplinary departments, Public and Community Service Studies itself became an interdisciplinary academic department in 2007 (see Hudson and Trudeau 1995; Battistoni 1998, for a more complete history). To date, almost 150 students have graduated with a degree in Public and Community Service Studies, and another 125 have graduated with a PSP minor.

The major requires eleven core courses (thirty-three credit hours), completed over a student's undergraduate experience, which include:

- PSP 101: Introduction to Service in Democratic Communities
- PSP 202: Foundations of Organizational Service
- PSP 303: Community Organizing: People, Power, and Change
- Cultural Diversity/Cultural Boundaries in Community Service
  (A number of courses can be used to satisfy this cross-cultural competency requirement)
- Philosophy 301: Ethics, Moral Leadership, and the Common Good
- Theology 376: Catholic Social Thought
- PSP 320–321: Practicum in Public and Community Service Studies (full year)
- PSP 450: Internship in Community Service
- PSP 480–481: Capstone Seminar in Public and Community Service (full year)

In addition to this core set of courses, each student designs a three-course track or concentration, reflecting her or his public policy issue focus (for example, education, health care, migration, or environmental sustainability), or an area within public service in which the student wishes to develop specific skills (for instance, not-for-profit management, philanthropy, youth development, or nonviolent conflict mediation and resolution). For the PSP minor, students take the first five courses and a senior independent study, which can take the form of an intensive, community-based internship or an action-research project.

A Sustained, Developmental Approach to Public and Community Service

The curriculum is designed so that, as students move through the major, both the content of their courses and the intensity and complexity of their work in the community deepens, as does student analysis and reflection on their public service work. The academic program encourages students to experience different kinds of community service or engagement, as well as to view their community work from a number of vantage points.

In addition, as students progress, their opportunities for leadership, initiative, and decision making increase. For example, in PSP 101, students engage in direct service (in teams) and critically examine the key concepts of service, community, and democratic citizenship through readings, oral presentations, and written assignments. PSP 202 offers students an introduction to the concepts of organizational management and theory that provide the context within which public and community service takes place. Through community work that combines observation and practice, students come to understand the organizational structures and processes essential to effective service. PSP 303 exposes students to the history, theory, and skills of community organizing, and over the course of the semester students identify and implement their own organizing project. In the full-year PSP Practicum, students assume major responsibilities as Community Assistants (CAs), liaisons between the campus and community-based organizations, where they also write grants, troubleshoot, and conduct detailed issue and organizational analyses. In the full-year PSP Capstone Seminar, students are asked to explore in much greater depth—and fully articulate for themselves—the central concepts and issues concerning community, service, civic vocation, social justice, and public ethics that were raised in a more elementary way in earlier course work. The capstone experience also allows students to spend the year executing a major action-research project in collaboration with a community partner and in consultation with a faculty adviser.

Each graduating class constitutes a cohort of PSP majors who connect and reconnect over the duration of their curricular and community experiences. Depending on when students declare the major, they may be together throughout their four-year undergraduate career, but all students go through the two intensive, one-year experiences in practicum and capstone as a unit. This cohort model of learning has implications for students' identity as public servants and for their commitment to lifelong action and service as alumni.

The story of Tylea Richard's journey through the PSP major offers an example of the kind of impact a sustained, developmental, cohort-based program can have. Tylea, who graduated from Providence College in 2004, entered the PSP program with "a suspicion that things were not right in the world," and a commitment to working collaboratively with the communities she was serving. In her practicum year, Tylea was a Community Assistant at Southside Community Land Trust, an organization dedicated to sustainable, organic, community gardening and environmental education in Providence. She deepened the themes of learning developed in the practicum year with a five-month field study and internship experience in Costa Rica and Nicaragua; she returned for her capstone year dedicated to the dual causes of worker justice and environmental sustainability. With the support and the challenge provided by her cohort group of majors, Tylea linked these values with a previous interest in fashion design, and for her capstone action-research project she researched and started a program for local adjudicated youth in socially responsible fashion, in which the youth designed t-shirts and other pieces of clothing and produced them for retail sale under responsible, sweatshop-free, and environmentally sustainable conditions.

In her final Philosophy of Service assignment (see a later section in this chapter and Appendix B for further discussion), which she titled "manifesto for being," Tylea understood that "my previous anger, frustration, and disappointment came from an inability to see past the horrors haunting me in order to express my vision of change with others. This year I have found my peers as well as organizations that are walking this same line of revolutionizing the world through revolutionizing people's lives in their communities" (Feinstein Institute, unpublished Philosophy of Service assignment). After graduation, Tylea helped start the Nicaraguan Garment Workers Fund, a not-for-profit organization committed to the eradication of sweatshops, partnered with a women's sewing cooperative in Nicaragua, and recently completed an individualized master's degree program in social entrepreneurship and socially responsible fashion. Looking back on her undergraduate experience in the PSP major, Tylea reflected recently that "those four years gave me a place to sort it all out. It was a laboratory to understand and articulate the problems and figure out where I could best plug in" (T. Richard, e-mail communication, September 28, 2009).

Contributions to the New Leadership

The PSP curricular program features three major elements that make it unique in terms of student leadership development. The first is the commitment to a practice-based and democratic pedagogy within a community of learners. Over their four years in the major or minor, students act in increasingly complex situations, take on major responsibilities, and provide feedback to and learn from each other as well as from faculty and community educators. This opportunity for "horizontal" as well as "vertical" communication provides students with the kinds of skills necessary for leadership in a democracy (Battistoni 1997). The second element is the significant opportunity for student voice and leadership, at different stages of the curriculum and often in collaboration with community members. In the Community Organizing course, for example, students identify their own organizing project, based on their values and interests in addressing a particular community issue. In the Practicum, student's work as Community Assistants requires them to take on important leadership roles, both in the community-based organization and with their peers in the classroom. Finally, the diversity of members and perspectives encouraged by the program forces students to reflect critically on their own values and commitments as they work in communities and discern their vocations as agents of social change.

Deepening Community-Based Leadership Education: Core Principles and Practices

We argue that new leadership education, with its key focus on civic identity and civic action, is best done in sustained, developmental, cohort-based programs such as the three described in this chapter. But what is it about these three programs that leads to the kind of civic engagement and leadership discussed throughout this volume? Our response is that these model programs contain four fundamental principles that help produce students with an enhanced civic identity and the skills necessary for relational, action-oriented leadership: student voice, community collaboration, engaged scholarship, and a commitment to reflective practice.

Student Voice and Leadership

Recognition and inclusion of student voice have been identified as constituting a catalyst for political engagement (Longo et al. 2006). Through a democratic pedagogy that cultivates student voice through shared facilitation, dialogue, and accountability, civic agency is fostered. All three programs employ collaborative pedagogies that represent a commitment to students as equal colleagues and coeducators.

Education for the new leadership requires opportunities and experiences in which students see themselves as actors in the process of change, so these programs operate in ways that honor the knowledge and experience students bring with them. Each program asks its students "what they can do" to address public concerns (Boyte 2008) and expects students to act. Students are frequently and formally invited to share their advice, to suggest changes, and to develop experiences that shape the programs for themselves, their peers, and the students who follow them. They often serve as classroom facilitators, coaches, and coteachers. They pursue research and community-based projects that build capacity for self-directed action and collaborative work.

A good example of this commitment to student voice is Providence College's Practicum in Public Service, through which students spend a year serving as Community Assistants (CAs), who are liaisons between the campus and community-based organizations. As students help to staff agencies and schools, and as they orient, supervise, and lead reflection with service-learners coming from different courses, they also advise faculty as they revise elements of the curriculum or partnerships. In the Practicum itself, students write grants, conduct organizational analysis, and are encouraged to practice problem solving and to frame the challenges they face, whether they be conflicts at their organization, disputes within their own learning community, or major policy debates underlying the community service being done (Kelly and Lena 2006). For student Angela Kelly, the grant assignment in particular epitomizes the Practicum's approach to student voice and leadership, because "it gives [students] a chance to create and lead a project of their own design . . . draws on the many relationships the CAs form [and] entrusts the CA with leadership while also encouraging collaboration with students, faculty, and community partners and members" (Kelly and Lena 2006, pp. 126–27).

Respecting student voice requires that we encourage students to figure out for themselves how they may best contribute, and that we challenge students to be responsible for their actions and to persist despite obstacles (Chickering and Reisser 1993; Boyte 2008). These skills are key to building civic leadership.

Community Voice and Collaboration

The recognition and inclusion of community partners in a civic engagement curriculum must move beyond making an agency a site for student learning, toward a relationship in which community members are fully integrated into the program (Mitchell 2008). Collaboration with community leaders and partners leads to greater solidarity, creates real understanding of the issues and concerns that students are asked to tackle in their civic engagement work, and, most importantly, ensures that the curriculum accurately reflects the needs, desires, and expectations of the community agencies who have agreed to be partners. For example, all three programs examined in this chapter employ community representatives as coteachers in some fundamental way.

A good example of this commitment to meaningful community collaborations can be found in the Citizen Scholars Program. Students in the CSP are encouraged (but not required) to work with a single community-based organization (CBO) for their four terms in the program. Long-term service assignments lead to students and community partners' developing deep mutual understandings. Early on, students use both participant observation and external research to gain a solid understanding of their CBO and how it works. By the end of the first year, students have a firm grasp of their partner organization's constituency; administrative structures (staffing, budgets, funding sources); vision and mandates; leadership; organizing challenges; and efficacy. This partnership culminates in a jointly designed capstone project that includes both a public policy and a community-organizing component. For example, Lindsay McCluskey worked with PHENOM (the Public Higher Education Network of Massachusetts) throughout her two years in the program. As part of her capstone policy project she researched MASS-GRANT, the Commonwealth's signature need-based financial aid program. She then organized a statehouse rally and a lobbying day devoted to supporting MASS-GRANT and other legislation promoting financial aid in public higher education. During the following semester she worked, in collaboration with PHENOM, to found Massachusetts Students United (MSU), a statewide student organization dedicated to mobilizing students to promote affordable public higher education in Massachusetts.

Throughout this process community partners work closely with the CSP staff in order to enhance the preparation of CSP students who will serve in their agencies and to think more ambitiously about capstone projects that will serve both the educational needs of the students and the pressing needs of the organizations. Collaboration with community also creates opportunities to engage with diversity, explore interdependent work, and build authentic relationships. As our students come to be trusted through their work in and with community, their roles become more complex, more involved, and more integrated into how they see themselves as community members and leaders, which is a continual aim of civic identity development.

Engaged Scholarship

All three programs discussed in this chapter place a premium on engaged scholarship, as evidenced by the very word "Scholars" in the titles of the Stanford and UMass programs. For the purposes of this discussion, engaged scholarship is defined as "research in any field that partners university scholarly resources with those in the public and private sectors to enrich knowledge, address and help solve critical societal issues, and contribute to the public good" (Stanton 2008, p. 20). As a model of inquiry, engaged scholarship links theory and experiential knowledge with concrete action. Accordingly, the student or faculty member who performs research is not a solitary, disinterested observer but rather an engaged, dialogical being who collaborates with community partners in the production of knowledge. Not surprisingly then, practitioners of engaged scholarship utilize a variety of participant-centered methods of data generation (for instance, informal interviews) and knowledge dissemination (for example, community-based workshops and presentations).

Reconceptualizing research in this way requires students to unpack conventional assumptions about the purpose of research, the role of the researcher, and the very nature of knowledge itself. What, for example, constitutes valid knowledge? As Stanton observes, "Advocates of engaged research point to the fact that when it is truly responsive to community information needs, as identified by community members, and collaborative in its approach, it yields knowledge that is field-tested and more likely to 'work' than traditional research outcomes" (2008, p. 27). Engaged scholarship thus expands validity criteria to include consideration of the direct and indirect benefits of research for particular communities and the public good. This model prompts students and faculty to think critically about the practice of research, as well as the potential for their research to effect positive change. The latter, in turn, instills a sense of civic agency and cultivates a disposition toward public action.

While students in all three programs carry out engaged scholarship, the Stanford model is exemplary in this regard, in large part due to its culmination in an honors research thesis. Reflections from Stanford students capture the transformative quality of engaged scholarship and the meaning of "research as service." For example, Andrea Romero, a political science major who studied the effectiveness of community-based health-care initiatives in Mozambique, finds that "Research as service connects students with the 'real world.' Students learn what it is like collaborating with organizations and watch their service provide something for a cause bigger than themselves. It not only provides them a means of gaining experience, but also of discovering something they can imagine themselves doing after school and beyond." For Anjali Dixit, a biological sciences major who focused on the health attitudes and behaviors of Indian immigrant women living in the San Francisco Bay Area, research becomes service "by spreading information gathered to change the way people think about a certain social issue, or even by informing the researcher herself to change the way that she thinks about and interacts with the world" (Haas Center 2009, p. 12).

All three programs demonstrate a similar commitment to faculty members who are engaged scholars. Indeed, the PSP department at Providence College recently revised its tenure and promotion guidelines to recognize that community engagement is basic to the teaching and scholarly work of all faculty. Drawing upon the guidelines of the National Review Board for the Scholarship of Engagement, the scholarly agenda and products of faculty are expected to "grow out of [their] teaching and community based experiences, and be developed in dialogue with local, regional, national, and/or international community partners" (Public and Community Service Guidelines for Evaluating Faculty 2008, p. 3).

Since faculty interaction fosters identity development in students (Evans et al. 1998), the role and responsibility of faculty in these civic engagement programs cannot be underestimated. Having faculty as engaged scholars who are connected to these civic engagement programs provides students with consistent and reliable feedback on their work, provides important examples and role models for leading a life consistent with one's values, and offers mentoring to students struggling to make meaning out of their classroom and community experiences. These opportunities often lead to collaborative scholarship by students and their faculty mentors, increased autonomy in academic work, and more willingness to take ownership and responsibility for learning (Boyte 2008).

Commitment to Deep, Reflective Practice

The process of developing civic identity requires critical reflection that affords the opportunity to think deeply on the process, actions, and outcomes associated with community practice. Knefelkamp contends that civic identity requires "active reflection," including "time to reflect with others, active discussion about choices and their possible consequences, and imaginative exercises that help students commit to a better and more just society" (2008, p. 3).

To respond to different learning styles and needs, multiple opportunities for reflection must exist to optimize identity construction and deconstruction. Students should have opportunities to reflect alone or in groups and should utilize multiple methods, such as journals, small-group and paired conversations, and artistic expression, to create as many different experiences as possible to help them understand how their ideas, experiences, and understandings have changed during their time in the program.

Each of the three programs discussed earlier in this chapter explicitly emphasizes the importance of critical reflection. In Stanford's PSSP, students complete weekly reflections designed to capture their thoughts regarding class discussions and their research activities. These reflections provide a valuable outlet for self-expression and prompt lively exchanges among students when permission is granted to share them. Students also use their weekly reflections to clarify their personal values with respect to a host of ethical concerns inherent in their research practice. In the UMass CSP, students are pushed throughout their time in the program to think in terms of praxis — of linking the theory and intellectual work of the classroom to their real-life experiences in the community (and vice versa). This is facilitated though weekly reflection exercises, guided and independent, written and oral. In Providence College's PSP program, critical reflection is exemplified in the Philosophy of Service assignment (see Appendix B). First, all students in PSP 101 are given the assignment of writing their own statement of the role of service in public life. They revisit and rewrite this assignment in both their junior and senior years, in the practicum and capstone courses.

This process of retrospective reflection affords participants the time and space to make "sense of contradictory options" and resolve "difficult tensions" (Youniss et al. 1997, p. 630), in order to develop a personal framework for citizen action (Roholt et al. 2009). A commitment to deep, reflective practice embodies a commitment to continued evaluation of what it means to contribute meaningfully to the greater good. It is a recognition that civic identity cannot be stagnant but evolves as the conditions and circumstances that create and sustain social problems change. This ability to be critically self-reflective (and reflexive) is an indelible skill of the new leadership.

Challenges to Instituting a Sustained, Developmental Approach to Student Civic Leadership

With all of the obvious benefits to creating sustained, developmental, cohort-based civic engagement programs in higher education institutions, we recognize that there are many challenges to doing this. The very length and coherence of such a sustained academic program is a challenge in itself. It is no small coincidence that most service-learning and civic engagement initiatives are one-course, one-semester experiences for students. The kinds of sequencing, student-cohort creation and development, and curricular interventions required by the examples described in this chapter are difficult to accomplish. In order to create academic programs like these, universities need to start from scratch, with ultimate student-learning outcomes in mind, rather than piecing together something from already-existing curricula. And the need for faculty and administration approval of new curricular programs, not to mention additional resources, presents yet another obstacle to overcome in creating such long-term developmental leadership impacts for students. The commitment of students to such sustained academic programs often means their forgoing the choice of other courses or concentrations.

An additional challenge lies in the commitment from faculty that such an approach to leadership education entails. The kind of time commitment necessary from faculty, in terms of curriculum and student development, long-term community partnerships, and assessment of programs and students, is much greater in programs like these than in other courses or programs, even those aimed at engaged student learning. Furthermore, support for engaged scholarship among faculty may be difficult to generate given the prevailing academic culture, particularly at research universities. A central feature of this culture is the reward structure that favors traditional academic research, that "places emphasis on research for its own sake, recognizes [faculty] for its publication in scholarly journals as a primary way of knowing, and rewards [faculty] primarily for the creation of new knowledge, and not necessarily for its utilization through training, consultations, and technical assistance" (Checkoway 2001, p. 136). Under these circumstances students may struggle to find faculty mentors willing to support the kinds of engaged scholarship projects generated in academic programs such as the three explored in this chapter. Furthermore, the sustained effort required to incorporate fully community partners into the research process relies heavily upon faculty in longstanding community partnerships. Their numbers may be limited when few incentives to forge such partnerships exist.

There is also the challenge posed by community partners, even to the sustained and community-oriented approach exemplified by these three programs. A commitment to student voice and leadership may often be in tension with community leadership in defining public problems and their solutions. And regarding students' community-based research or organizing in the advanced stages of such academic programs, questions are raised about how directly and concretely students' research or activism ought to benefit a community. For students whose action plans or research questions arise out of their own interests or are driven primarily by their disciplines, the identification of communities or organizations likely to benefit from their research can be challenging. The academic program, therefore, must serve as a key resource to help students integrate community voice and collaboration into their research, organizing, or action projects. The nature and scope of engagement are not easily defined, however. Indeed, as Rice argues, "engagement with public issues and intellectual independence stand in a delicate balance and the relationship has yet to be worked out" (2003, p. 19). And in so doing, students are likely to confront resistance from those inclined to dismiss engaged scholarship as partisan.

In addition, the student-centered, democratic pedagogy at the heart of programs like these not only is a challenge to create and sustain but also may create cognitive dissonance with more traditional approaches to teaching and learning in the rest of the student's curriculum. Students may end up resisting a more "liberatory education" when their other classes assert more traditional approaches to knowledge and intellectual rigor, and faculty may find themselves marginalized by their more traditional colleagues when they attempt to empower students to think critically or "to come to voice" (hooks 1994).

Finally, a somewhat related challenge is posed when students take leadership and act on the values and with the skills developed in these programs, especially on campus. What happens when we are successful? In their separate treatises on grassroots organizing, Stout and Horton both note that successful challenges to power are likely to be met with violence (Stout 1996; Horton 1998). Our students' mastery of principles of civic leadership has led to activism on campus that, while not received violently, nonetheless has not always been welcomed by campus administrators, and in a few instances has been met with retribution. At Providence College, PSP majors have led efforts on two occasions to pressure the administration to pay its food and custodial service employees a just, living wage, creating tensions with institutional authorities.

At UMass, CSP students or alumni have served as prominent leaders in several campaigns, including the successful 2007 Student General Strike (United Student Action 2007). The strike was precipitated by a number of grievances shared by graduate and undergraduate students at UMass, for example, escalating tuition and fees, reduced student services, undercover police in the dormitories, and increasing privatization and commercialization of space funded through student fees. The action by nearly two thousand UMass students included a one-day boycott of classes, a series of teach-ins, and an impromptu, brief occupation of the UMass administration building. These activities led to months of amicable negotiations between the students and the interim UMass chancellor that ultimately resulted in the university's meeting a number of student demands (United Student Action 2007). Among the demands met was an annual administrative contribution of $50,000 to support travel for service-learning classes. The following year, the administration closed the campus Office for Community Service Learning, putatively as part of a reorganization to cut costs. After a one-year hiatus, the office was reopened under a new, part-time director and with a much-diminished mandate. While the university administration never acknowledged the closing as retributive or connected to the strike, rumors and leaks from within the administration abounded, suggesting that individuals within higher levels of the administration held CSP students (and some of the staff) responsible for what they regarded as an unjustified and embarrassing uprising. Students' joy at their successful and civil negotiations with the interim chancellor was eventually tempered by the aftermath of (the perceived) backlash. This, too, was a valuable lesson in the realities of challenging power and points to perhaps a different definition of student leadership than the one held by the university administration.

Beyond Single-Course, Single-Semester Approaches

Challenges acknowledged, we believe colleges and universities need to move beyond the kind of scattershot, single-course or single-semester approaches that dominate the field of civic engagement and service-learning. For truly effective education for civic leadership to happen, campus administrators and faculty need to examine their existing curricula, with a view to enhancing the ability of students to develop strong relationships and take public action on matters that concern them. This requires linking course work to community-based service or research in order to create a sustained program that builds skills and develops value formation in students over time. In addition, colleges and universities should look to create community, particularly among student participants, but also with faculty and off-campus partners, through the establishment of cohorts that work and learn together over a sustained period of time. The three programs discussed earlier in this chapter offer different options, from a one-year, research-based capstone program to a four-semester sequence to an interdisciplinary major.

What is also needed to move toward more sustained, developmental, cohort-based models of leadership education is a stronger research agenda for evaluating the short- and long-range impact of civic leadership programs. The uniqueness of programs like these, with their sustained, developmental, and communal nature, requires unique approaches to measuring performance and assessing achievement. All three programs, using a collaborative and democratic process, have arrived at a set of outcomes for civic learning and leadership.

At Stanford, the PSSP program director recently developed adaptations of the outcomes for civic learning about self, communities and cultures, knowledge, skills, values, and public action that have been formulated by the Civic Engagement Working Group (Musil 2009, pp. 62–63). In order to forge authentic relationships with community partners, students must be aware of and respond to their positionality as researchers (related to learning about self and values), demonstrate cultural humility and curiosity (related to learning about communities and cultures), recognize the socially constructed and contested nature of knowledge and the politics of evidence (related to learning about knowledge), communicate and cooperate effectively by learning to listen first (related to learning about skills), and follow through on the implementation of a public service plan that counters the extractive nature of much non-community-based research (related to learning about public action). The program also has addressed the need to evaluate the process and impact of engaged research and offers Guba and Lincoln's authenticity criteria (1989) — including fairness, ontological authenticity, educative authenticity, catalytic authenticity, and tactical authenticity — as practical alternatives to more narrowly defined epistemic criteria.

At UMass Amherst, program leaders very early on formulated a set of desired learning outcomes that have driven the curriculum and, more recently, assessment efforts (Polin and Keene 2009). These learning outcomes span three categories: Knowledge for Citizenship, Skills for Citizenship, and Vision for a More Equitable Society. Within each category there are additional subcategories of knowledge that each student needs to master (see Appendix A). These intended outcomes are the result of the collaborative thinking of CSP students, faculty, and staff, and are reviewed, evaluated, and revised annually at program retreats. But the long-term goal of the CSP is to prepare students for lives as active citizens in a vibrant and diverse democracy. The ultimate measures of performance, then, are to be found in how CSP graduates live their lives after they leave UMass. Are they informed, active, engaged, and effective citizens in their communities, and has each of them, in her or his own way, assumed leadership with respect to meaningful issues? Are they conscious of their own agency? Do they feel empowered to act?

At Providence College, faculty, students, and community partners recently developed and implemented a set of student "core competencies" against which the program's overall performance and impact on students could be judged (see Appendix C). With these competencies in place, the PSP program is combining a rigorous self-assessment process with a collective faculty and community partner evaluation process to determine how each student is meeting these competencies. These measures are seen as both formative and summative, so students will soon be asked to assess themselves during the practicum course in order to determine what gaps in the core competencies they need to fill during the final, capstone year of the program.

Each program has produced some evidence of impact on conceptions of civic leadership and action, through course assignments, student self-evaluations, exit interviews, and sporadic reports from alumni after graduation. But now that each program is over a decade old, we recognize the need and the opportunity to evaluate the impacts of our programs longitudinally. As a result, we are planning to conduct a systematic, qualitative research effort, consisting of both individual interviews and focus groups, to document and assess the long-term outcomes of our programs.

The PSP program had a less ambitious study of nearly thirty graduates, conducted in 2006, which unearthed the following themes: that deep relationships with faculty and community mentors have been key to discerning directions to take the public service ethic developed during their time at Providence College; that the relationships with fellow students encouraged by our cohort model continue to support and challenge them in their postgraduate lives; and that the major—particularly the full-year practicum and internship opportunities—gave them the "hard" and "soft" skills necessary for effective community work. This study also revealed the development in students of notions of vocation or civic calling through the program and its opportunities for intensive community experience and reflection. The education in the major, the study concluded, "centered on the clarification of personal values and greater understanding of who they are as people. Often these ideas were framed in terms of how one will make a difference in the world" (Grove 2006, p. 4).

What curricular programs and interventions are likely to yield the student civic leaders this book advances as a new model? The three programs described here make a compelling case for adopting a sustained, developmental, cohort-based approach to curriculum development. Faculty and staff who have struggled to create the current array of single-course, single-semester models for civic engagement may wonder that they may be asked to do more. But if we care about the civic leadership capacities of our students, we can do no less.

APPENDIX A

Intended Outcomes for the Citizen Scholars Program

Learning Category: Knowledge for Citizenship

1. *Political knowledge for democratic citizenship*
   - Elementary conceptions of the functions of government and the roles of citizens in a democracy
   - Conceptions of the ways that citizens can influence the status and actions of government

2. *Service-learning*
   - An understanding of service that locates it within a broader framework of civic engagement, recognizing political action as a related and parallel form of engagement
   - A comprehensive understanding of different models of service, contrasting approaches of charity and justice
   - Service grounded in mutual and reciprocal relationships

3. *Social theory, social analysis, and social justice*
   - A basic introduction to social theory
   - An understanding of why social analysis is necessary; a fundamental understanding of power relations and of manifestations of social injustice in America and beyond. Students will not necessarily develop a comprehensive social analysis within the program but will develop the knowledge necessary to see the need for such analysis and the motivation to seek it in specialized courses in other programs (economics, political economy, social justice, anthropology, sociology, political science, literary criticism, public policy, and so forth).
   - A basic understanding of different conceptual models of justice (for example, distributive justice)
   - A sophisticated understanding of the root causes of at least one major social problem (for example, housing, health care, hunger, AIDS, and so forth) and an elementary understanding of several others
   - Knowledge of the diverse communities in which students serve;

knowledge of communities, societies, or institutions that operate on assumptions different from students' own

- Elementary theoretical and cognitive foundations for understanding and negotiating difference (for example, understanding the concepts of culture, relativism, ethnocentrism, culture shock, privilege, and so forth)
- Exploration by each student of his or her own values, beliefs, assumptions, and life goals within a civic context. Each student understands her or his own social and cultural identities, including the relative privilege or marginalization that such identities entail. Students can locate themselves within a larger set of communities. Students can answer the question: who am I, and what do I stand for?

4. *Tools for change*
   - An understanding of leadership
   - A basic knowledge of many of the tools that an engaged citizenry can use to work for structural change, including, but not limited to, the following: policy analysis and advocacy, grassroots organizing, group and organizational dynamics, oral and written communication, and contemplative practice
   - An understanding of how these tools for change work and how and when each might be effectively used

5. *Communities and community organizations*
   - Knowledge of diverse communities
   - Detailed knowledge of how at least one community organization addresses community problems. This knowledge will include understandings of mission, budget, resources, programs and operations, staffing, clients, and policy—and of how all these elements interact as parts of a system within larger systems to yield both successes and challenges.

Learning Category: Skills of Citizenship

Critical thinking and reading

The ability to:

- construct and define problems in a complex way
- read across many texts, synthesize arguments, and find connections
- engage the ideas of others with one's own original ideas
- engage in dialogical analysis
- look at local community problems and connect them with their root causes

Ethical thinking and reasoning

The ability to:

- assess alternative actions in relation to one's core values, and to select the alternative that best aligns with those values

Inquiry and scholarship

The ability to:

- place issues and interests in a context of scholarship, to recognize that useful ideas, information, and models may already have been formulated by others, and to look in appropriate places to join conversations about the issues of concern
- frame and pursue significant questions about community needs and aspirations, and about public policy and citizen action, using appropriate research methods effectively (using library and internet sources and working directly with people)

Communication

The ability to:

- communicate complex ideas clearly, both orally and in writing
- write for many audiences
- switch codes and knows when this is appropriate (that is, to engage in formal academic or legislative discourse as well as popular or community discourse)

Cultural competence

The ability to:

- hear, consider, and engage points of view that are different from one's own
- work within a community that is different from one's own
- recognize and appreciate cultural difference
- make strides toward seeing the world through the eyes of people who live according to cultural assumptions that differ from one's own
- enter a community (unlike one's own) as an effective ally
- enter and exit a community in ways that do not reinforce ethnocentrism or systemic injustice
- competently participate in work defined as valuable by the community

Leadership and teamwork

The ability to:

- take responsible initiative
- deal with power: sources, kinds, forms that are useful; prescribed versus self-initiated

- see beyond what one knows to be true
- work with others using principles of reciprocity, collaboration, and negotiation; compromise, build consensus, and work in teams in the absence of consensus to facilitate group discussion and deliberation
- take on leadership roles (formal and informal) and also to follow the leadership of others
- decide when to compromise and when not to compromise
- create solutions that are not simply compromises between positions and that do not require compromise

Praxis

The ability to:
- translate thought into action (demonstrated by successfully deepening one's work at a service site and by implementing an organizing project)
- engage in reflective practice; analyze and question one's own beliefs, values, and assumptions while developing an understanding of the beliefs and values of others
- design and implement public policy and community-organizing projects grounded in collaboration with community stakeholders use political skills to recognize, acquire, maintain, and use political power

Social analysis and systems thinking

The ability to:
- link social problems to their root causes
- see social problems as complex and the product of multiple and interrelated causes
- understand complex strategies for addressing social problems

Learning Category: Vision of a More Equitable Society

Commitment and accountability
- Passion for social justice or for civic engagement, in the present and in the course of one's life beyond the university
- Willingness to take responsibility for following through on one's commitments

Compassion and empathy
- Sense of compassion for and connection to the world beyond one's self and one's family
- Desire and capacity to take the perspectives of others, to stretch oneself toward the experiences of others
- Conviction: the belief in one's ability to make a difference; the intention to live with integrity and to act in accordance with one's ethical vision

Philosophy of Service Assignment (PSP 101 version)

At the beginning of the semester, you were asked to construct your service autobi-ography. At the end of the semester, we are asking you to take this one step further, to articulate your "philosophy of service." In its final form this will be a one-para-graph statement of your philosophy of service, followed by a narrative of three to five pages explaining the paragraph statement. Since this assignment is the culmi-nating one for the course, among the things you might want to consider are: your definition of service; what values, motivations, or goals underlay your understand-ing of service and the service you choose or want to do; the relationship you seek to establish with those whom you serve (including how you understand the people being served, their "needs" and "assets," how you prepare for entering and exiting service, how you confront the various critiques of service, and so forth); how you understand "community" and how that impacts your philosophy of service; and how, if at all, issues of citizenship or politics enter into your philosophy of service. In the narrative portion of the paper, you should identify readings or class discus-sions that were transformative for your thinking about service or the development of this statement.

Core Competencies of the Public and Community Service Studies
Curriculum and Major

Over the past two years, faculty, students, and community partners of the Feinstein Institute have been working on identifying and defining a set of core competen-cies or capacities that we believe should emerge from the Public and Community Service Studies curriculum. Descriptions of the competencies have been left in-tentionally general, so that future students, faculty, and community partners may bring their own experiences to bear on each area and thus add further definition to the competencies as they have been developed to date. The PSP faculty sup-ports the idea that students' senior portfolios and presentations will be evaluated against the competencies described below.

1. "*Eloquent listening*" *competency.* We borrow the term "listen eloquently" from Langston Hughes. This first competency refers not just to what some call "ac-tive listening," but to a capacity Nell Morton describes as "hearing people into speech." The ability to listen eloquently allows someone to discern the interests of others in conversation, as well as find common ground in working for com-munity change (see Margaret Wheatley's ideas about "simple conversations [to] change the world").

Specific skills and experiences: storytelling, the ability to find common interests in one-to-one conversations, use of field notes as practice in observation and as the basis for reflection (ethnography), conflict resolution, stakeholder analysis, community mapping.

2. *Organizational competency.* Over the years we have found that college-age students, especially ones coming into this major, have an antipathy to institutions, organizations, and organizational thinking. They seek to intervene directly in the world and its problems, through service and other forms of direct action. The ability to engage in organizational analysis, however, is critical, if one is to act effectively. Public and Community Service Studies majors require the ability to think institutionally and systemically, to consider the organizational (power) structures and imperatives within which service and other human interventions take place.

    Specific skills and experiences: budgeting and financial analysis and development; power mapping; volunteer management; strategic planning; general knowledge of organizational models and analysis of systems; skills in group process, organizing, advocacy, and conflict resolution.

3. *Cross-cultural competency.* While it may be impossible to be completely competent across cultural boundaries, it is possible to achieve "cultural humility," and to be competent at "crossing borders" (to use Gloria Anzaldua's phrase) of race, class, gender, religion, and culture. This requires a self-knowledge of culturally influenced fears and biases, an articulated understanding of difference, and the ability to overcome fear of the other. It also includes a global awareness (the ability to link locally and globally).

    Specific skills and experiences: a range of experiences, readings, and especially dialogues with others from different backgrounds; communication across cultural differences; foreign language exposure.

4. *Personal competencies.* In 2006, Maggie Grove conducted interviews with twenty-five PSP senior majors and alumni going back to the first graduating class. In her conversations with these public service students and alumni, the primary outcome of participating in the major, for all of them, was their ability to develop and clarify personal values related to service, career, and making an impact on the world based on passions and principles. This area of personal competencies continues to be central to the PSP curriculum.

    Specific skills and experiences:
    - Authenticity: being true to oneself, which involves knowing oneself; alignment of personal values and organizational mission; discernment of one's personal and civic calling

- Confidence: being honest, open, and clear; the ability to step into fears
- The ability to move out of one's comfort zone; maintaining a sense of oneself when off balance and in new situations
- Knowing how to use trial and error
- Values clarification
- Reflective ability and critical thinking

5. *Writing and public speaking.* Communications skills are essential to any undergraduate major, and to citizenship in a democracy more generally. But Public and Community Service Studies majors need to be able to communicate their thoughts and actions, both vertically to community and world leaders, and horizontally to fellow students and community members.

Specific skills and experiences: the ability to write well, which includes editing and proofing skills and the ability to write to specific audiences. Public speaking involves not only the capacity to speak to different groups but also the ability to converse one-on-one and to present visual materials in public.

6. *Specific issue and content competency related to "track."* In addition to the core curriculum, each PSP major chooses a "track" that ideally reflects the student's interest and passion in a specific area related to public service and community development or change. We expect students to be able to develop specific competencies related to this passion or interest.

Specific skills and experiences:
- Analytical skills related to a specific issue or area
- The ability to identify and develop mastery of an issue or interest area (for example, public health or immigration), from charity to policy
- Research skills
- Familiarity with a relevant literature in a specific field (and the definition of that literature if necessary)
- Systems analysis and thinking
- Writing and presentation

REFERENCES

Addes, D., and A. Keene. (2004). Grassroots community development at UMass-Amherst: The professorless classroom. In *Students as colleagues: Expanding the circle of service-learning leadership,* ed. E. Zlotkowski, N. Longo, and J. Williams, 227–40. Boston: Campus Compact.

Battistoni, R. (1997). Service learning as civic learning: Lessons we can learn from our students. In *Education for citizenship: Ideas and innovations in political learning,* ed. G. Reeher and J. Cammarano, 31–49. Lanham, MD: Rowman and Littlefield Publishers.

———. (1998). Making a major commitment: Public and community service at Providence College. In *Successful service-learning programs*, ed. E. Zlotkowski, 169–88. Bolton, MA: Anker Publishing Company.

Bernstein, R. (1983). *Beyond objectivism and relativism: Science, hermeneutics, and praxis.* Philadelphia: University of Pennsylvania Press.

Bickford, D. M., and N. Reynolds. (2002). Activism and service-learning: Reframing volunteerism as acts of dissent. *Pedagogy: Critical approaches to teaching, literature, language, composition and culture* 2 (2): 229–54.

Boyte, H. (2008). Against the current: Developing the civic agency of students. *Change* 40 (3). Retrieved on July 31, 2010, from: http://www.changemag.org/Archives/Back%20Issues/May-June%202008/full-against-the-current.html.

Bronfenbrenner, U. (1993). The ecology of cognitive development: Research models and fugitive findings. In *Development in context: Acting and thinking in specific environments*, ed. R. H. Wozniak and K. W. Fischer, 3–44. Hillsdale, NJ: Erlbaum.

———. (1995). Developmental ecology through space and time: A future perspective. In *Examining lives in context: Perspectives on the ecology of human development*, ed. P. Moen and G. H. Elder Jr., 619–47. Washington, D.C.: American Psychological Association.

Checkoway, B. (2001). Renewing the civic mission of the American research university. *Journal of Higher Education* 72 (2): 125–47.

Chickering, A., and L. Reisser. (1993). *Education and identity.* 2nd ed. San Francisco: Jossey-Bass.

Colby, A., E. Beaumont, T. Ehrlich, and J. Corngold. (2007). *Educating for democracy: Preparing undergraduates for responsible political engagement.* Stanford, CA: Carnegie Foundation for the Advancement of Teaching.

Evans, N. J., D. S. Forney, and F. Guido-DiBrito. (1998). *Student development in college: Theory, research, and practice.* San Francisco: Jossey-Bass.

Freire, P. (1970). *Pedagogy of the oppressed.* New York: Continuum.

Goldstein, K., M. Marino, and C. Mathewson. (2005). Chronicling the evolution of PSSP: A community of scholars. Accessed August 24, 2009, at: http://vpsa-web.stanford.edu/sites/default/files/haas/files/CommunityofScholars_HWP.pdf.

Guba, E. and Y. S. Lincoln. (1989). *Fourth generation evaluation.* Newbury Park, CA: Sage.

Haas Center for Public Service. (Summer 2009). *Commons.* Stanford, CA: Haas Center for Public Service.

Haas Center for Public Service. (n.d.). "Public Service Scholars Program." Available from: http://vpsa-web.stanford.edu/haas/pssp.

hooks, b. (1994). *Teaching to transgress: Education as the practice of freedom.* New York: Routledge.

Horton, M. (1998). *The long haul: An autobiography.* New York: Teachers College Press.

Hudson, W., and R. Trudeau. (1995). An essay on the institutionalization of service-learning: The genesis of the Feinstein Institute for Public Service. *Michigan Journal of Community Service-Learning* 2:150–58.

Jacoby, B., and Associates. (2009). *Civic engagement in higher education: Concepts and practices.* San Francisco: Jossey-Bass.

Kahne, J. E., and S. E. Sporte. (2008). Developing citizens: The impact of civic learning opportunities on students' commitment to civic participation. *American Educational Research Journal* 45 (3): 738–66.

Kecskes, K., and S. Kerrigan. (2009). Capstone experiences. In B. Jacoby and Associates 2009, 117–39.

Kelly, A., and H. Lena. (2006). Providence College: The community assistant model. In *Students as colleagues: Expanding the circle of service-learning leadership*, ed. E. Zlotkowski, N. Longo, and J. Williams, 121–33. Providence, RI: Campus Compact.

Klein, N. (2007). *The shock doctrine: the rise of disaster capitalism*. New York: Picador.

Knefelkamp, L. L. (2008). Civic identity: Locating self in community. *Diversity and Democracy* 11 (2): 1–3.

Longo, N. V., C. Drury, and R. M. Battistoni. (2006). Catalyzing political engagement: Lessons for civic educators from the voices of students. *Journal of Political Science Education* 2 (3): 313–29.

Meade, J. (2009). Connecting community service learning and radical engaged pedagogy to the recovered factory movement in Argentina: An anthropological reflection. Capstone experience manuscript archived at Commonwealth College, University of Massachusetts Amherst.

Medoff, P., and H. Sklar. (1994). *Streets of hope: The fall and rise of an urban neighborhood*. Boston: South End Press.

Mitchell, T. D. (2007). Critical service-learning as social justice education: A case study of the citizen scholars program. *Equity and Excellence in Education* 40 (2): 101–12.

———. (2008). Traditional vs. critical service-learning: Engaging the literature to differentiate two models. *Michigan Journal of Community Service-Learning* 14 (2): 50–65.

Musil, C. (2009). Educating students for personal and social responsibility: The civic learning spiral. In B. Jacoby and Associates 2009, 49–68. San Francisco: Jossey-Bass.

Polin, D. K., and A. S. Keene. (Under review). Bringing an ethnographic sensibility to the assessment of service learning: The evolution of evaluation in the Citizen Scholars Program.

Public and Community Service Guidelines for Evaluating Faculty. (2008). Tenure and Promotion Guidelines for Department of Public and Community Service Studies, Providence College.

Renn, K. A. (2004). *Mixed race students in college: The ecology of race, identity and community on campus*. Albany: State University of New York Press.

Rice, R. E. (Fall 2003). Rethinking scholarship and engagement: The struggle for new meanings. *Campus Compact Reader*, 1–9.

Roholt, R. V., R. W. Hildreth, and M. Baizerman. (2009). *Becoming citizens: Deepening the craft of youth civic engagement*. New York: Routledge.

Stanton, T. (2008). New times demand new scholarship: Opportunities and challenges for civic engagement at research universities. *Education, Citizenship and Social Justice* 3 (1): 19–42.

Stout, L. (1996). *Bridging the class divide and other lessons for grassroots organizing.* Boston: Beacon Press.

United Student Action. (2007). Available from: http://www.unitedstudentaction.org.

Weick, K. E. (1995). *Sensemaking in organizations.* Thousand Oaks, CA: Sage Publications.

Youniss, J., J. A. McLellan, and M. Yates. (1997). What we know about engendering civic identity. *American Behavioral Scientist* 40 (5): 620–31.

Sarah McCauley, Nicole Nicotera, Eric Fretz,
Sarah Nickels, Charla Agnoletti, Hannah Goedert,
Emelye Neff, Taylor Rowe, and Russell Takeall

7

Civic Leadership and Public Achievement at the University of Denver's Center for Community Engagement and Service Learning

Our ideas in this chapter approach leadership within a framework of community organizing and public work that we practice through our work at the Center for Community Engagement and Service Learning (CCESL) at the University of Denver. We locate our definition and practice of civic leadership within a citizen-centered model of community organizing, specifically the community-organizing tradition that was originated by Saul Alinsky in Chicago in the 1940s and that has been subsequently developed through the Industrial Areas Foundation (IAF) and other national organizing groups such as the Gamaliel Foundation.

This tradition of community organizing in the United States is rooted in cultural pluralism, the struggle for social justice, and the involvement of ordinary people in important public issues. Community organizing as it was laid out by Alinsky and carried on by the IAF finds and cultivates local leaders, activates the talents and capacities of ordinary people, and facilitates grassroots efforts to make communities better places in which to live. And contrary to what tends to be the popular view of community organizing, this model of civic leadership is not about organizations and institutions' mobilizing citizens to accomplish their work, nor is it about engagement in 1960s-style protest politics.

Conventional leadership theories (Kouzes and Posner 2002; Heifetz 1999; Chrislip 1994) pay little attention to community-organizing principles, focusing more on an individualistic approach to leadership in which the group attends to some leader at the top of a hierarchy, often one powerful person. By contrast, community organizers and civic leaders who embrace a citizen-centered approach to community problem solving encourage group members to act as leaders and agents in their own right. They invest in the important public activities of strengthening their community and creating social change by encouraging leadership among members as a means of fostering each person's development into a civic leader. Ultimately civic leaders and organizers cultivate the power of ordinary people to transform their lives, create strong communities and local change through democracy, and practice what Harry Boyte describes as "everyday politics" (2005).

This chapter exemplifies how students develop the public skills to engage in these everyday politics. Five of the authors of this chapter are students in Public Achievement, a civic engagement program at the University of Denver (DU). First we discuss the process of working with these students. Then, through the writing of these students, we arrive at a definition of civic leadership that was cocreated through this very process. Finally, we conclude with concrete ways for colleges and universities to work with students to develop the public skills and understanding necessary for civic leadership.

Students Cocreating Civic Engagement: The Writing Process

Public Achievement (PA), an initiative founded by the Center for Democracy and Citizenship at Augsburg College, focuses on building civic agency among young people by enabling high school and college students to collaborate on public work projects that produce tangible community results. (For a fuller treatment of DU's PA project, see Fretz and Longo 2010; see Boyte 2005; Boyte and Shelby 2008, for a detailed explanation of Public Achievement as an international movement; see also the Public Achievement Web site: http://www.publicachievement.org.) Currently, the DU Center for Community Engagement and Service Learning (CCESL) trains forty students each year to act as PA coaches in one of the five school partnerships that have been developed throughout the Denver public school system. CCESL has run and managed a Public Achievement program since 2003. Public Achievement at the University of Denver is supported through institutional and external resources. The bulk of the support for PA comes from the Provost's Office, which supports a full-time Associate Director in the Center for Community Engagement and Service Learning to run PA and other school-based civic engagement programs. Additional funds are leveraged through the Federal Community Work Study program, AmeriCorps Education Awards, and a variety of local foundations. (For more information on how PA is supported at DU and how you might develop and sustain PA at your institution, contact us at ccesl@du.edu.)

Public Achievement engages college students with groups of middle school and high school students to identify issues that they care about and to find ways that they can effectively act for change. College students act as coaches for the younger students, helping them to navigate the process of public action. The coaches and students in PA learn the public skills that they need to produce public work. They also practice a different way of looking at the world, not as something imposed upon them, but as something that they can mold.

Throughout the process, coaches build public relationships with the students in their groups, challenge their students to build powerful public relationships with community members outside their schools, and engage others in public issues through one-to-one interviews, house meetings, power mapping, facilitation, and public dialogue. They learn the importance of identifying and understanding self-interest, both their own and that of the people with whom they work. Together they learn to understand power as power *with* and power *to*, rather than power *over*. As they learn to practice politics, coaches and students engage with tension, learn to negotiate difference, and develop critical and active listening skills. Public Achievement fosters a collaborative learning environment, valuing the knowledge that each person brings to the table. As a result, coaches and students learn these skills and lessons together.

Public Achievement is not about tutoring, mentoring, or teaching K–12 students from a transactional or banking model of education (Freire 1993). Rather, PA is about activating self-interests, political agency, and the ability that we all have to accomplish public, tangible work in communities. A typical PA session begins with the coach's helping the group establish roles. In order to develop active agency and personal responsibility, each PA session has a designated facilitator, evaluator, recorder, timekeeper, and encourager (for more on roles, see Erlanson and Hildreth 1989). The facilitator works with the group to establish an agenda for the day, and then the group moves into work mode. Attention is focused on students' local knowledge, or what they know and understand about the issue, as well as relationships they have with others who also care about the issue. Public Achievement groups often invite adults and community members who are working on the same issues to visit and engage with students in collaborative ways, but not to teach. On any given day, in any PA group, students are constructing "power maps," conducting one-to-one relational meetings, calling and e-mailing people who care about or understand the issue they are working on, developing surveys, or doing research on the issue their group has chosen.

In the past five years of PA at the University of Denver, students have produced tangible public products that have improved the communities in and around their schools. In 2005, students at Cole Middle School created a student newspaper focused on things students cared about in their community in order to address the issue of youth voice. In 2006, Bryant Webster Middle School students delivered a presentation to the Denver Public School Board and received funding for a learning landscape that transformed the grassless field behind their school. Bruce Randolph School students ran an antidiscrimination commitment and Know Your Rights campaign in their school in partnership with the Colorado Progressive Coalition in 2007. In 2009, North High School students held an event to address the issue of parent involvement in their school by engaging students and parents together to understand and use the resources at North High and the surrounding community. Most recently, South High School students have created a peer mentoring program to address access to and preparation for higher education. All of these projects were produced by groups of students, with college coaches helping to guide and facilitate the process of civic engagement.

Our group of writers for this chapter developed from different levels of the PA program: Fretz directs the Center for Community Engagement and Service Learning, where PA is housed at the University of Denver, and McCauley is the Student Civic Engagement Coordinator there. Nicotera, Associate Professor of Social Work, and Nickels, a PhD student in social work, have experiences in youth civic engagement development. Agnoletti, Goedert, Rowe, Neff, and Takeall, the major contributors to this chapter, are undergraduate civic engagement practitioners and students at the University of Denver who used their experiences as PA coaches to reflect on the meaning of civic leadership.

Each of the student contributors was asked to write an essay about the lessons they learned from their PA coaching experiences as they related to PA's core concepts (public work, politics, self-interest, power, citizenship, democracy, freedom, free spaces, diversity, accountability, learning from each other, tension, and vulnerability), and its broadly conceived definition of civic leadership. The students used the context of a critical incident that they had experienced in their work as coaches to reflect on how those experiences helped them to develop into specific types of leaders. (For full versions of their critical incident journals, see: http://www.du.edu/ccesl/student/publicachievement.html. See also Cooper 1998 for a detailed pedagogical example of how critical incident journals can be used in a service-learning classroom.) As the students developed their essays, the entire team of writers met weekly and often read their draft essays aloud. This process fostered lively conversations about the core concepts of PA, the development of polished essays, and a linking of the core PA concept with the students' experiences. In addition to the weekly meetings, students learned how to apply a qualitative approach to analyzing one another's essays for pertinent quotations related to the core concepts, in order to consider the commonalities and differences among their individual experiences as PA coaches. These processes resulted in a focus on three defining characteristics of civic leadership: self-interest, politics, and power, which we explain in the following section.

The process of writing this section of the chapter has been unique and inspiring. This is the most dialogical writing project in which any of us have ever participated or developed. Because there were so many writers, the process was messy and energizing, frustrating and rewarding. The final product reads like a set of reflections on Public Achievement and community organizing and uses PA student writing to produce a full-fledged definition of civic leadership. We present the results of this collaborative writing effort and definition within the context of the Alinsky model of community organizing. In the next section, we review the literature that defines these core concepts of civic leadership in order to facilitate the reader's understanding of the connections between the concepts and students' experiences as voiced in their essays.

Student Civic Engagement through Community-Organizing Models

The student writers' experiences in Public Achievement and their practice of civic leadership led the team of authors of this chapter to identify self-interest, power, and politics as three important aspects of civic leadership often overlooked in traditional leadership theories that draw directly from the organizing tradition of Saul Alinsky. Much has been written about Alinsky and the community-organizing tradition that he developed through his work in Chicago and through the IAF (Bailey 1974; Lancourt 1979; Finks 1984; Horwitt 1992; Warren 2001; Osterman 2002; Gecan 2004). Over the years, as the United States has become increasingly polarized over political issues, Alinsky and the entire community-organizing tradition have frequently been co-opted by ideologically driven groups on the left and right, misread by academics and journalists, crammed into "management" models, and generally thought to produce senseless rabble-rousing. As a result, Alinsky's tactics (humiliating public officials, organizing street protests, and so forth) as they are described in *Rules for Radicals* are often overemphasized, and his fundamental principles of social justice, civil rights, and the pursuit of a fair and equitable society, which are more clearly articulated in his first book *Reveille for Radicals*, are neglected or forgotten by the public. Following Alinsky's death in 1972, his ideas "grew up" through the thinking and practice of his successors in the IAF, Ernesto Cortes and Edward Chambers. Nowadays, while the IAF and other organizing institutes are surely indebted to the legacy of Alinsky, their public tactics are significantly more relational and civil, and less reactionary.

Next, we define Alinsky's ideas of self-interest, power, and politics as they motivate the way we talk about and practice civic leadership. This background should be clear from the student writings that follow.

Self-interest is what makes a particular person or group connected to (or interested in) an issue or problem in his or her community. Understanding and working with self-interest was one of the cornerstones of Alinsky's organizing model. Self-interest is the foundation of public action and social change; it is, as Alinsky wrote, the "prime motivating force in man's [sic] behavior" (Alinsky 1971/1989, p. 53) and concerned the self among others. Uncovering self-interest is accomplished through one-to-one interviews: strategic meetings to figure out another person's self-interest, ideas, motivations, and visions and to identify where they intersect with one's own. Chambers describes a one-to-one as "one organized spirit going after another person's spirit for connection, confrontation and exchange of talent and energy" (2004, p. 44). The first step in community organizing is understanding and tapping into the self-interests of local leaders. "You start with the people, their traditions, their prejudices, their habits, their attitudes, and all of those other circumstances that make up their lives" (Alinsky 1946/1989, p. 78). Alinsky understood that approaching people on the "basis of common understanding" was the first step in activating ordinary people's sense of political agency (Alinsky 1946/1989, p. 93).

Power is an ability to act. As Chambers and Cowan write, power is "given to us at birth. Power is our birthright, our inheritance. [Power] is the basis of our capacity to address differences through politics" (2004, p. 27). In today's world, where the concept of power is highlighted as part and parcel of privileged social and cultural identities and is upheld by systemic oppression, the idea of a power as a birthright can be viewed as problematic. Therefore, we emphasize that power as a birthright is an essential component of the agency inherent in all individuals and communities, from which they find the strength to stand against social injustice. This power is the power to act *with* and *to*, as opposed to power over others.

Politics, the third concept of civic leadership, refers to creating public strategies for addressing and solving community problems with others through relationships, negotiation, tension, power, and democracy. Each of these concepts, self-interest, power, and politics, will be woven throughout this chapter as we arrive at a definition of civic leadership, especially through the narratives of students' struggles with power, privilege, and oppression in their work as PA coaches.

Charla Agnoletti

Charla Agnoletti was born and raised in Denver, Colorado. She attended the University of Denver and worked in the Denver Public Schools (DPS) as a PA coach for four years. Charla graduated from DU in 2009 with a degree in Spanish and Sociology and now teaches middle school English with Teach for America. Charla explains her motivation for participating as a PA coach as having always been rooted in her own experiences of the education gap that exists in the Denver community and in this nation. She holds the belief that if youth are the future, then they must be given meaningful educational opportunities and opportunities to express themselves as leaders and cocreators of their realities and communities. She worked with PA groups that focused on student life at Manual High School.

In the following section, Charla discusses how civic leaders understand and practice power and work with tension. PA coaches practice power as a negotiated, relational process that is acted out through public voice and that, when exercised authentically, elicits strong public relationships through which people act on their political agency. PA coaches and their students discover that real power is power with others and power to act toward a goal, rather than power over others. Charla's piece demonstrates the importance of civic leaders' recognizing and skillfully working with the tension that occurs as individuals move from ideas of power *over* to those of power *with* and power *to*. Tension, in this regard, requires that leaders be vulnerable and listen critically to what they are hearing from other individuals. Tension is viewed as an opportunity for the growth and negotiation in which our biggest successes are born. Charla describes how civic leaders create innovative and inclusive actions and goals by engaging in tension and finding collaborative solutions.

The critical moment during my experience as a PA coach dealt with power, but not a positive type of power among or of power to act. This was a classic power struggle. My co-coach and I were working with three different groups of students. One group was trying to reform school lunch policies, another was working on updating the school lounge, and a third was examining the school dress-code policy. One day, we decided to work with the students in one big group, since each group was researching its own issue. On this particular day, the students were unfocused and unengaged. My fellow coach confronted the students, "Do you guys want to do this?" she asked. "If you don't want us to be here, you need to tell us." Shocked, the students became silent and dropped their gazes to the floor. When they finally responded, they expressed a disbelief in their ability to change anything at their school, making statements such as, "nothings gonna change anyways."

At that point, an ROTC group passed by, and our students started talking about how cool it was that the ROTC members got to practice with guns at school. I got mad and said, "If you wanted to practice with guns, then you should have joined ROTC, but you did not, so pay attention." The students were, rightly, offended. They gave me dirty looks, and I felt ashamed. I reacted badly to their lack of respect, and I realized that I had missed the opportunity to be proactive in a negative, resistant situation. My reaction fueled a negative tension within the group.

I could have been more effective as a coach by applying my understanding of power as an ability to act and by working with the tension and frustration rather than letting it get to me. I could have addressed the student disrespect or created a space in which to open up a conversation about the specific incident, as well as larger issues of power and respect, to highlight for the students and coaches how power and its dynamics affect each of us in both negative and positive ways. It is important to be confrontational, yet at the same time to be so in a way that encourages participation.

When I reacted to the students, I was not practicing authentic power. In this particular situation I felt that I was being disrespected and sought to regain power through authority. Authentic power creates egalitarian relationships, inspires confident action, and changes the lives of individuals and communities for the best. Authentic power comes from being proactive in addressing difficult situations, in a way that does not demean others but works to foster a more respectful and productive environment and community. This critical moment during my PA work allowed me to understand power in its negative context, providing an opportunity to address the common tensions that arise in PA groups. It is often difficult for a student coach to know how to manage behavior and disrespect. However, through a recognition of the importance of experiencing power struggles, I am able truly to understand power and how best to practice it in the PA program. Central to being an effective PA coach and civic leader is the ability to recognize and address tensions as they occur; dealing with power in politics is not always clear-cut and positive, but through PA work authentic power can be understood.

After this critical incident, I was able to exercise power in different and more effective ways. I began to cultivate power in the relationships between myself and the youth. We were able to have conversations about our differences, our similarities, and our common understanding of our own power as community leaders. One specific instance occurred during a reflection at the end of the year, when our time together was structured as an open dialogue regarding power, public work, and the outcome of our PA work together. Students were given the opportunity to express their new impressions of power and themselves. In this instance they exercised their power through meaningful conversations; as coaches, we had shown them how to access power and then provided the safe space for them to realize and reflect on that power within themselves and each other.

The results of the PA work in which I engaged came in many forms. Of course there are the tangible results: a student-produced video about drug prevention, a school assembly about gang prevention, student-led meetings with principals about school-based issues, and the possibility of opening a school store. However, the most powerful results of my involvement with PA work have been the changes that this type of public work has made on the attitudes and actions of youth. I have built relationships with youth who have found their own capacity to exercise power and transform their worlds into the places where they want to live and thrive. I have seen youth change from apathetic individuals into community leaders. Public Achievement has instilled, within me and the many youth with whom I have worked, the importance of public work and leadership in education.

Hannah Goedert

Hannah Goedert is a third-year real estate and finance major at DU and has been a PA coach for two years. In 2009, she was recognized by the governor of Colorado for her community work. Hannah's motivation for Public Achievement comes from her passion for helping kids get to college. She loves to empower young voices because she believes that they are our future and deserve all of our focus. During Hannah's first year as a Public Achievement coach, she worked with a group of tenth-graders at Bruce Randolph School on racism and discrimination. These issues are very personal for all of the Latino youth at that school. The project of Hannah's second PA group centered on getting more of the group's peers to attend college.

In the following narrative, Hannah Goedert couples the one-to-one interview with an exercise called a "privilege walk," to get at her students' self-interests and to uncover difficult issues of identity and diversity. Hannah's experience speaks to the need for civic leaders to be comfortable with ambiguity and to trust that engaging diverse voices and self-interests within the group will yield positive outcomes.

My PA group was working on the issue of racism against teens. Before I began my work as a PA coach, I enjoyed images of all of my students getting along, inspired and excited to accomplish their community work. Those images were quickly dashed. The fresh, smiling faces I imagined turned out to be frustrated and blank. My co-coach and I tried many different ways to engage the students. Sometimes we caught glimpses of their true feelings, but more often than not we were met with indifference. I talked with the students enough that I knew they were interested in enacting their agency and making a good life for themselves, but when I asked them why they chose to work on the issue of racism against teens, they would produce superficial answers that were obviously worded to free them from any emotional obligation. They tried to distance themselves from their true feelings because otherwise they would have to take action, which they saw at the time as pointless. It seemed to me that they silenced those thoughts because it was ingrained inside of them that they lacked power over the issue they chose. This, in turn, made me feel powerless.

Almost all of the students in my PA group were Latino, with roots in Mexico. It made sense to me that they cared about the issue of racism; they felt it every day, everywhere they went. I, on the other hand, was born and raised in Golden, Colorado, and I enjoy the privileges of being white. I never traveled much, and I never really spent time with people who were very different from me. When I began to reflect on these differences between my PA students and me, I started to realize why they might not want to talk to me about racism in their lives.

As a way to get at these differences and to form a stronger collaborative bond with our students, my co-coach and I decided to engage in a privilege walk. The members of the group stood side by side as a unit, and then each person took a step forward every time he or she answered "no" to a question, including such questions as: Do you feel you have ever been treated unfairly? Has anyone ever judged you because of the way you look? Do you ever feel like people do not listen to what you have to say because of your background? The more steps you took, the more privilege you enjoyed. There were about seven of us participating, and after the first few questions about unfair treatment in the past we were pretty much all on the same level. As a group, we started to recognize the similarities that we had and how common it is for people to feel discriminated against. At the end, no one was more than a few steps apart, but the kids who were the most reluctant to participate (and who were, by and large, Latino) ended up in the back of the line.

I followed up the privilege walk by conducting one-to-one relational meetings with each of the students. This was important because, while the privilege walk is a good way to highlight difference, it can also leave people feeling, on the one hand, isolated and alone, or, on the other hand, guilty. For example, I met with a young man named Pablo, who was one of the students at the back of the line by the end of the privilege walk (all high school students' names have been changed to protect their privacy). Pablo talked about the bullying that he and his friends had experienced because of his race. He noted that everywhere he went he felt that people were saying things behind his back or even to his face. Pablo had developed strong negative feelings of his own against people and authorities of other races due to the treatment he received.

The one-to-ones came at a crucial time in our PA group. They, along with the privilege walk, allowed us to talk openly about the things that separated us, so that we could work together to address the issue of racism. Few of the kids understood what building public relationships really meant before Public Achievement. Eventually each student recognized the meaning of her or his presence in this group and understood that these experiences gave him or her the power to initiate change in his or her community. Without all of the experiences of our group members I do not think that respect and consistency would have been established. After working extensively on the issue of racism and discrimination for a year, the group that I worked with finally felt comfortable recognizing and admitting the problem at hand. The problem was very up close and personal for almost every student at the school, so the group wanted to figure out a way for students to become more accepting of one another and to work together to confront the way their race was treated in the community.

After learning how much racism and discrimination affect the lives of so many individuals, from children to adults, the students really felt empowered and yearned to make a difference. For their final project they wanted to do something to bring this topic to the attention of as many people as possible, to force people to think about how they acted on a daily basis. One of the members was an excellent artist, so he designed a t-shirt to get the message across and included some helpful tips on dealing with police discrimination, which was one of the topics they learned more about. Another member spoke to the Colorado Progressive Coalition to seek financial support for printing as many t-shirts as possible. Then, as the culmination of the work, each member of the group stood up during the lunch hour at school, encouraged every student to sign a pledge to stop racism and discrimination, and handed out the t-shirts. This project not only gave these few students a voice and empowered them to make a difference. It also showed their peers what they can do and made them aware of an important issue. It ignited a fire in many students when they put on the t-shirts and embodied the goal of the whole project.

Hannah's experience with the privilege walk shows the importance of understanding how social structures of racial privilege and oppression influence the work of civic leaders. It also demonstrates that vulnerability is tantamount to gaining enough trust to access individuals' self-interests, so that they move themselves to action. Hannah's insights into the experiences of her students, as well as her own social location, allowed her to work with them and to motivate the group to affect change at their school.

Taylor Rowe

Taylor Rowe is a sophomore at the University of Denver working on a major in international business and a double minor in Spanish and legal studies. She began working with PA during her freshman year at DU because she believed the program to be an excellent way to learn about community involvement beyond volunteerism. Her PA groups worked on issues including gangs, police harassment, and school lunches. The group she wrote about addressed police harassment against youth and minorities by successfully working with the Colorado Progressive Coalition to create a video raising awareness about "Knowing Your Rights."

My co-coach had prefaced our first PA meeting by remarking, "Taylor, one of the girls is on house arrest," and "they have piercings and tattoos and they're freshmen in high school!" When I stepped in the room for the first time, all I could see were dark brown eyes staring back at me. We began with introductions. I talked excitedly about my life and my interest in getting to know them and working with them, and I was met with blank stares and an obvious lack of respect. The next few meetings turned into an unstated, silent battle for power. My credentials and background were not impressive to these students, and my lack of understanding of their culture, ways of talking, and ways of being together presented an unavoidable dilemma. When I asked them questions about themselves and their communities, they would mumble, "You don't know, miss." And they were right; I did not know.

Despite all this, I was still affected by these students, and I soon began to reflect on the idea of diversity as I saw how this sometimes elusive and abstract concept was part of our group. We went wrong when we allowed our differences to build tension and conflict, rather than using those differences to work collaboratively and assist in making a difference in the community. I needed to figure out how to work through the inevitable tension to negotiate difference.

One of the ways I accomplished this was through conducting one-to-one relational meetings with the students. An example is the one-to-one I did with Maria, a very talented but attitude-ridden leader of the group. I motioned for her to leave the room with me. As soon as we entered the girl's restroom, she broke down in tears and laid her head against me. I was so moved by her new actions of vulnerability that we stood in silence for a while. Eventually, she shared her story with me, not forgetting any detail. I struggled to give advice: Should I make myself vulnerable? Should I advise her? Should I be her friend? As the story continued to unravel, I found myself thinking less and listening more. During this interview, I learned that exploring diversity of perspective and using its resulting tension to develop a successful group can yield relationships and positive results. So the one-to-one was successful in that I was able to build a personal relationship with Maria, but the PA program is not just about personal relationships. As a coach, I had to figure out how that personal relationship could be translated into a public relationship that would allow Maria and me to work together.

The following week, Maria's participation in class was positive and representative of the work the group performed: she had transformed her role. Her peers responded to Maria's behavior immediately, and the team began working to incorporate the ideas of all the students to achieve a cohesive goal. My co-coach and I were astonished by Maria's transformation and abilities. Maria's change of perspective led the way for her attitude to change the course of the group; my preconceived judgments and fight for power dissolved as I opened myself up to the group.

I learned that civic leadership is a constant struggle and that respect is earned by understanding others' experiences. In the realm of civic leadership, power cannot be assumed but rather is developed over time. In order to create a group that has a positive impact on group members and the community, it is necessary to build relationships based on this knowledge.

Taylor demonstrates how self-interest and the exercising of power, public voice, and politics are intimately connected to issues of diversity and multiculturalism. Civic leaders understand the role that diversity plays in a strong democracy and see diversity as connected to real work being accomplished by people who come from different places and perspectives. Taylor's piece also illustrates this hard fact: optimism in community-engaged work often is cut down at the knees. It is an unpleasant aspect of community work that good civic leaders know how to deal with, and Taylor demonstrates some techniques for handling these challenges.

Emelye Neff

Emelye Neff, a senior majoring in geography and international studies at the University of Denver, has been with the PA program for just over three years and has enjoyed working on a range of critical issues with students. These projects have included a basketball game depicting the impact of gang violence on communities, a formal presentation on the history of immigration in America, and an educational music video on American civil liberties. After graduating, Emelye hopes to continue her work as a youth advocate and volunteer in war-torn areas of the Middle East and North Africa.

In the following section, Emelye illustrates how civic leaders practice politics. For civic leaders, practicing politics involves creating free spaces for ordinary people to act as political agents. Agency means that people do not need permission to act and do not need to wait for others to do things for them; they find power within themselves to act on their self-interest, and they organize others who care about the same issues. As civic leaders (the PA coaches) develop, they begin to see politics through a lens of community organizing, in which every interaction is a chance to practice politics by working with those who are different from themselves, negotiating that difference, forming relationships of solidarity and trust, and creating public, tangible products that strengthen their communities. In civic leadership, practicing politics is also about valuing the individual in a public landscape. Students who practice civic leadership acknowledge the talents and experiences that every person brings to the table. Emelye shows how local knowledge and the experiences that contribute to each person's self-interests and passions have a role in creating collaborative public organizations that create stronger communities.

I have been a PA coach for three years, and over that time, I have coached student groups working on issues of immigration policy, gang violence, and police brutality. Throughout the research, development, and implementation of these PA projects, I have learned a great deal about group dynamics, power structures, education reform, and youth voice. However, I have only recently stumbled upon the classroom politics of gender that firmly dictate social behavior, peer expectations, and the right to creative expression.

The majority of my students have been young men. I never worked with young women in the PA program until this year. This may seem insignificant; one might argue that all students are eager to subscribe to a cause or student movement regardless of gender. This is not the case. As an outspoken feminist, I am naturally conscious of gender relations and sensitive to social cues that direct conversation, attention, and action. Thus, my introduction to "gendered education" has led to an ongoing struggle to counteract codes and norms that limit women's classroom dialogue to a slurry of comments such as "I don't know" and "whatever he said." I noticed at the initial stages of our project that, when engaged in class discussions, the young men were more likely to offer their thoughts promptly and confidently, even if what they said negated the entire conversation. Conversely, the young women—even though they outnumbered the men—fiercely guarded their thoughts and even consulted their male peers before adding to the discussion.

A story illustrates this point: Maya had fallen into the habit of speaking only when she was called upon and only if it corroborated someone else's position. Frankly, I didn't blame her for developing this inconspicuous approach, because I had noticed that other female students, who had a greater awareness of their abilities, received an onslaught of antagonism from their male counterparts when sharing an opinion, despite its relevance, legitimacy, or feasibility. Some boys resorted to name-calling, while others—eager to rile up the women in the room—directly attacked a young woman's argument with a slew of adamant negations such as, "What are you talking about?" or "Nooooooooo, that's not true!" Despite all of this, you could tell Maya had a great deal of untapped wisdom, creativity, and energy brewing behind her silent exterior, especially when her occasional comment deviated from the customary "I don't know, Miss."

One occasion stands out as marking the dramatic transformation of Maya's role. It had been a fairly difficult afternoon with our students. Fearing that we had hit a wall with our class, my fellow coaches and I devised an impromptu scheme to enlist their help and spur discussion. Together, students and facilitators outlined class roles and assigned jobs to every student and coach. Andrea became the historian, the coaches became assistants, Carlos took on the position of group representative, and Christine volunteered as the go-to artist. Interestingly, Maya requested the spot as the discussion leader, who was responsible for molding and offering questions that provoked thought, expression, and action among group members. The first few minutes after this activity were nerve-racking and strained, as students struggled to identify their newfound responsibilities and act accordingly: "Miiiiiiss, this is dumb." "Miiiiiiss, I don't want to be team leader." "But Miiiiiiss, I don't have any good ideas." The room quickly fell silent as the students plotted a hasty departure from the classroom. Then I desperately called on our new discussion leader to reinvent the current situation.

Maya thought for a moment and then spoke: "We could make a play about immigrant rights and try raising money for ESL teachers so that kids of immigrants can get help." The students nodded in agreement. Carlos was beside himself with approval. Maya's comment launched the group into a whole new world of opportunities, plans, and commentary. Minutes after Maya had shared her idea, we had outlined a project demonstrating our research and passion for our issue and had identified key student and faculty leaders who could help us perform.

Maya has never been a misplaced wall flower since that time. She continued to volunteer her thoughts, time, and energy to every activity. In fact, she single-handedly crafted the group's mission statement. While she still received backlashes from her male peers, she countered opposition with poise and a polite smile, without compromising her intelligence and voice. She represents a growing contingent of young women who can translate the language of the oppressor into a call for public agency. Each young activist we coached contributed a unique set of talents and experiences that channeled our collective efforts in fascinating and inspiring directions. The students in Maya's group wrote, produced, and performed a rap-music video that teaches the value of knowing one's civil rights and calls on our police forces to act responsibly and compassionately.

Civic Leadership Defined

We set out to develop a definition of civic leadership based upon the written experiences of our students. Looking backward now, we can posit a set of qualities that civic leaders possess and practice:

- Civic leaders understand their self-interest and the self-interest of others and use this understanding to motivate their public actions
- Civic leaders build relationships that allow them to act and to practice power with, not power over
- Civic leaders practice politics by addressing social justice issues and building leadership and capacity for action in others
- Civic leadership requires understanding and practicing the concepts of self-interest, power, and politics

Over the years, we have presented many students with these concepts and consistently reflected with them about their practice of the concepts at their PA sites, as a means of building students' confidence in and understanding of how to lead in communities. However, as the student essays demonstrate, presenting and reflecting on the concepts are not sufficient for building confidence and understanding. Only through the PA coaches' real struggles to put these concepts into action did their skills and confidence emerge.

The student narratives in this chapter are a testament to the constant struggles of good civic leaders. Those leaders negotiate their leadership positions and have responsibility for democratic decision making and playing a role, while ensuring that everyone's voice is heard and valued in the process of democracy. This means that civic leaders understand the self-interests of the people with whom they work. Strong civic leaders also have a demonstrated ability to deal with emotional challenges within community settings. They recognize agency not only as the power to act and continue to act but also as an ability to interact and be affected by the people and situations around them. They are vulnerable because they allow themselves to be changed by the power of others, so that their work is based on relationships and their actions are taken with others to meet collective self-interests. At the same time, they never lose their connection to the core principle of working for social justice and the broad political participation of ordinary people.

The exercise of power can often lead to tension, and sometimes to conflict. This in particular is something our students have struggled with as they have practiced and worked with concepts of power in PA groups. Tension and conflict will always challenge civic leaders, but, as we look back to the legacy of Alinsky, he provides some insight into the role of conflict in community organizing: "Conflict is the essential core of a free and open society. If one were to project the democratic way of life in the form of a musical score, its major theme would be the harmony of dissonance" (1971, p. 61). In this way, Alinsky describes the integral role of conflict in creating systemic change in any society. It is, in his words, dissonant and often tense, but it is through this conflict that progress leads to public outcomes. Our student essays clearly reflect this struggle with conflict, as well as the skill and confidence gained in negotiating this tension throughout the PA process.

Civic leaders practice a relational politics that is located in the agency of ordinary people and a collective public voice. As Hannah Goedert has demonstrated, her relationships with students were the key to the PA team's moving toward political action as a group. We can see that, by building those relationships, her group began to practice what Alinsky described: "When people are brought together, or organized, they get to know each other's point of view; they reach compromises on many of their differences, they learn that many opinions which they entertained solely as their own are shared by others, and they discover that many problems which they had thought of only as 'their' problems are common to all" (Alinsky 1946/1989, p. 55). Civic leaders understand the role they play within the larger context of a democratic society. Like Tocqueville and Addams, civic leaders understand that America's mediating institutions — its schools, places of worship, and voluntary organizations — are critical to the evolution of a strong democracy. They also insist that ordinary citizens and citizen-organizations realize and act upon their political power as their birthright.

Our students' experiences have shown us that effective civic leadership requires an understanding of the core concepts of self-interest, power, and politics in order to organize communities to address important issues. In order to practice self-interest, power, and politics, civic leaders and community organizers ask questions, facilitate discussions, and organize ideas as they relate to multiple perspectives. They recognize the agency of individuals and foster the development of public voices in people, they negotiate tension and work within conflict to create better communities, and they listen to and engage with people of multiple perspectives as they practice relational politics. These public skills allow them to lead and organize, to develop their own leadership skills as they simultaneously build strong, vibrant, democratic communities.

Developing Civic Leaders in Higher Education

Self-interest, politics, and power are not skills fostered in most community environments. They are not skills that come naturally to most, but rather must be learned through practice and reflection. How do we in higher education work with students so that they use these skills in their communities to address the issues that they care about effectively? How can we develop young adults whose worldviews are such that they build powerful public relationships and see potential for positive change through strong civic leadership? In *Rules for Radicals*, Alinsky wrote that we all go through life and things happen to us: "happenings" as he calls them. What happens next is the important part: "Happenings become experience when they are digested, when they are reflected on, related to general patterns, synthesized" (Alinsky 1946/1989, p. 69). In the development of civic leaders and community organizers, it is important to provide structures within which students may digest and reflect on happenings and turn them into experiences that they will use to work with others. This chapter is just one example of that digestion process with our students.

At CCESL, we train our students to work in three phases when doing public work in the community. The first phase is Relationship Building and Issues Selection. The second phase is Researching the Issue, and the third phase is Action. Throughout all our student programs, there are a number of tools that we use to engage our students in important conversations, to build relationships and power, and to practice public skills. (For more information on community-organizing models and the public skills our students practice, see the full CCESL Community Organizing Handbook at http://www.du.edu/ccesl/communityorganizing.html.)

The Relationship Building and Issues Selection phase is critical to the community-organizing process. During this phase students build relationships with community members, leaders, businesspeople, and other students and begin to identify the issues that matter to people in the community. In Public Achievement, student coaches spend about one third of their year building relationships with the students in their group, trying to figure out what the students care about, before the group chooses an issue on which to work. In this phase students apply the self-interest assessment and one-to-ones to learn about the self-interest of every person involved. They use house meetings to begin conversations about important public issues that affect each member of the group. Each of these tools is explicitly defined:

- *Self-interest assessment and one-to-ones.* This tool guides students through the process of identifying their own self-interest, as well as the values and experiences that play a role in its development.

- *One-to-one interviews.* This is a tool that enables students to discover the self-interest of another, motivate others to identify their self-interests, find connections between the self-interests of different people, and begin organizing communities.

- *House meetings.* One way for civic leaders to make their work public and to begin practicing politics is to conduct house meetings with people who share similar concerns about an issue or converging self-interests.

In Researching the Issue, the second phase of the community-organizing process, our students start to research the issue and build their local knowledge. Part of this phase involves working with community members to identify root causes of the issue and analyzing the power and structures that surround the issue the community has selected. In Public Achievement most students do this through meetings with community members, surveys, and power mapping. Students in some of our other civic engagement programs use the one-to-one model, discussed earlier, to have conversations with key power players and also conduct more traditional research through surveys and interviews. Again, these tools may be explicitly defined:

- *Power mapping.* Students can more strategically practice politics and approach public solutions by finding all the power players involved in their issue. Power mapping helps students to identify and strategically target their actions with power players.

- *Community-based research.* Community-based research means digging up information within the community and conducting research with people in neighborhoods. It's a time-intensive process, but the goals are to dig deeply into issues that affect communities and to have intentional conversations that allow one truly to understand what community members know and think about issues. When as much information as possible has been collected, it is analyzed and used to design the third phase — action.

The third phase, Action, is about creating real, sustainable change in a community through a tangible product. In the Action phase, organizers develop and implement a plan for creating change on the issues they chose in the first phase. These choices are based on the information gathered in the research phase. Sometimes the products are events, campaigns, or policy changes, and sometimes they are permanent structures such as the playground that the Bryant Webster students brought about at their school. In any case, action is about leveraging the power one has built through relationships and research to meet the collective self-interest of the community. Students also critically reflect on and evaluate their progress with the community throughout this phase. The tools associated with the Action phase are: public actions, critical reflection, and public evaluation and assessment. Each of these is explicitly defined:

- *Public action.* This is an important step in moving an issue into the public arena and getting others involved in a solution. Public actions should include and speak to stakeholders from all sides of the issue. This step in the process is often difficult for students who have previously been limited to written assignments and private actions. Going public is one of the most important parts of the process.

- *Critical reflection.* As discussed earlier, students translate their "happenings" into experiences through reflection. By continually reflecting on self-interest, successes, failures, political learning, and the negotiation of power and tension, students learn to become stronger and more effective civic leaders. Critical reflection also helps student leaders to take responsibility for strategically addressing the problems that arise in the first and second phases of the process. Reflection before, during, and after community engagement should address many different forms of learning, including academic, personal, community, and emotional knowledge. Sensitivity to the different lessons learned in different areas is important to help students gain the most from their experiences.

- *Evaluation and assessment.* "If it isn't worth evaluating, it isn't worth doing." We evaluate everything that we do as organizers. Evaluation allows students and practitioners to look at how any part of the process went and to determine how it could be better. We believe that public evaluation fosters the democratic process that organizing is built on, so our students end every meeting and action by evaluating together how things are going.

All of the tools described in this section, and the many more included in the CCESL Community Organizing Handbook (http://www.du.edu/ccesl/docs/CO_Handbook_2009_Pri.pdf), play an important role in helping students develop in their practice of civic leadership. While students do not become civic leaders by reading and following the directions for using these tools, the tools are important resources for guiding the active development of public skills, including an understanding of the important concepts of self-interest, power, and politics. Reading and following directions are not enough to build civic leaders. They must be accompanied by real-world struggles and the taste of failure and success.

REFERENCES

Alinsky, S. D. (1946/1989). *Reveille for radicals.* New York: Vintage Books.

Alinsky, S. D. (1971). *Rules for radicals.* New York: Random House.

Bailey, R. (1974). *Radicals in urban politics: The Alinsky approach.* Chicago: University of Chicago Press.

Boyte, H. C. (2005). *Everyday politics: Reconnecting citizens and the public life.* Philadelphia: University of Pennsylvania Press.

Boyte, H. C., and D. Shelby. (2008). *The citizen solution: How you can make a difference.* Minneapolis: Minnesota Historical Society Press.

Chambers, E. T., and M. A. Cowan. (2004). *Roots for radicals: Organizing for power, action, and justice.* New York: Continuum International Publishing Group.

Chrislip, D., and C. Larson. (1994). *Collaborative leadership: How citizens and civic leaders can make a difference.* San Francisco: Jossey-Bass.

Cooper, D. (1998). Reading, writing and reflection. New Directions for Teaching and Learning, no.73 (Spring): 47–56.

Erlanson, B., and R. Hildreth. (1989). *Building worlds, transforming lives, making history: A coach's guide for public achievement.* Minneapolis: Center for Democracy and Citizenship.

Finks, P. D. (1984). *The radical vision of Saul Alinsky.* New York: Paulist Press.

Freire, P. (1993). *Pedagogy of the oppressed.* New York: Continuum Books.

Fretz, E., and N. Longo. (Forthcoming). Students co-creating an engaged university. In *Handbook of engaged scholarship: Contemporary landscapes, future directions,* ed. Hiram Fitzgerald et al. East Lansing: Michigan State University Press.

Gecan, M. (2004). *Going public.* New York: Anchor Books.

Heifetz, R. (1994). *Leadership without easy answers.* Cambridge, MA: Belknap Press of Harvard University Press.

Horwitt, S. (1992). *Let them call me rebel: Saul Alinsky, his life and legacy.* New York: Alfred A. Knopf.

Kouzes, J., and B. Posner. (2002). The leadership practices inventory: Theory and evidence behind the five practices of exemplary leaders. Retrieved March 5, 2007. Available by subscription at: http://www.lpionline.com.

Lancourt, J. E. (1979). *Confront or concede, the Alinsky citizen-action organizations.* Lanham,MD: Lexington Books.

Osterman, Paul. (2002). *Gathering power: The future of progressive politics in America.* Boston: Beacon Press.

Warren, M. R. (2001). *Dry bones rattling: Community building to revitalize American democracy.* Princeton, NJ: Princeton University Press.

Elizabeth Hollander, Kei Kawashima-Ginsberg,
Peter Levine, Duncan Pickard, and Jonathan Zaff

8

Assessing the Effects of Institutional Culture on Leadership Education at Tufts University

There are strong theoretical reasons to believe that a college or university that provides substantive, enriching civic experiences for its students will encourage the development of active citizenship in its student body. That is the basic assumption that has persuaded many institutions to provide programs, courses, internships, counseling services, events, extracurricular opportunities, and other supports (such as offices to coordinate community partnerships) as strategies for enhancing their students' civic engagement.

Researchers have tested this theory to a degree, finding that well-implemented service-learning programs can have a positive effect on the civic skills, attitudes, and behaviors of participating students (Astin, Vogelgesang, Ikeda, and Yee 2000). The best of these studies have ranged from large-scale longitudinal studies of several thousand students spread across numerous universities, and spanning their years in school (Astin and Sax 1998; Astin, Sax, and Avalos 1999; Vogelgesang and Astin 2000), to more modest, quasi-experimental evaluations of students on one campus (Myers-Lipton 1998).

Meanwhile, as noted in the Introduction to this volume, leadership education is a burgeoning field. One way to put civic education and leadership education together is to enlist students as leaders in providing civic opportunities for their peers.

At Tufts University, this combination is an explicit strategy—with some additional elements. We are concerned with the overall civic culture of the institution, as well as specific courses and programs, and we are committed to measuring our impact in order to improve our work.

Although focusing on programs, courses, majors, events, and the like is useful, it can miss the effect of the broader university culture on students' development of their civic identity. A consensus statement by scholars and practitioners found little research on the civic effects of campus cultures. The report called for scholars to "focus on relevant characteristics of institutions: not just size, type, mission—for which data are easily available—but also campus culture; policies (such as promotion and tenure criteria, allocation of the faculty to first-year courses, campus work-study allocations, and financial-aid policies); institutional leadership at all levels from the department to the university as a whole; and the array of civic engagement opportunities provided across each campus and community for full- and part-time students and for students in different fields of study" (Carnegie Foundation for the Advancement of Teaching and CIRCLE 2006). Tufts is committed to creating a strong institutional culture for civic education; in this chapter, we call it a *civically promoting culture*.

Moreover, Tufts enlists students to advance civic education broadly defined. Student leaders are expected to create, lead, or influence specific programs for civic education at Tufts and also to influence the whole campus culture to be more civically promoting. In turn, effective programs and a positive overall culture should help to cultivate student leaders for civic engagement. There is also an important relationship between the campus and its surrounding community. Students' civic work should benefit the community, and the community should challenge and educate students and enrich the campus culture. Important aspects of programs at the Jonathan M. Tisch College of Citizenship and Public Service include careful orientation to the geographical communities around Tufts and training on how to work respectfully and effectively in partnership with community organizations.

So we may summarize the Tufts student leadership model visually (see fig. 8.1).

A final distinctive element of our strategy is a strong commitment to self-evaluation and measurement. We recognize that a university can be blessed with students who score relatively high on measures of civic engagement and leadership, yet the institution might not be doing as much as it should to enhance their civic engagement or leadership. We are committed to maximizing our impact; to make sure that happens, we try to self-evaluate constantly.

Because the model shown above has many parts, evaluation is a complex business. For our ongoing *Civically Promoting Culture* study (outlined in this chapter), we have focused on four primary aims:

- Document the civically promoting culture that Tufts has created
- Examine the effect of that culture on current students' and alumni's civic attitudes and behaviors
- Evaluate the impact of student leadership on the campus culture
- Determine the additional capacity that Tufts' civically promoting culture provides to its surrounding communities

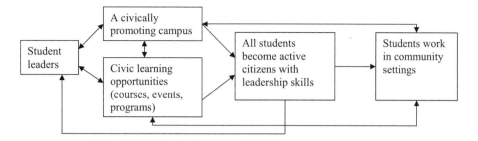

FIGURE 8.1

Background of Tisch College

In 1997, the president of Tufts University, John DiBiaggio, a leader of Campus Compact and a proponent of civic engagement, decided to launch an ambitious initiative that would make Tufts a national leader among engaged universities with civic missions. He argued that Tufts already had many relevant programs and people (faculty, staff, students, and alumni) and that integrating their work into a new institution would add substantial value. His original idea of a graduate school devoted to public service evolved, after a two-year deliberative planning process, into a "virtual college" that would infuse civic learning into all the activities of Tufts colleges, undergraduate, graduate, and professional (Hollister, Mead, and Wilson 2006).

In 1999, the trustees voted to create the University College of Citizenship and Public Service (UCCPS). The college was soon endowed by Pierre and Pamela Omidyar with a $10 million gift. In 2006, Jonathan M. Tisch gave an additional $40 million, and the college was renamed after him. From early on, the work of the college focused on faculty, students, community partnerships, and alumni.

Faculty were originally given seed grants to develop curricula and to conduct research related to civic engagement. The Faculty Fellows became a community that met regularly for substantive discussions. Certain faculty grants turned into ambitious institutional initiatives. For example, Professor Doug Brugge of the Tufts Medical School has led the creation of the Tufts Community Research Center (TCRC), an ongoing collaboration among Tufts faculty and community partners dedicated to research. TCRC's seed grants have led to several federal grants for community research on topics such as highway pollution and obesity prevention, funded at more than $1 million each. These projects meet needs identified by Tufts' host communities and involve both cutting-edge science and community input and participation.

Students can engage with Tisch College through various programs that involve experiential learning and leadership for active citizenship. Tisch aims to reach the entire student body with certain activities, events, and messages, such as the first-year book (available to all *incoming* undergraduates for discussion and study) and a corps of residence hall advisers who focus on active citizenship. In 2009, Tisch launched *honos civicus*, the nation's first graduation honors society for active citizens. Tisch provides more sustained and demanding opportunities for about 20 percent of students, who volunteer in various ways to participate; it enlists about 5 percent of students as civic leaders who not only develop their own civic skills and dispositions but also enhance the civic engagement of their peers. The flagship undergraduate program for leaders is the Citizenship and Public Service Scholars Program. This is a multiyear, intensive leadership course that also provides students with stipends. Additional intensive opportunities include Active Citizenship Summers (a community internship program), the Civic Engagement Fund (minigrants), the Media & Public Service Program (an academic minor), and postgraduate public service internships. (This is an incomplete list of student programs; Tisch staff also do behind-the-scenes work assisting professors, advocating for policies, and supporting networks within Tufts.)

Community partners provide placements for Tufts students, advise on community issues, and collaborate with Tufts faculty and students on joint research projects. Tisch College's most active community partners—mainly leaders of nonprofits in Somerville, Medford, and Boston's Chinatown, which are the locations of Tufts's main campuses—are increasingly organized into advisory committees and hold seats on the Tisch College Board of Advocates. The Lincoln Filene Center for Community Partnerships (LFC) is a center within Tisch College that works to build and maintain strong relationships with these partners and coordinates university-community partner activities. The LFC is engaged in directly supporting service-learning courses, community-based collaborative research, and cocurricular community service, and in developing the partnering capacity of university staff, students, and community partners. For both faculty and students across the university, trusting, open, collaborative relationships are important resources, without which they cannot do certain kinds of research and educational activities. Just as the library is part of the research infrastructure of a university, so is a diverse network of community partners who are used to collaborating with professors and students.

Alumni are active as sponsors and organizers of internships, as adjunct professors in special courses, as career mentors, and as visiting lecturers.

Measuring Impact

Since the creation of Campus Compact more than two decades ago, universities throughout the country have been increasingly interested in developing and documenting the systems-level processes, regulations, and programs that theoretically lead to a civically promoting culture on campus. To this end, Campus Compact initiated the Indicators of Engagement Project to determine the specific systems-level factors that define such a culture. The Carnegie Foundation for the Advancement of Teaching built on the Campus Compact initiative and, in 2005, launched a pilot version of its Carnegie Foundation Community Engagement Classification System. University applicants answer questions about institutional identity, curricular engagement (opportunities through class work for students and faculty to address community-defined issues), outreach, and partnerships (Driscoll 2008). In 2006 and 2008, a total of 196 campuses, including Tufts, were approved for one of the three classifications.

Project Pericles, founded nearly ten years ago by Eugene Lang in the hope of integrating disparate civic projects on campuses into cohesive, campuswide experiences, has five policies by which Periclean institutions must abide:
- Institutional Commitment (a formal resolution of the university board to make education for responsible and participatory citizenship a key aspect of university life)
- Program (the specific campus and community programs that encourage citizenship)
- Constituency Involvement (ensuring that all stakeholders at a university, from administrators and faculty to students and alumni, play a role in creating a civically promoting culture)
- Central Administration (supervision of all programs by a central director who reports to the president of the university)
- Cooperation and Collaboration (collaboration between the university, the community, and civic partners)

Despite these laudable efforts to document systems-level factors that make up a civically promoting culture, we unfortunately do not know when or whether these factors lead to strong engagement among students, during their time on campus and after they graduate, or whether communities benefit from university policies. A similar dynamic is seen in the research on community collaboration. Although there is much to be said about what a strong collaboration comprises and how these relationships are formed (Community-Campus Partnerships for Health 2004; Rubin 2000; Vidal et al. 2002), there is relatively little rigorous, systematic research on whether collaborations lead to better outcomes in the community.

Tufts students, and especially participants in the Scholars program, have high average levels of engagement, by national standards. Compared to a national college student annual volunteering rate of approximately 24 percent (Marcelo 2007), 47 percent of Tufts seniors volunteered within the past twelve months, according to a survey conducted before graduation. On average, Tufts seniors contribute 144 hours annually to community-based volunteering services, and 25 percent say that they "often" or "very often" engage in volunteer service activities. Furthermore, 39 percent of seniors say that they plan to volunteer often, and 81 percent are willing to volunteer at least occasionally, after they graduate from Tufts. In the 2008 election, according to a careful study that involved checking voter records, the voter turnout of Tufts undergraduates was roughly 74 percent (based on actual voting records), compared to a self-reported rate of 59.7 percent for all currently enrolled college students in the United States.

Merely documenting that students at a given university such as Tufts are highly engaged does not show that the institution has made a difference. There may be selection effects (students who are already engaged choose to attend that college), peer effects (engaged students encourage one another simply by virtue of being concentrated in one place), life-cycle effects (people generally become more engaged as they move from age eighteen to age twenty-two), class effects (students from upper-income backgrounds, who are on a path to higher incomes, tend to be more engaged), and effects from the various individual courses and experiences offered at the college. Our evaluation of civically promoting culture begins to assess whether the institutional culture at Tufts adds value beyond these other factors.

The following section on evaluation methodology is divided into components aimed at documenting the systems-level factors that create a civically promoting culture, student-level data that assess the civic experiences of students at Tufts, and community data that assess the potential increase in capacity that Tufts and its students provide to community partners. We provide some early findings from some components of our study. In conducting this evaluation, we are able to leverage many existing data systems that were created by Tisch College and the Office of Institutional Research and Evaluation at Tufts to assess the civic attitudes and behaviors of students, faculty, and staff.

Systems-Level Data: Building the Ethos of a Civically Promoting Culture

For this portion of the evaluation, we are examining and documenting the structures in place at Tufts and in specific schools and colleges within the university, such as Tisch College, that form a civically promoting culture. We draw from the frameworks produced by Campus Compact and the Carnegie Foundation Community Engagement Classification System to guide this work. More specifically, we are first documenting the university-level policies that reflect a civic culture, such as the mission and vision statements of the school, strategic plans for the university and individual colleges, and committees that are tasked with promoting a civic culture to students. Next, we are examining current civically oriented programs and classes offered at different schools and colleges, as well as existing campus organizations at Tufts, both college- and student-created.

To begin this process, we are determining the criteria for defining policies, programs, and classes as civic. We are fortunate that Tisch College has previously gone through the process of obtaining a community-engagement classification from the Carnegie Foundation and therefore has thought this through. We are reengaging the partners involved in that application, including department heads across the university, and are working with other Tisch leaders and affiliated faculty to develop and confirm the criteria. We believe that engaging multiple stakeholders in this definitional process is essential for obtaining buy-in from faculty and staff for a formative evaluation and for ensuring that we are using valid and reliable standards for defining a civically promoting culture.

This year, we are inviting faculty to consider and designate their own courses as civically oriented. All faculty members received a letter requesting that they nominate their own courses as civically oriented, with reasoning. This new system allows Tufts students to select courses that are civically oriented, and it also provides faculty an opportunity to frame and teach their courses in a civic manner. Finally, this effort provides useful information on how civically oriented the university's academic programs are.

Student-Level Data: Effects of a Civically Promoting Culture on Students' Civic Behaviors and Attitudes

We are using surveys (complemented by focus groups) to assess the civic engagement and leadership of Tufts students and to gain some insight into the impact of the Tisch College "infusion" strategy. Three major sources of survey data are available:

1. *Schoolwide surveys.* When Tisch College was created in 1999, Tisch, in collaboration with the Office of Institutional Research and Evaluation, developed a set of assessment instruments to determine changes in civic attitudes and behaviors while students progressed through their college years. Civic measures are now included in existing student surveys that capture a large majority of undergraduate students, as well as in surveys that target specific graduate programs. These surveys include a New Student Survey of incoming freshmen, the Sophomore Experience Survey, the First Year Engineering Advising Survey, and the Tufts Senior Survey.

   Fielded since 1986 as an exit survey for graduating seniors, the Tufts Senior

Survey documents the seniors' postbaccalaureate plans. Because the survey has become a step toward preparing for graduation, response rates typically exceed 90 percent. Now, in addition to soliciting the postbaccalaureate information, the survey also asks students about their undergraduate experience and their perceptions of and satisfaction with the university environment (D. G. Terkla, PhD, Executive Director, Office of Institutional Research and Evaluation, correspondence, May 26, 2009). Since 2003, the survey has included civic measures. The Sophomore Experience Survey has included civic measures since 2006. Thus, we can currently conduct a time-lag longitudinal analysis on the senior survey to examine the trends in various civic attitudes and behaviors over the past six years. A more modest, three-year analysis can be conducted on the Sophomore Experience Survey.

2. *Community experience surveys.* Beginning in the spring of 2009, we have been fielding a semiannual survey of students who participate in community engagement programs at various levels through Tisch College. These students typically begin their community experiences during the fall semester. We are therefore capturing the pre- and postprogram civic attitudes and behaviors of students. Because the students who participate in community engagement programs come from various backgrounds and work in diverse ways, we hope to gain a better understanding of the relationship between intensity and duration of experience and civic outcomes. Data from this survey have not yet been analyzed, but the effort is an important part of our assessment plan.

3. *The Civic and Political Activities and Attitudes Survey* (CPAAS). A cohort-based, sequential, longitudinal study of a sample of Tufts students has been conducted since 2003 (Terkla et al. 2007). In such a study, several subsequent classes of students are each followed for several years, allowing the investigators to distinguish the effects of moving through the program (in this case, Tufts University) versus the effects of outside historical events (such as the 2008 election). The outside events influence each class at different times and so can be isolated from program effects.

   The study's purpose is to examine the relationship between students' civic activity participation and their civic attitudes, as a means of assessing Tufts's work to transmit civic knowledge, skills, and values to the student body. Importantly, the study was also designed to examine the differential effects of the Tisch Scholars Program on civic outcomes as compared to the civic outcomes of students who are not a part of the Scholars program. The Web-based survey instrument has been administered to four successive cohorts of freshmen since 2003, thus representing samples from the 2007 through 2010 graduating classes. The cohorts are surveyed at the end of each of their four years and for their first two postgraduate years, for a total of six years of data collection.

At this point, there are complete data for all cohorts through junior year, data through senior year for three of the cohorts, data through the first postgraduate year for two cohorts, and data through the second postgraduate year for the 2007 graduating class. The initial samples for each cohort were drawn from the broader Tisch College Participant Survey. All freshmen were encouraged to participate in the survey, and the respondents became the population from which the samples were drawn. A purposeful, representative sample was then drawn from this population for each of the cohorts, resulting in a total sample size of 272 across the four cohort years, that is, the classes of 2007, 2008, 2009, and 2010. In addition, the participants were identified as high-participators ("high school highs"), low-participators ("high school lows"), or Scholars. The high-participators and low-participators designations referred to the level of civic involvement during high school, as assessed by the Tisch College Participant Survey. The Scholar group referred to those who were Tisch College Scholars. The questions in the survey were adapted from CIRCLE's Young Citizens Survey, the Americorps Baseline Survey, the Social Justice and Diversity attitudes subscales of the Civic Attitudes and Skills Questionnaire, the Community Service Self-Efficacy Scale, the Public Service Motivation Scale, and the Social Responsibility Inventory. The survey was supplemented by an in-depth, semistructured interview with four students from each cohort while they were sophomores and seniors.

There are many ways to investigate these data; we have just begun to analyze the survey results that we have while we await more data. One strategy is to trace growth curves for all the classes combined. We would expect the Scholars to be the most engaged when they first arrived at Tufts, followed by the high school highs and then the high school lows. Because of the special opportunities afforded the Scholars, we would hope that they would improve on their strong baseline scores of civic engagement. Finally, in part because of the Scholars' leadership, and in part because of Tisch College's infusion strategies throughout the university, we would hope that the other groups would also show growth. Thus, whether civic engagement is defined in terms of service, membership, voting, or any basket of such measures, we can construct an ideal longitudinal graph (see fig. 8.2).

If the essential purpose of the Tisch Scholars program were to provide civic leadership to other students, then we would expect the gap between the Scholars and the other two groups to narrow thanks to the Scholars' impact. But civic leadership in regard to the rest of the undergraduate student body is only one of several purposes of the Tisch Scholars program. The Scholars are also expected to

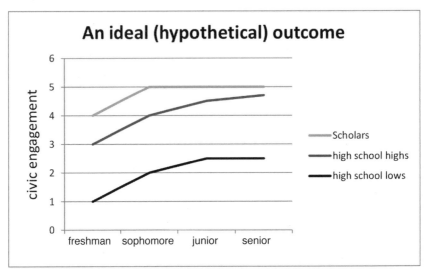

FIGURE 8.2

serve community groups and to enhance their own civic skills. Hence, in the ideal graph, all the groups show growth but the gap remains.

Such a result would not prove that Scholars caused the increase in the other groups; many other factors might be responsible. But this is the result that we would want to see if the campus culture in general, and the Tisch Scholars leadership program in particular, enhanced all Tufts students' civic engagement.

The reality is bound to be more complicated, because many other factors intervene, from junior years abroad to the difficulty of finding service opportunities after graduation to the mounting demands of course work. (The last factor may especially affect the high school lows, who have the lowest cumulative GPAs of the three groups.)

Consistent with the goals of the program, we do find that the Scholars are leaders. By senior year, 83 percent of them lead a community service organization other than a Scholars group. In contrast, 21 percent of the high school highs and 12 percent of the high school lows lead such organizations. Thus, when non-Scholars perform service, many are led (and perhaps recruited and motivated) by Scholars. Scholars are also most likely to lead other sorts of groups (for example, cultural or identity organizations), but they are not as far ahead of the high school highs and high school lows on this measure. Apparently, Scholars focus their leadership on community service to a considerable degree. This suggests that the leadership strategy is working.

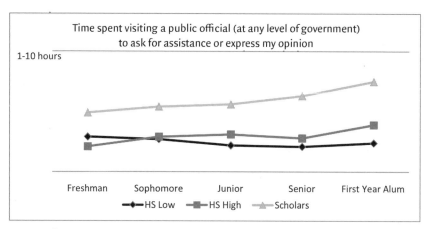

Time spent visiting a public official (at any level of government) to ask for assistance or express my opinion

1-10 hours

Freshman Sophomore Junior Senior First Year Alum

HS Low HS High Scholars

FIGURE 8.3

Scholars are also far more likely than other Tufts students to be involved in political activity. In fact, we find something like the ideal result when we focus on contacting or visiting public officials (see fig. 8.3). Especially if the upward trends seen in alumni continue, this looks like a positive result. Community service, however, shows a different pattern (see fig. 8.4).

For all groups, community service rises from freshman to sophomore year, presumably because students are finding their way to civic opportunities in a new community. Service then falls in junior year, perhaps because many Tufts students take that year abroad. Engagement rises again in senior year, but not quite to the sophomore level. (Seniors may be increasingly focused on job searches.) Consistent with national data, a decline in service and volunteering rates occurs after graduation — probably because young graduates temporarily lack the institutional structures that enable them to connect to service groups. The gap between the Scholars and the others narrows, but only because the former reduce their volunteering rates.

Just as the results shown in the ideal graph would not prove that Tisch Scholars were responsible for boosting the civic engagement of other students, the volunteering graph shown above does not prove that the Tisch Scholars program fails to benefit non-Scholars. Volunteering rates may be higher than they would be otherwise, because of the Scholars program. High school highs and high school lows who perform community service are often led by Scholars. The fact that Scholars do not increase their rates of service may be attributable to many external factors: a time squeeze from demanding course work, a high level of civic engagement at baseline that makes it difficult to improve, foreign travel, and the like. Still, it

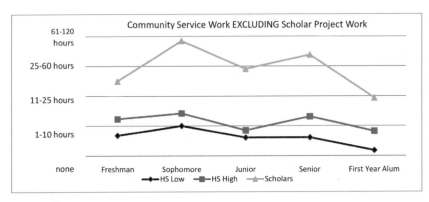

FIGURE 8.4

would seem that the Scholars program is very effective at identifying and developing service leaders, but there is no evidence that it increases service rates across the campus.

In 2009, Tisch staff were adjusting the student leadership strategy. The Tisch Scholars program was being shortened and simplified. Members of the staff have developed a new initiative called Leaders For Change (L4C) in collaboration with the Office for Campus Life. L4C will be a series of hands-on training sessions for any Tufts students who wish to participate, in which they will practice and expand their skills as leaders. The workshop topics planned for the 2009–2010 academic year included maximizing impact, recruiting and managing volunteers, writing grants, the ethics of speech in community, "challenging the process" (the focus of which is diversity), and sustaining organizations when leaders change. These workshops draw on experiences in the Scholars program but will be more directly accessible to all Tufts students.

Community Data: Effect of Tufts on the Civic Infrastructure in Partner Communities

To assess whether the civic activities of Tufts and its student body are benefiting the surrounding community, we administered a survey to 105 members of numerous community organizations with which Tufts students work during the school year and over the summer. Sometimes, more than one staff member from the same organization received and completed the survey, because staff members worked in different capacities or departments. In most cases, however, one staff member represented each organization. These organizations range from community-based groups and K–12 public schools to municipal agencies addressing community needs such as immigrant issues, affordable housing, education (English as a Second Language programs, job and vocational training, and college access programs), youth services, domestic violence, health, and much more. We conducted a systematic survey with all of the community partners, and focus groups that followed up with a subset of these organizations, in order to reflect on the findings from the surveys. The survey had both practice and research goals. The questions asked how, if at all, Tufts students' involvement contributed to the organization's capacity building, equity of partnership, experience with university-community collaborative research, satisfaction with the students who worked with each organization, satisfaction with the Lincoln Filene Center for Community Partnerships, and general communication between the organization and LFC. We define the benefit to the community organizations as an increase in capacity that is provided by Tufts students and other support from Tufts.

Overall, the survey results suggest that Tisch College has built and maintained positive and collaborative relationships between community organizations and various parts of Tufts University. These results suggest that Tufts students did contribute to the organizational capacity of many community-based organizations, by, for example, providing committed and meaningful service, bringing new energy to agencies, and acting as a bridge between community-based organizations and Tufts. Almost all (96 percent) of the responding partners felt that Tufts students came into the community well prepared to work with their constituents in a respectful and culturally competent manner. Many saw themselves as mentors to the students and had built positive relationships with them. In a further testimony to the collaborative nature of the partnership, some partners have asked to take on roles as coeducators in the Scholars program, to review Scholars applications, to become more involved in the selection process, and to help match students' assets with community needs. Although not all partners show this level of involvement, it is nonetheless highly indicative of the commitment and sense of responsibility demonstrated by some of our partners.

The challenges revealed in the survey and focus group included the following:

1. Finding agency resources to train and supervise students adequately
2. Coordinating students' busy schedules
3. Aligning an agency's needs with academic schedules (Students are gone once the semester ends.)
4. Ensuring that all students come to the community culturally and professionally prepared
5. Improving communication between Tisch College and partners, and between partners themselves

Partners also asked for more information about the resources available at Tisch College and Tufts University and desired more workshops, especially to learn more about working with students well. Although many partners identified areas for further improvement, a majority (79 percent) of partners said that their experience with Tisch College and Tufts students had made them more interested in developing and extending their partnerships with Tufts.

To understand the breadth of Tisch's reach into partner communities, we are beginning to use an innovative technology to map its connections. YouthMap software allows many users to collaborate to build one evolving diagram of the connections in a community's civil society. Starting in 2008, the Corporation for National and Community Service, a federal agency, provided Tisch College with funds to enlist college students throughout the Boston area to build a diagram or map of the entire civil society of the region. The map will allow institutions, including Tisch College itself, to understand how they fit into networks of other organizations, people, and issues. Over time, if Tisch College is successful with its community partnerships work, the network that includes Tisch will become visibly denser and larger. Fewer organizations within the network will be isolated from one another, and there will be fewer divisions within the network along lines of demographics, geography, or issues.

A Student's Perspective

The authors of this chapter think it is important to suggest what the Tisch College of Citizenship and Public Service means to students who go through the program. Duncan Pickard was asked to draft some reflections on his experience, both positive and negative. Duncan is a rising senior and a Citizenship and Public Service Scholar, also known as a Tisch Scholar. He served as president of Tufts's student senate in his junior year and as a Synaptic Scholar at the Institute of Global Leadership (an undergraduate research colloquium). In the latter capacity, he did fieldwork in the Dominican Republic and Peru in the spring and summer of 2009. Duncan was news editor at the *Tufts Observer*, the student magazine, during his sophomore year, and was also the campus public editor, the ethics watchdog for student journalism. He spent the summer after his sophomore year in Jordan studying Arabic and traveling extensively, and the summer after his junior year in an internship at the U.S. Embassy in Damascus, Syria.

Duncan says he chose to come to Tufts "for the academics and because it was close to home. I had heard the active citizenship focus about Tufts, but I heard that from a lot of places. From conferences I have attended and what I know about other institutions, I do believe that Tufts is a national leader in this kind of work, but Tufts didn't emerge from the pack then as it does for me now. I knew I was looking for somewhere close to home. I also chose Tufts because it offered a great liberal arts education that would develop, I was told, practical skills. The admissions and pre-matriculation materials all touted the active citizenship focus, but I still didn't really know what that meant until I got here."

During his three years at Tufts, Duncan's experience has provided him several major benefits. It has given him an intellectual underpinning to his civic engagement; has helped him to think through tough issues of democratic leadership; has provided him opportunities to try out, reflect on, and integrate many different civic leadership experiences in a safe setting; has given him opportunities for experience in the global community; and is helping him to shape his specific interests in addressing global citizenship.

1. *Intellectual underpinning to civic engagement.* "The greatest advantage of many Tisch College programs," Duncan writes, "is the expectation that students engage with material in the classroom before beginning a project. For example, to enter the Scholars program, students must take a semester-long course that introduces the communities in which we will be working, complicates traditional understandings of service, challenges us to consider our own background in the work we do, and teaches some social theory."

2. *Availability of faculty to help think through tough issues of democratic leadership.* "Tisch provides resources for students and faculty to meet and feel comfortable talking about difficult issues. For example, I took a Critical Race Theory seminar. I thought, as a reasonable college student, it would be pretty easy. I found that I could define and explain the concepts we were learning, but in retrospect I kept the issues at arm's length, unable to engage with them in a personal way. I think this might be because it was uncomfortable for me to accept the way my white identity can contribute to social inequity without my being aware of it. It was easier for me to keep these theories in the academic realm instead of applying them to real life. The required journals were the first opportunity for me to successfully combine race theory, my own identity, and my civic leadership opportunities, and it was a challenge."

3. *Opportunities for reflecting on and integrating many different experiences, learning about leadership, and trying out different approaches in a safe setting.* "I expanded on my interests in student government and journalism at Tufts. I served as student body president and as an editor at a campus magazine. Government and journalism provide two different perspectives on any society — the first provides and allocates resources, and the second uncovers the beauties and the beasts that impact the community. Each requires different questions and different answers, and they encourage people to engage with different corners of the community.

   "What Tisch helped me to do is find the intersections between these interests, to understand why I am particularly motivated to engage civically through government and journalism. I believe that we develop civil societies when two people, seemingly opposed or in conflict, can make connections and learn together. Government is at its best when it promotes cross-cultural dialogue, and journalism can reflect on peoples' interactions. I have tried to foster this dialogue in the senate among the student body, and I have written about the ways in which we can be more engaged with one another."

4. *Opportunities for engagement abroad and reflection on global citizenship.* "Tufts also gave me opportunities to be engaged outside of the United States and [to] think critically about my experiences. I have had opportunities to travel and meet other people, and these experiences all help me develop a critical perspective wherever I go."

5. *Increasing civic learning skills.* "Some of my best experiences at Tufts have shaped my understanding of civic leadership and my own strengths and weaknesses as a leader. The senate has given me a life-changing leadership experience, in leading an executive board of six people, a senate of thirty-five, and a campus of 5,000. I was responsible for keeping the senate together, under the scrutiny of thousands of voices. This was probably the most intense and powerful learning experience it is possible to have during two semesters in college.

   "The senate presidency was powerful for me because it was challenging, and at times it was incredibly stressful. People would rightfully question my own leadership, and we were confronted with some important decisions to make in a short amount of time. Tisch helped me think about and define leadership. At Tufts I learned that leadership is bringing out the best in others in moving toward a common goal."

In reflecting on the ways in which the Tufts program could be improved, Duncan calls for better integration of academic and civic experiences, along with more sustainable community experiences:

1. *Need for better integration of academic experiences.* "Tisch advertises itself as a program that horizontally integrates all the pieces of the university, challenging others to focus on civic engagement in the work they are doing. This is a wonderful goal that encourages people to think critically in serving communities. But often people interpret this goal as not a horizontal integration, but another vertical addition to everything else students have to juggle. The required class for the Scholars program is wonderful, but it is also the only credit we receive for the work we do in the community. I do not suggest Scholars should receive credit for their projects. But rather, perhaps there should be a seminar on civic engagement, or an independent study, in which professors can encourage their students to integrate their course work and their projects in the community.

The times I have used my experiences in the community to inform my course work are rare, but the opportunities and potential for learning are abundant. For example, in the work I did with immigrant communities, I could have referred to classes I had taken on race politics in political science, or social theory from anthropology. Professors and students should share responsibilities for integrating community work into the classroom. Instead, my Scholars project feels like something else that I do, and the connections between it and my course work are not immediately clear unless I sit down and think about them. My criticisms of Tisch come when it tilts to the vertical.

"At Tufts, civic engagement has become prestigious. Community activism in the past has stereotypically been below the ivory tower. But here 'saving the world' is something you want to do when you graduate, what you can write on a résumé or a Facebook page. There are selective programs and scholarships for civic engagement. Sometimes it's something you do to fit in, not to challenge traditional models of education. Tufts should provide opportunities for practical experiences, tout it as a goal, encourage critical thinking in the classroom, but not create an environment in which 'engagement' is necessary to fit in. Tisch is essential in providing those opportunities for engagement, but it should also work with faculty to integrate civic thinking—not necessarily just action—into our curriculum. Tisch tilts toward [the] vertical when it creates 'new' civic engagement opportunities that aren't rooted in what's already going on. Civic engagement doesn't work when it's destined for the résumé.

"I believe the divide between civic engagement and academic rigor is false, and that this new perspective on active citizenship is a product of the pitting of the two. We shouldn't balance work in the community and course work; we should merge the two. Civic engagement is one important hook upon which knowledge is hung. Work in the classroom is important, but seeing the friction behind the theories we study is the best way to better understand the world.

"I think that Tufts can be misinterpreted as advocating civic engagement without the academic rigor. This is a dangerous misinterpretation. People should be engaged in their communities, and it is important for me to understand how my work impacts particular communities in ways that are beneficial and problematic, sometimes simultaneously. College is a great place to do that work—and explore it more in the classroom. College should never lose its function as the academic underpinnings of the future work of civic leaders."

2. The Tisch approach still stresses student experiences that may not be sustainable in the community and must always keep the community's needs foremost in mind. "I also want to work with the Civic Scholar community to understand better how we can make our projects sustainable. Our projects require positive energy to make them

sustainable, since the forces stacked against us (graduation, study abroad, breaks) all hurt the prospects of sustainability. Senior Scholars have the opportunity to work on their own projects without community partners, and I think this is a bad idea. There have been some wonderful projects that have endured beyond the Scholar who started them, but more often than not, new projects die at graduation. Either the program ends, the conference is forgotten, or the final report sits on a shelf. The benefit for the student is unquestionable, but the benefit to the community diminishes. We need to think more clearly about action steps after we graduate, and we need to make sure that community partners are engaged with every project so that local leaders can take up these issues — if they are important — once we are gone."

Tufts has tried to create more than a series of courses, projects, and programs that teach active citizenship experientially. Through Tisch College, Tufts has tried to infuse themes of active citizenship in all the educational and research programs of the university, and to build what we call *civically promoting culture*. Furthermore, we have enlisted students as leaders in creating this culture. Whether our efforts across the institution add value above the net of the various programs (for a student body that enters with strong skills and commitments) really remains to be seen. But Tisch College has begun an ambitious evaluation process that will answer that question and provide guidance — whatever the answer is — on how to improve its impact. For our peer institutions, we recommend this combination of programming, culture change, leadership, and evaluation.

REFERENCES

Astin, A., L. J. Vogelgesang, E. K. Ikeda, and J. A. Yee. (2002). *How service learning affects students: Executive summary.* Los Angeles: Higher Education Research Institute, UCLA.

Astin, A. W., and L. J. Sax. (1998). How undergraduates are affected by service participation. *Journal of College Students Development* 39 (3): 251–63.

Carnegie Foundation for the Advancement of Teaching and the Center for Information and Research on Civic Learning and Engagement (CIRCLE). (2006). Higher education: Civic mission and civic effects. Retrieved from the CIRCLE Web site at: http://www.civicyouth.org/PopUps/higher_ed_civic_mission_and_civic_effects.pdf.

Community-Campus Partnerships for Health. (2004). Making a positive impact. Seattle: author. Accessible at: http://depts.washington.edu/ccph/pdf_files/ccph_brochure_00250_03764.pdf.

Driscoll, A. (2008). Carnegie's community engagement classification: Intentions and insights. *Change: The Magazine of Higher Learning* 40 (1): 38–41.

Hollister, R. M., M. Mead, and N. Wilson. (2006). Infusing active citizenship throughout a research university: The Tisch College of Citizenship and Public Service at Tufts University. *Metropolitan Universities Journal* 17 (3): 38–54.

Marcelo, K. B. (2007). College experience and volunteering. CIRCLE fact sheet. Retrieved from: http://www.civicyouth.org/?cat=15.

Myers-Lipton, S. J. (1998). Effect of a comprehensive service-learning program on college students' civic responsibility. *Teaching Sociology* 26 (4): 243–58.

Rubin, V. (2000). Evaluating university-community partnerships: An examination of the evolution of questions and approaches. *Cityscape: A Journal of Policy Development and Research* 5:219–30.

Terkla, D. G., L. S. O'Leary, N. E. Wilson, and A. Diaz. (2007). Civic engagement assessment: Linking activities to attitudes. *Assessment Update* 19 (1).

Vidal, A., N. Nye, C. Walker, C. Manjarrez, and C. Romanik. (2002). Lessons from the community outreach partnership center program. Washington, D.C.: Urban Institute. Available at: http://www.oup.org/files/pubs/lessons_learned.pdf.

Vogelgesang, L. J., and A. W. Astin. (2000). Comparing the effects of community service and service-learning. *Michigan Journal of Community Service Learning* 7:25–34.

9

Community Colleges Returning Home
Community Institutions for Community Leadership

In 2007 I left my job in investment banking at Bank of America to join the world of community activism and engagement. I had been involved in the community for some time while working at the bank; however, I craved more hands-on involvement in helping address some of my communities' biggest problems. I was a graduate of Leadership Charlotte, a program that trains community business leaders to get involved in their communities.

Yet, at the age of twenty-four, I was the youngest of our group of business leaders by nearly ten years and was in a different place in my career than the more experienced executives who were my classmates. However, I felt confident that there was no difference in my ability to contribute to the community. During this experience I decided that, instead of seeing community service and civic leadership as an extracurricular activity, I wanted to make them my full-time job.

This realization led me on a new journey that ultimately brought me to Generation Engage and now Mobilize.org, where I have worked to increase young people's civic participation. This journey also helped me see the importance of community colleges to the health of a community.

I saw that in Charlotte, like too many other communities, we outsourced solving our community-level issues to the business community and others with money or corporate resources. I was grateful for my experience as a Leadership Charlotte member. However, I recognized that community leadership couldn't be hierarchical: we need to create ways of empowering every level of our community with the resources to get involved, not just facilitate the business elite and their checkbooks as the sole community problem solvers.

Likewise, we must provide high school students with the same opportunities that Leadership Charlotte graduates are afforded. And most importantly for this chapter, we must provide to community college students curriculums that not only prepare them for the workforce but also connect them to their roles as civic and community leaders. This provides the kind of new leadership model described throughout this book, in which the responsibilities for community leadership are not left to community notables, but are taken up by ordinary citizens and community members, the native leaders who so often attend our nation's community colleges. I have found that this group of local leaders can have the greatest impact on addressing community problems. We just need to give these students more opportunities to take on these responsibilities as part of their education and beyond.

I was positioned to have a nice, comfortable career in finance and to make a lot of money, yet I wasn't satisfied. Through my participation in Leadership Charlotte I was afforded access to a conversation and to resources that many of my peers didn't know existed. I had mentors who instructed me on how to get things done, including whom to talk to and how to talk to them. After spending eight years at Bank of America (four as an intern in college, and four as an associate) I craved using this kind of access to do good in the world and trying my hand at being a civic leader, a community activist. It was then that I asked a mentor, who allowed me to join in meetings, and with whom I discussed business deals, to recommend me for a community leadership position.

His reply caught me off guard. He said, "You don't have enough experience." I was taken aback, even though it made sense to me. At the time I was working on a trading desk managing billions of dollars, was serving on multiple boards, and was involved in the community, but apparently I still hadn't reached the mysterious threshold of being ready to contribute. I was qualified, but the ability of many people in our communities to contribute was controlled by an old leadership hierarchy that made community service a club requiring some vague criteria for participation.

Like many people of my generation, I rejected this idea. I knew I was ready to contribute as a leader and also to catalyze the talents and skills of other young people.

I soon quit my job at the bank and figured that, if I wasn't experienced, I needed to get busy getting whatever he meant by experience. After leaving the bank I joined a grassroots engagement initiative called Generation Engage, where I was tasked with connecting noncollege youth with civic education opportunities and facilitating increased civic participation.

As I moved into my role with Generation Engage and worked in the community, I soon found many young people just like me, who craved an opportunity not only to give back but also to learn and share as they were doing it. Young people, especially those in marginalized populations, contrary to the perception of many in society, have a passion for making their communities better and seek opportunities to incorporate this passion into the way they live their everyday lives, not just in one-off, extracurricular activities. Many of these young people experienced community-level issues not by reading the front page of the paper, but by walking out their front door.

The first partner I sought when I started community work was the local community college. I searched out these institutions for a number of reasons, but the most important was the fact that they hold the very people the community thinks can't contribute. In high school we talked about community colleges as the places where "lost people go," as places for those who had no contribution to offer the community. My experience leaving the bank was a transformative one, and I realized that community leadership was not predicated on a degree or intellectual capacity; rather, the foundation of community leadership is *the application of perspective and experience.*

Too often we use an established community leadership hierarchy based on economic status. But, as the recent economic recession illustrated, this is not a sustainable way to exist. Shortly after I left the bank, the bottom fell out of the economy, and in one-industry towns such as Charlotte the infrastructure of the community was shaken. Bank of America would struggle to stay alive, and Wachovia, another bank located in Charlotte, would soon falter. Our community and the traditional leadership model were badly shaken, and those who suffered the most as a result were those beholden to this socioeconomically based civic structure.

Not long after I started my work with Generation Engage, everyone jumped on the community college bandwagon, not just in Charlotte but also across the country, led by lofty presidential goals to improve college graduation rates and an economy on the verge of collapse. From retraining and certificate programs to low-cost education, our community colleges became the pillars of struggling communities and meeting places for community redefinition.

In this chapter, I briefly review the purpose of community colleges and then discuss how my experience working with Central Piedmont Community College and Miami Dade College was an exciting opportunity to institute curriculum-based leadership development, which made community problem solving that extends beyond campus a principal component of the academic experience. Working with these institutions, we expanded the utility of the community college from satisfying a community's economic and development needs to providing a place for innovation and solution building for the community's social and civic problems. These examples are part of a larger trend and an evolution at community colleges that have been acknowledged by the Obama administration and are part of the historic role played by community colleges.

The Community College: An Overview

Community colleges, or junior colleges as they are sometimes called, are over one hundred years old and exist in multiple forms. The label "community colleges" applies to the array of institutions providing vocational programs, skills certification, preprofessional certificates, and contemporary liberal arts education ending in an associate's degree or a transfer to a four-year college or university. Community colleges come in all shapes and sizes: public, private, proprietary, and even online.

Community colleges have an expressed commitment and connection to the communities they serve. The 1947 President's Commission on Higher Education, which gave community colleges their official moniker, inspired the concept of "the community college." The commission stated that "the term 'community college' be applied to the institution designed to serve chiefly local community educational needs. Its dominant feature is its intimate relations to the life of the community it serves" (President's Commission on Higher Education 1947, p. 3).

Also incredibly important is the Carnegie Commission on Higher Education (1970), which established that community colleges should be within commuting distance of every adult. These commissions, together with the Higher Education Act of 1964 and amendments in 1972, enabled community colleges to grow into more than schools, into community institutions that would drive the pulse of communities.

The contribution of the community colleges has evolved from workforce development to community development. As adaptive institutions that take their cues from the pulse of the community, they are now evolving once again with the economic downturn and the political and social instability of our growing democracy.

Most community colleges are open-admission institutions, which means they are open to anyone who seeks to attend. Their often lower cost and part-time options, when compared to those of four-year institutions, make them the only realistic option for many people. The diversity of options available at community colleges has been one longstanding and attractive feature of these educational institutions. As the cost of higher education continues to increase and the technology economy evolves, the need for an institution with the resources and flexibility of the community college will continue to rise (Education Encyclopedia 2010).

Community Colleges in the New Century

Community colleges are growing, and the Millennial Generation is fueling their growth. The Millennial Generation is the most ethnically and racially diverse generation yet. The diversity of this generation isn't yet represented on four-year campuses: most of the browning of America is taking place at community colleges. They enroll 43 percent of all postsecondary students, including 45 percent of African American postsecondary students, 53 percent of Latinos, and 52 percent of Native Americans (American Association of Community Colleges 2010).

Millennials are on pace to become the most educated generation in American history. This is not a feat that is being accomplished just because they want to stack up degrees; the demands of an ever-evolving information age require the new generation constantly to acquire skills and knowledge for immediate application. The number of Millennials attending college has reached an all-time high, and almost half of this increase has been due to community college enrollment (Pew Research Center 2010).

The Millennial relationship to education is changing due to the economy and the redefinition of work. Millennials are acquiring skills, not just degrees, for a number of reasons, but primarily because they will be different from their parents. Millennials will switch jobs or careers multiple times during their lifetimes; therefore their relationship to education has undergone a remarkable shift that has only fueled the utility of community colleges.

Generation Engage and Community Colleges

The faces of our next generation's leaders will be much more diverse, and those leaders will as a result have a much different relationship with the institutions of society, which were created in a much different world. The relationship will move from institutions that shape to ones that will be shaped by this new generation of leaders. This is what makes creating opportunities to lead so important, and where community colleges uniquely come into play. These institutions have a physical and experiential diversity that, coupled with programs to build leadership capacity, can ensure that the baton of this democracy is handed off cleanly to a generation that is capable, informed, and already acting.

Through my work with Generation Engage, I was able to observe the work of three community colleges — DeAnza Community College, Central Piedmont Community College, and Miami Dade College — and their attempts to teach leadership and speed the evolution of community colleges as community institutions. Our theory of leadership was rooted in making leadership and citizenship a real thing, something the students recognized in their everyday actions, not just in what they saw on television or on the news.

After the 2004 election it became evident that the playing field for civic engagement and leadership development was not level. Low voter turnout, especially among youth not bound for college, along with apathy toward public issues, led to national efforts to identify ways to mobilize young people to become involved in public life. Many of these efforts, however, were focused on four-year campuses, often ignoring the socioeconomically disadvantaged.

Slightly more than half of those ages sixteen through thirty have no college experience or access to four-year institutions. Research done by CIRCLE at Tufts University shows that the lack of access to four-year institutions in itself will virtually guarantee fewer civic opportunities, as well as fewer opportunities to develop crucial skills that are necessary to participate fully in our democracy. Research shows that the lack of opportunities to volunteer continues to be a barrier for largely marginalized communities (Volunteering and College Experience 2009).

As a result, Generation Engage, now a project of Mobilize.org, was created to address the civic opportunity gap for young people who had not attended a four-year college or university. We based our efforts on three assumptions:

- Young people suffer not from a lack of interest, but from a lack of access
- Our democracy should be a dialogue, not a monologue
- The best investment we can make in the health of our democracy is in young leaders at the local level

Our community college partners all had mechanisms to fund their work. However, the most important investment that scaled our leadership programs was that of the community. We depended on community resources and opportunities to create transformations and education for students in civic leadership, as well as ways to connect civic leadership to their development academically.

We also had strong presidential leadership. People such as Eduardo Padron of Miami Dade College and Brian Murphy of DeAnza Community College see the role of their service-learning centers and student life departments as extending the community college as a community institution. Working with our partners DeAnza Community College, Central Piedmont Community College, and Miami Dade College (the latter two of which are described below), we developed a learning process for participants that informed them about specific public policies, connected them with other young people to share perspectives, and then brought civic and political leaders to the table, bridging the divide between the issues students cared about and the people effecting change on those issues.

The most important aspects of Generation Engage were to facilitate participation and build leadership. Many young people are used to being acted on, instead of having others work with them to connect their experiences and perspectives to leadership skills and to ways of becoming involved in their communities.

Using the Civic Health Index, developed by the National Conference on Citizenship (NCOC) to measure citizen-centered engagement, we were guided by the fact that civic leadership opportunities often are inaccessible to community college students. Young people at community colleges are often working full-time, have dependents at home, and are low-income, yet they are actively working to attain an associate's degree or a skills certificate. Leadership development and civic life are luxuries they can't afford in terms of money or time. Students who are commuters, juggling busy working lives while taking courses at community colleges, have no interaction with the civic resources for addressing community-level problems or the many things that affect their lives. One of the participants in our program used the analogy that "we are a dart board just waiting for things to hit us, with no control over anything."

Yet through Generation Engage we established formal partnerships with our community colleges in three cities and saw these partnerships develop into high-impact tools for creating not only better students and workers but ultimately citizen-leaders who will form the foundation for their communities' future. By creating a pathway to civic engagement and leadership training, we were able to change the paradigm of the community by introducing new actors on community issues who have unique, ground-level perspective, and whose solutions will therefore be much more authentic and efficient.

The Program: Inform, Connect, Act

For the two-year period from the fall of 2007 until the spring of 2009, there were a total of 7,000 participants in the program from DeAnza Community College, Central Piedmont Community College, and Miami Dade College who attended events, meetings, policy discussions, and volunteer opportunities. In our work with these institutions our role was to be a partner to connect the work of the students with opportunities to take their leadership off campus. This was especially important given the challenges of the community college student, who is almost always a commuter. The local program was based on a three-step model called Inform, Connect, Act.

Inform involved meeting with participants to discuss particular issues in their community from their perspective. We brought these discussions to them, often asking for a meeting room on campus during lunch, bringing pizza, or holding a meeting at a conveniently located coffee shop nearby.

Connect involved direct conversations and communication with elected officials, policy experts, or actors dealing with the issues we were discussing. In the process of leadership development one of the most transformative elements of our program was the opportunity to show that decision makers are everyday people just like the students. The only difference is the title they hold. As a citizen, the student has a responsibility and opportunity to hold them accountable by sharing experiences with them or explaining how their decisions, policies, or organizations affect the student's life.

Act is the most important part, because it is where we develop the new leaders for our community by providing them an opportunity to act on what they have learned and experienced. Just as students work jobs and internships hoping to gain experience in a career or specific job, we held the same concept for civic participation. Continuously identifying opportunities to get involved, participate, and effect change on the issues one cares about not only is preparation for active citizenship but also is the work of democracy.

Central Piedmont Community College: Taking Leadership to the Classroom

Central Piedmont Community College (CPCC) is located in Charlotte, North Carolina—my hometown. When I was growing up, the institution was very much the place where one took classes, and then one went to work, nothing more, nothing less. Central Piedmont Community College was the perfect partner to begin this three-step process of engagement and action because many of the students, having committed to continuing their education, are eager to learn, but many have not had the ability to see themselves as future leaders. Applying this model may result in new leaders for a community that needs them.

CPCC is guided by a change in the curriculum model. The Learning College has two guiding questions: Is it good for our community? Is it good for our students? This evolved over time, and the administrative leadership of the institution has embraced a new relationship between knowledge and its application. Knowledge is not just for work, it is something that should facilitate our communities' growth. The skills students attain can help the community.

The goal is for every graduate of Central Piedmont Community College to demonstrate mastery of the core competencies (communication, critical thinking, personal growth and responsibility, and information technology and quantitative literacy), in addition to the requirements of individual programs. In the development of leaders within community colleges, there must be leaders at the administrative level who are committed to shifting their institutions from worker-development institutions to risk-taking institutions trying to develop leaders who also work.

Citizen Designer Course

Working with Kenn Compton, Chair of the Graphic Design Department at Central Piedmont Community College, we designed a curriculum in which students would gain an understanding of the communities' civic infrastructure while pairing this knowledge with their course work in graphic design. The project course was called Citizen Designer, and its focus was the exploration of how graphic design can be used as a tool of civic engagement. Instead of students doing random projects from a course manual or via an online curriculum, Generation Engage staff and the instructor (Compton) worked together to design a key community partnership to allow students to learn about their communities and then to show them how they could contribute locally with projects linked to their skill sets.

Through several project challenges, the students had to use their natural design thinking to understand and develop solutions whose impact was for the greater good. At the end of this project, the students would be able to analyze a target market to determine the best way to reach them with a specific message; utilize the design process to develop multiple solutions; evaluate proposed solutions against project objectives; and communicate the process, problem, and results verbally and visually.

The project had several phases:

1. *Research.* In addition to independent research, students partner with an agency involved in the issue they choose to work on. Students are expected to spend a minimum of ten hours with the agency, learning from it about the issue and existing responses to that issue. Students must interact with people affected by the issue; they are the target audience. The agency may ask students to do limited design work for it; this is to be completed outside of the ten hours and is not a part of the final project.

2. *Creative exploration.* What is the problem the students are trying to affect? How many different approaches can be generated? For example, creating an awareness poster would be one approach. But it does not directly engage the people affected by the issue.

3. *Conceptualization.* Generate several conceptual approaches and thumbnail them. Always ask, what else can I do? Make certain that the concept or message is directed at helping people affected by the issue.

4. *Presentation.* Pitch the best concept to the agency partner and client.

The result of this project was that a group of students who gained a skill first through their classroom instruction and then through our partnership were able simultaneously to see how that skill translated into ways for them to be active and engaged citizens in their community. The goal of this program partnership between the community college and Generation Engage was to create a pilot program to make community leadership not just a class but an aspect of everything the community college does. These students were working toward associate's degrees, and some were attempting to earn certificates. When we entered the class, many of them had never thought that their experience in the course would also include leadership development. This partnership produced not just better graphic designers but also citizens who had gained leadership skills and a road map for applying them every day.

Miami Dade College

In Miami, Florida, as we worked with the Miami Dade College Center for Community Involvement, we identified students who normally don't have opportunities to participate locally in activities. We created a leadership model that was about education and empowering them to scale what they learned in their communities.

Partnering with the City of Miami and the Office of Sustainable Initiatives, we taught a group of fifteen Miami Dade students about the city's climate action plan and gained their feedback.

The engagement plan the city was previously going to execute was significantly altered after the meeting with these students. These students worked to create a plan that was more relevant to varying perspectives and that accomplished the goal the city had laid out, to reduce its carbon footprint. With the City of Miami, these students created a campaign called "Switch and Save," in which they convinced a local hardware store to donate energy-efficient lightbulbs and then created an on-campus campaign empowering students to green their homes with free, energy-efficient bulbs if the students switched out their inefficient bulbs. The program seemed very simple, but its impact was amazing: it allowed students to be educated on an issue and then to take ownership of a process.

This process became our Active Citizens program within the Center for Community Involvement at Miami Dade, a program that derived from work with the Corporation for National and Community Service (see http://www.nationalserviceresources.org/initiative-active-citizens), and it grew into a structured program. The Active Citizens program recommends that organizations incorporate training for citizenship in their outreach programs. The goal is further to expose participants to the democratic process in their communities and impress upon them both their role in those communities and opportunities for leadership. Generation Engage didn't follow the exact model displayed in the Active Citizens 101 program but used it to develop the Generation Engage Active Citizens program, which includes:

- *Talking politics*: Each month staff organize a small group of students for a conversation with a local elected official on issues affecting their community.

- *Community cinema film screenings*: In partnership with Independent Television Service (ITVS), Miami Dade College hosts monthly film screenings, which include documentaries focused on addressing national, social, and political issues. These film screenings enhance the cultural landscape with the voices and visions of underrepresented communities and reflect the interests and concerns of a diverse community.

- *Volunteer opportunities*: Each month local staff offer students hands-on volunteer service opportunities hosted by local nonprofits in each Generation Engage community. Generation Engage acts as the connection to other community organizations in order to offer unique service opportunities for students, which they might not otherwise be connected to.

- *Personal leadership*: Each Generation Engage community has a personal leadership program. This program may focus on different issues in each community, but each program centers on empowering students to take action in their community. Students learn to develop their advocacy skills in order to affect change at the local and national levels.

- *Video conferences*: Generation Engage organizes a multitude of national speakers from Washington D.C., and each local community hosts a video conference at which students have the opportunity to lead an informed conversation with important national, political, and civic leaders.

These experiences showed us that facilitating the opportunity for students to be actors, instead of those always being acted upon, not only produced increased engagement but also created the foundation for a new population of community problem solvers and leaders.

With regard to leadership within this growing population of community college students, it is important that we find ways to provide authentic, challenging opportunities to lead that also provide a road map for sustainability. Earlier discussion of leadership has justifiably concerned volunteer service that solves an immediate need; the new conversation needs to be about leadership that is sustainable and that evolves with the demands of our local communities. Our democracy is counting on this.

The Future of Community Colleges

Through these programs, students have developed a concept of democracy that has been built into their individual curriculums, but these programs have also removed the barrier between these students and their role in our democracy. They have become actors, not just those acted on by a system. This is the new definition of leadership.

And community colleges will be at the forefront of the next generation of our democracy's leaders. The hallways of our community colleges are the best representation of this country's diversity, providing a way for immigrants to make the transition into the country. As American society becomes increasingly diverse and four-year institutions continue to increase in cost, community colleges will be the way for more and more people to pursue higher education. Now making up almost half of all higher education institutions in the United States, community colleges present a unique opportunity. They have the ability to combat and significantly reverse the social inequity in many of our communities, through their academic programs and through their increased role as leadership developers, bridging the civic gap within the millennial generation.

Community colleges are the canvas on which we will paint the new image of our American democracy. They are the new community institutions holding the keys to economic renewal through job retraining programs, innovation centers, and skills development. The students who find a home on community college campuses are most often firsthand witnesses to the deficiencies of our democracy and until recently have not been engaged in the process to fix them. The opportunity within community colleges to build systems of engagement and action within their student populations is not only unprecedented. It is the necessary ingredient to ensure the sustainability of our democracy and guarantee that local communities are capable of supporting the growth and development of their citizens.

The previous examples describing the work at community colleges to create leadership training are but two small stories of engagement and leadership development. When we think about building the next generation of leaders, community colleges are our training camp, the basic training on which we can create a foundation of young people who can ensure our local democracies are effective.

For too long we have focused our civic opportunities on four-year students when leadership development and civic information would be better and more efficiently directed at community college students, who may have a more direct relationship with institutional inequity, poverty, and the many other issues this next generation will be tasked with correcting. Many community colleges are responding by adopting leadership development programs across multiple certificate programs and curriculums. They must not be alone in this; communities must adopt their community colleges as the investment vehicles of the communities' future.

Community colleges, their leadership, and their structures of support, must understand that we must institute shared strategies to build citizens who are ready to lead in this new society. These students will return to their communities not just as workers but also as citizens who are engaged, active, and informed, with the undoubted results of better communities, a better democracy, and increased opportunities for future generations.

As I entered the world of community organizing I saw community colleges as training grounds for the new crop of sustainable leaders who will form the foundation of our communities. As the tsunami of the economic recession has hit our communities across the country, our community colleges can become proverbial community reconstruction companies, helping both to repair the economic infrastructure and also to provide the next generation of community leaders.

Though our country may have backed into an understanding of the importance of community colleges, there is an opportunity to turn our default realization into an intentional strategy for community repair and excellence. And this new strategy needs to be rooted in building leaders from community colleges and empowering them with the keys to driving our communities.

The community college is one of the finest creations of our American democratic experiment and the institution best situated to stimulate the next generation of leaders in our communities. It is an apolitical institution that is flexible, large, and adaptive, with an express purpose of helping communities by providing locally tailored resources for local educational needs. The next generation requires a sustainable force of leaders across the country who are invested in their communities, knowledgeable, and ready to contribute through participation and leadership.

REFERENCES

American Association of Community Colleges. (2010). Community college fact sheet. Retrieved from: http://www.aacc.nche.edu/AboutCC/Pages/fastfacts.aspx.

Carnegie Commission on Higher Education. (1970). *The open door colleges: Policies for community colleges*. New York: McGraw-Hill.

Education Encyclopedia. (2010). The history of community colleges. Retrieved at: http://education.stateuniversity.com/pages/1873/Community-Colleges.html.

Pew Research Center. (2010). Millennials: A portrait of generation next. Retrieved from: http://pewresearch.org/millennials/.

President's Commission on Higher Education. (1947). A report of the *President's Commission on Higher Education*. Washington, D.C.: Government Printing Office.

Volunteering and College Experience. (August 2009). CIRCLE fact sheet. Retrieved from: http://www.civicyouth.org/?p=350.

IV Moving Forward

Adam Weinberg, Rebecca Hovey,
and Carol Bellamy

10

Exploring Leadership through International Education
Civic Learning through Study Abroad in Uganda

Leadership education in the twenty-first century cannot ignore the global risks, opportunities, and realities of our interconnected world; so too international education cannot avoid its responsibility to provide the knowledge and vision needed to resolve critical issues we will face as a global community. A model of international education is needed that acknowledges the diverse global community in which institutions are based and learning takes place. In linking leadership and international education, we propose an alternative approach to both based on recognition, reciprocity, and responsibility toward others. Basing our work on the concept of an "ecology of learning" to describe community-based education (Longo 2007), we refer to a "global ecology of learning" in which students learn through deep cultural immersion in communities through international education (Hovey and Weinberg 2009). Educational opportunities based in local communities, or learning ecologies, offer insight into how societal problems are constructed, perceived, and resolved through the actions of local citizens. In particular, we address the internationalization of undergraduate education as a way to think about and act upon leadership development as a dimension of moral responsibility and democratic civic engagement in an increasingly globalized world.

Over the past two decades, notions of leadership in the United States have been profoundly shaped by the unexpectedly swift collapse of the Soviet Union between 1989 and 1991 and a rebirth of American exceptionalism in response to the attacks of September 11, 2001. Within U.S. higher education, both of these historical events stimulated policy efforts to enhance our knowledge of global affairs and of the emerging and uncertain realities that would follow such dramatic shifts in our world order. Many of the current initiatives to internationalize U.S. higher education were formulated in response to these events and the perceived need to strengthen our national security, economic competitiveness, and democratic leadership through education (Hovey 2004). However, as many internationalization initiatives sought to assert U.S. competitiveness, other voices raised questions regarding the need for peaceful coexistence and collaboration in the face of common threats such as climate change and global health pandemics. The Simon legislation, named in honor of Paul Simon, the former senator, acknowledges both concerns with its claim that "We are unnecessarily putting ourselves at risk because of our stubborn monolingualism and ignorance of the world" (NAFSA 2003, p. 1).

At the same time, globalization trends beyond the control of U.S. national security have been altering the landscape of higher education around the world. Knight makes the following claim regarding internationalization of higher education: "Since the 1990s, it has become a formidable force for change, perhaps the central feature of the higher education sector" (Knight 2008, p. 3). Knight's analysis of five key elements of globalization—the knowledge society, information technologies, market economies, trade liberalization, and changing governance structures—emphasizes the fluid context of institutional change and its relationship to new economic, technological, and political forces at play in the world.

The rush to internationalize higher education, however, lacks a sound understanding of the kind of leadership needed for the social challenges we face in the twenty-first century. Students born after the fall of the Berlin Wall and raised in a Web-based media society already understand the arbitrary nature of borders, nations, and information. What is not addressed in this rush to make sure our students and faculty "know the world" is the more profound question of how "to be in the world." This is not merely an existential question, for we must learn to be with others in a global civil society and to create the social fabric of this new society. International education needs more explicitly to address the need for alternative approaches to leadership. To do so involves learning from how others lead.

A Shift in Thinking

As a starting point, we posit that our ability to prepare students to be leaders in the twenty-first century requires shifting our thinking about higher education in four fundamental ways. First, we have to position civic education as a central driver of higher education. Clearly, higher education has civic roots. American colleges and universities were founded to produce informed citizens (Colby, Erlich, Beaumont, and Stephens 2003; Colby, Beaumont, Erlich, and Corngold 2007). However, it is also clear that, throughout the twentieth century, civic education was not a driving priority for colleges and universities. This has shifted over the last twenty years.

On most campuses, faculty participate in civic engagement efforts through ser-vice-learning and community-based research projects. Many campuses encour-age this work through programs, strategic institutional plans, and affiliation with Campus Compact. That noted, there has been growing concern among civic edu-cation proponents that our progress has slowed. John Saltmarsh, the director of the New England Resource Center for Higher Education (and formerly of Campus Compact), recently wrote what many of us have been thinking: "while the move-ment [to date] has created some change, it has also plateaued and requires a more comprehensive effort to ensure lasting institutional commitment and capacity" (cited in Boyte 2008, p. 10). Institutions that are not committed to civic life will not be capable of producing civic leaders.

If the civic education movement has plateaued, what is needed to develop civic learning further? Saltmarsh has previously urged educators to attend to the civic knowledge, skills, and values that link education to the community: "An under-standing of the community's history is essential to effectively participating in it as well as effectively shaping its future. Further, it is important to conceive of civic knowledge as knowledge that emerges from community settings. Civic knowl-edge, in this framework, emphasizes the role that the community, in all of its com-plexity, plays in shaping student learning" (Saltmarsh 2005, p. 54).

Significantly, though, this revitalization must not be only a replication of the early service-learning experiences. As emphasized by Lewin and Van Kirk, such community-based learning approaches to civic education must address the ques-tion: "How can we engage students in a way that facilitates the greatest commu-nity impact?" (Lewin and Van Kirk 2009, p. 555). Similarly, educators are asking how such learning can motivate students for sustained civic engagement.

One answer is to revive civic education with a greater link to the active peda-gogies of civic engagement and high-impact learning. A recent report of the As-sociation of American Colleges and Universities (AAC&U), using data from the National Survey of Student Engagement (NSSE), identifies service-learning and community-based learning as among the most effective learning practices for making an impact on students' personal and professional growth (Kuh 2008). Most of the other practices identified as effective come about through commu-nity engagement efforts, including study abroad, internships, undergraduate re-search, diversity or global learning, learning communities, and capstone projects. A related project is the Bringing Theory to Practice (BTtP) project, an independent initiative funded by the Charles Engelhard Foundation in partnership with the AAC&U. Over fifty institutions affiliated with the BTtP project have been exploring ways that engaged student learning improves the quality of students' education, development, and health. Their empirical work suggests that active pedagogies engage students in learning through reflection, in ways that contribute to the resiliency and health of students and hence to better learning outcomes (AAC&U 2009).

Second, we need to change how we conceptualize leadership education. Traditionally, leadership has been conceived of as the heroic individual who achieves the remarkable through charisma. This is an outdated and not very useful conceptualization. Leadership has shifted, as the world has shifted. Today, we are preparing students for what Longo and Shaffer call "leadership for the diverse democracy of the twenty-first century" (Longo and Shaffer 2009, p. 155). For Longo and Shaffer, leadership education is about helping students develop the capacity for the collaborative problem solving needed to address public issues in the twenty-first century. The leader-follower dichotomy is replaced with leaders who know how to facilitate groups to act collectively, across the community and over a sustained period, to identify and solve public problems. The role of higher education in preparing leaders is crucial. As Longo and Shaffer emphasize: "[It] must be integrally connected to the kind of learning that asks students to see themselves as creators and agents actively shaping local and global communities, rather than as passive consumers of their education and the broader culture" (Longo and Shaffer 2009, p. 155).

Third, we need to shift how we see public issues or social problems. The issues that our students will face in the twenty-first century are clearly global in scope, even if they require action within the local context. As Skelly puts it, "We know what the challenges are, and they are global in nature: climate change; poverty; environmental degradation; militarism; and increasing hunger, among a myriad of others" (Skelly 2009, p. 21). But Skelly also points out that while the mission statements of higher education institutions acknowledge this change, few programs "fundamentally address the problems our students, and humanity more broadly, will face in the decades to come" (p. 22).

Finally, we need some orienting concepts to ground this approach. We propose civic agency and public work as key concepts. Civic agency refers to the "capacities of communities and societies to work collaboratively across differences like partisan ideology, faith traditions, income, geography, and ethnicity to address common challenges, solve problems, and create common goods" (Boyte and Mehaffy 2008, p. 1). Higher education is essential to creating a pool of civic agents across society, because society is dependent upon higher education to graduate students who have the capacity and commitment to be community leaders who enhance civic agency. As Boyte states, "the central problem of the 21st century is the development of civic agency. Civic agency is the capacity of human communities and groups to act cooperatively and collectively on common problems across their differences of view" (Boyte 2008, p. 1). In essence, we are talking about preparing students to do public work as part of their everyday lives (Weinberg 2005). Public work can be defined as "sustained, visible effort by a group of people that creates things — material or cultural — of lasting civic impact, while developing civic learning and capacity in the process" (Boyte 2008, p. 1). This work requires the development of moral judgment and social responsibility that enables students to build strong affiliations and affinities in community, which prevent more instrumental or political abuses of public service.

How do we do this kind of work? We argue that international education, or study abroad more specifically, is one place where higher education can do a better job of preparing students for the public work that will enhance the civic agency of communities in the coming decades. International education has the ability to extend the institutional infrastructure of education beyond the classrooms and walls of the university. By linking students to the kind of learning that occurs in the real world, we connect them to civic life and direct encounters with public problems. Longo (2007), following a tradition associated with the education historian Lawrence Cremin, describes this extended world of education as an "ecology of learning" in which everyday life forms the basis from which knowledge is generated and acquired. Adapting this concept, we propose the notion of a "global ecology of learning" to describe community-based education in another culture, where language learning, cultural understanding, and awareness of alternative worldviews are gained through informal social learning integrated with more formal classroom instruction. The learning that takes place when education is seen as a global ecology involves recognizing the source of knowledge within the community and environment, developing reciprocal relations or partnerships between the community and the institution in order to sustain these relations over time, and, finally, instilling an ethic of responsibility among students, staff, and faculty to respond to local community issues and concerns (Hovey and Weinberg 2009, pp. 39–41).

Exploring Study Abroad

Clearly, U.S. colleges and universities are internationalizing. The number of American students studying abroad has quadrupled over the past two decades, reaching an all-time high of 262,416 in 2007–2008 (Open Doors 2009). Internationalization is a central theme in many college strategic plans. Despite this, the number of college students studying abroad remains appallingly low, less than 2 percent of the 18 million undergraduate students enrolled in degree-granting institutions (U.S. Department of Education 2009). Likewise, too many internationalization efforts are having impacts well below anticipated outcomes. For example, partnerships and projects often don't last very long or have far fewer students than anticipated. Efforts to bring more international students to U.S. campuses leads to too much parallel play, in which international students and U.S. students are on the same campus but rarely interact.

We start by distinguishing between two different kinds of study abroad. In one model, universities and programs send college students into the world, with little preparation, for culturally thin experiences. Students make minimal efforts to learn local languages or customs, travel in large groups, and are taught in classrooms that have only Americans. They live and go to bars with other Americans, often drinking too much and getting into trouble. They see local sights through the windows of traveling buses. Far from experiencing another culture deeply and on its own terms, these students (at best) simply get the American college experience in a different time zone. It is worth noting as well that many of the study-abroad destinations considered fun don't even require language study and offer relatively minimal challenges to students' sense of place and culture. These also happen to be the places with the highest percentage of students.

In a second model, programs are developed to ensure deep cultural and linguistic immersion. Students are oriented to understand and respect local customs and are encouraged to take responsibility for projecting a positive image of Americans. Such programs follow principles of cultural reciprocity and emphasize quality of experience over organizational efficiency. They emphasize sustainable, participatory, and community-based programming. In study abroad, such programs ensure that students become part of the culture by staying with local families and giving back to local communities. U.S. students attend classes but also participate in activities with local community members. They are taught by local staff who are paid fair wages and offer an inside view of the culture. Students return to the United States with the motivation to stay active in their relational learning in the community; to help others learn from their experiences; and to push for better understanding from their academic institutions, future workplaces, and political representatives with regard to the world beyond our borders. These students become young intercultural emissaries, global citizens able to adapt and contribute to a complex world.

Study abroad that starts with this focus on deep cultural reciprocity and linguistic immersion can help us develop leaders for the twenty-first century. In the next section, we use our SIT Study Abroad program in Uganda as a case study.

SIT Study Abroad: A Case Study

SIT Study Abroad offers academic programs in over forty countries around the world. SIT is the accredited higher education division of World Learning, which had its origins as The Experiment in International Living, the preeminent high school international exchange program, founded in 1932. Approximately 2,000 students per year currently participate in SIT Study Abroad's programs, which focus on critical global issues and many nontraditional study-abroad destinations.

SIT's experiential learning and cultural immersion model has served as a guide for many in the international education field (Batchelder and Warner 1977; Gochenour 1993); it has also lent itself to educational approaches to understanding inequality and social justice (Lutterman-Aguilar and Gingrich 2002). Increasingly, the extension of SIT's model into an ethnographic, fieldwork approach to inquiry has reinvigorated approaches to experiential learning by emphasizing its contribution to cultural documentation, policy studies, and knowledge construction (Ogden 2006; Hovey 2009).

This maturation of SIT's experiential, community-based learning also forms a basis for democratic education, global citizenship, and leadership for public work. The process of cultural immersion in a community-based learning model has a powerful impact on the civic identity and affiliations of U.S. students. Civic learning becomes even more powerful as students return home and find themselves both representing the host community from abroad and reinterpreting their own sense of belonging and citizenship at home. As students develop into young professionals and community members, they enact a role as citizen-diplomats, moving respectfully between cultures and building the connections needed for leadership in the global civil society of the twenty-first century (Hovey and Weinberg 2009).

SIT Study Abroad's programs in Uganda illustrate this experiential, community-based learning as a contribution to global leadership education. What makes the Uganda case unique? SIT's programs in Uganda evolved from our extended presence in East Africa during the 1980s and 1990s. Beginning with an excursion site from the SIT Kenyan programs, relationships with local community members and organizations (initially in Mbale, Jinja, Kampala, and other towns along Uganda's southern east-west corridor) offered a unique location to study critical approaches to development studies. Kevin Brennan, former Regional Director for African Programs and the Uganda program founder, at the time initiated an early shift in SIT programming, with a focus on local practicum experiences employing participatory research methods, identification of local intellectuals with alternative perspectives on development, and a focus on asking critical questions about our knowledge of the region. In his view, this shift was a move beyond cultural immersion for its own sake, with the result that students and staff actively engaged with communities in ways that could make a real difference because of the program's presence (K. Brennan, personal communication, September 30, 2009). For example, the SIT Uganda program developed the Uganda Resource Center in Kampala, a library open to local residents and an important local center for access to information, Internet services, and recent scholarly material relevant to development studies in Uganda. Kampala has become a burgeoning site of non-governmental organizations (NGOs), and the resource center offers a reciprocal exchange of resources with local activists and scholars by providing access to the library, along with multiple and diverse opportunities for students to interact with the local NGO community.

The growing worldwide attention to the civil war in northern Uganda and the barbaric abduction of children as child soldiers, along with the Rwandan genocide hearings held by the United Nations International Criminal Tribunal, are additional focal points in this region. They have contributed to making the larger Great Lakes region of Rwanda, Uganda, and Tanzania a site for understanding the human rights and social justice issues surrounding conflict transformation and reconciliation. The lessons from the frequently horrific accounts of violence and interethnic bloodshed are critical for understanding some of the very real obstacles to democratic civil society. The local struggles of East African communities to seek justice through both traditional and global human rights mechanisms, as well as to promote stronger and more accountable governance, offer models of local leadership needed to rebuild the social fabric of local communities. These examples of local leadership, alongside the presence of NGOs and multilateral institutions, from groups such as ResolveUganda (formed by former SIT Study Abroad students) to the International Criminal Court, offer insight into the challenges and possibilities needed for effective leadership in global civil society.

SIT Study Abroad currently offers three undergraduate programs in Uganda: the Kampala-based Development Studies Program, the northern Post-Conflict Transformation Program, and the Rwanda/Uganda Program on Peace and Conflict Studies in the Lake Victoria Basin. Each of these programs shares key components of SIT Study Abroad's community-based learning model. The programs are each led by Academic Directors (ADs) whose primary responsibilities involve administering the local program and, as faculty, facilitating the integrated course work, lecture series, field visits, and independent study work of the students. The following are the core components of the SIT model:

1. Intensive language study for communicative competence
2. Homestay with local families and sometimes with rural villages as a first-hand cultural immersion experience
3. Seminars on the theme of the program that introduce students to a variety of local academics, policy makers, activists, intellectuals, and other community representatives through lectures, site visits, research activities, and discussion groups
4. Some form of independent project

In the SIT Uganda programs, this fourth component is offered in three distinct ways. The Post-Conflict Transformation Program offers the typical SIT Independent Study Project (ISP), a four-week independent field project guided by a local mentor. The Development Studies Program offers an alternative, six-week practicum in which students serve as interns with local organizations and write policy papers based on their experiences. The practicum experiences correspond to one of four modules introduced during the thematic seminar: public health, human rights, gender, and grassroots microfinance. The Peace and Conflict Studies program, given its shorter length over the summer, allows for a shorter "mini-ISP" in which students can explore a topic of their own choosing.

Community-Based Learning

The SIT community-based learning model depends first of all on the integration of the community into the program. This is done through careful identification and selection of communities; meetings with appropriate groups of elders, local councils, or NGO leaders in which the program is clearly explained; the establishment of clear expectations on the part of the leaders, students, and host families; and ongoing follow-up and engagement with the community. Working through the local leadership is a critical element of community integration. The local elders and leaders play a role that is much more than just cultural gatekeeping: once they agree on common expectations, they assume the responsibility of building the program with the local community (M. N. Wandera, personal communication, July 10, 2009).

In some cases, community relations are facilitated by program lecturers. For example, the two-week Development Studies module on gender and development is coordinated by faculty at the Department of Gender and Women's Studies at Makarere University. During the first week, students attend lectures at Makarere University; during the second week, they are introduced to community organizations associated with projects connected with the Gender and Women's Studies faculty.

Dan Lumonya, a long-term Academic Director of the SIT Uganda programs, describes the five key principles of community-based learning that accompany student participation in community interactions: bottom-up leadership, inclusiveness, flexibility, cultural sensitivity, and culturally appropriate behavior (D. Lumonya, personal communication, July 14, 2009). These principles are applied throughout the program as students gain experience interacting and developing relationships with local individuals and organizations. For example, in the homestay experience, students learn to engage with the local community through the knowledge gained from their homestay family in program assignments such as constructing a family tree, drawing a village map, and debriefings with other students living within the same community.

As the students gain knowledge of their local context, they are better prepared to understand the larger themes of development and postconflict issues that are at the core of the programs. Uganda is a case study for learning about development and conflict in general; but, as Academic Director Martha Nulubega Wandera emphasizes, the first lesson of understanding development or conflict in practice is that it is important for understanding the local culture. The ADs create the structure of the program, but they want the students to learn from the "very people who do the practice" (M. N. Wandera, personal communication, July 10, 2009).

Participatory research is an important element of the fieldwork. Traditional interviewing, in isolation from context and with a set of structured questions, has limitations for understanding the full cultural context and meaning of development. Instead, the Development Studies program facilitates student participation in the rural activities of the community, whether this be planting, gathering water, or farming, and the use of this time to establish dialogue with members of the community. By talking, asking questions, and working alongside the community, students are able to grasp the cultural context and meaning of their responses. At the founding of this program, this approach was intentionally developed to follow action research methods such as Rapid Rural Appraisal to complement more typical ethnographic cultural research methodologies (K. Brennan, personal communication, November 9, 2009).

Leadership Education

William Komakech, Academic Director of the Post-Conflict Transformation Program, emphasizes that coming to Uganda to understand postconflict transformation is preparation not just for the students and their lives upon their return to the United States, but also for leadership critical for the global community. Leadership, democracy, good governance, and accountability are critical challenges in dealing with the impact of a decades-long civil war in Uganda and the genocide in neighboring Rwanda. Students learn about these challenges in their formal academic lectures in Uganda, but they come to understand the profound impact of these issues for local families through their homestays. Most of the homestay families are only now rebuilding their lives after years of displacement from their farms, life in refugee camps, loss of family members due to war and abduction, and the long, slow process of reconstructing their culture. Through their understanding of the academic, policy, and immediate life-worlds of postconflict transformation, students are better able to think through the implications of policy decisions made about Africa. Komakech tells students, "next time you hear about how decisions are being made about Africa, you can tell them what you have witnessed" (W. Komakech, personal communication, July 13, 2009).

The powerful significance of learning to listen to the people themselves can be a valuable dimension of foreign policy in the region. Charlotte Mafumbo, an Academic Director of the Development Studies program, reminds students of former President Clinton's foreign policy of "constructive engagement" in the region. When Clinton asked Africans what they needed from Americans, the response was that they needed Americans to come and learn from Africa. They needed decision makers and policy advisers to know from direct experience what the impact of their decisions would be (C. Mafumbo, personal communication, July 13, 2009). This message comes across repeatedly from families, community leaders, and Academic Directors: the students are witnesses and intermediaries who can inform the world at large and their own hometowns of the realities they encounter by living with communities in Uganda and Rwanda.

Komakech emphasizes that, while these experiences prepare students for leadership, the experiences also prepare local Ugandans. When student groups visit a community, the community becomes stronger through telling its story. This is particularly true among youth, who are eager to move past the conflict. They are determined to be in control of their own lives and obtain the education and economic activity needed to improve their lives. For Ugandan youth, having U.S. students who are learning from the Ugandans' own experiences gives them encouragement. They feel that if others come to Uganda to learn from them, they can emulate these students as well (W. Komakech, personal communication, July 13, 2009). The power of these educational exchanges is intense and immediate for these Ugandan youth, just as it is for the U.S. students who learn that hope and joyfulness of life can reemerge even after the trauma of war and genocide.

From a student's perspective, these exchanges can be seen differently, especially as students develop sensitivity to the overwhelming presence of international NGOs in the Ugandan context. One student responded to a question about examples of Ugandan leadership by stating she had observed a lack of agency among many Ugandans and a frequent dependence on the support of NGOs. From her perspective, this passivity is often created by the very organizations that purport to help Ugandans. Unfortunately, this creates a stereotype among the NGOs that the local population is passive, so when Ugandan youth attempt to initiate change, they are not viewed as emergent leaders by the NGO community. This student sees her work as an attempt to advocate for a local perspective on what appear to be global solutions (B.V.T. Ho, personal communication, July 13, 2009).

This student conducted her ISP on traditional justice models for the repatriation of formerly abducted persons (FAPs). Her research utilized qualitative research approaches of participant observation, focus group sessions, and individual interviews in Kitgum Province, northern Uganda. While multilateral organizations such as the International Criminal Court have called for the arrest and trial of brutal opposition leader Joseph Kony of the Lord's Resistance Army, the student found that an important faction of Ugandan reconciliation advocates opposed the arrest warrant as an imposed, "western" approach to justice through means of punishment. Instead they seek to practice local traditions of justice through truth-telling, forgiveness, and cultural renewal traditions. In writing of the painful struggles of families and communities to reintegrate formerly abducted persons who were forced participants in the violence of northern Uganda, the student encounters the profound need for the community to move beyond the self-perpetuating discourse of enemy and victim. She writes:

> Reconciliation in post-war Uganda encompasses innumerable aspects. It requires an aspect of wholehearted forgiveness: self-forgiveness, person-to-person forgiveness, and community forgiveness. It involves an active effort to reach out to individuals once perceived as 'enemies,' to provide support and to allow support to be given, and the restoration of relationships. It requires the genuine desire of a whole collective body to come together not as victim and perpetrator, but simply as neighbors, in an effort to rebuild the identity of the community and to regain stability. Post-conflict reconstruction is too often simplified to mean the rebuilding of physical infrastructure when the rebuilding of relationships and lives is of utmost importance. (Ho 2009, p. 31)

After completing her study in Uganda, the student continued her work on traditional justice through a summer internship with the Africa Faith and Justice Network, an organizational advocate for international traditional justice mechanisms. Her depiction of the northern Uganda efforts at reconciliation and reconstruction lies at the center of what Longo and Shaffer call for in a new approach to leadership for global challenges: leadership that is "relational, collaborative, community based, and perhaps most important, public" (Longo and Shaffer 2009, p. 155). Even the best efforts at leadership concerning social justice and human rights cannot be top-down and applied universally according to abstract principles. Leadership with respect to global challenges of such critical humanitarian dimensions can only be developed in collaboration with local customs, values, and community support, if it is to be effective. And the education for such leadership requires on-the-ground experiences and careful analyses such as those provided to this student and so many others in community-based learning programs abroad.

Multidimensional Aspects of Leadership Education

These examples demonstrate the multidimensional aspects of leadership education in an international context. Developing and administering programs that can promote understanding of how local communities handle development and conflict reconciliation involves constructing and supporting leadership in diverse and multilayered ways. Collaborative leadership needs to be practiced at several different levels:

- Through the institution's own training and support of local staff responsible for leading a community-based program

- Through the local staff's role in developing community relationships and encouraging the local population to emerge as leaders in local projects as they represent their community and find ways to integrate students in their daily lives

- Through access to activists and policy makers to learn about how leadership is practiced in specific contexts

- Through facilitating a process by which students gain the confidence to participate in the local culture and begin to develop a mind-set of mutual learning, appreciation of local moral norms, respect for community belonging, and responsibility for furthering their learning on their return home

Mary Lou Forward, former Academic Dean of Africa for SIT Study Abroad, describes the leadership approach to both education and program administration as one of learning to make connections, to bring resources together and to facilitate interactions with others. From the training of Academic Directors, to the cultivation of community leaders, to the preparation of students as future leaders, the lesson is that leadership "is not about you" and is not about "follow me." Instead she describes leadership in the following way: "Leadership education involves giving people a chance to feel part of something that is important and big, then having a chance to participate" (M. L. Forward, personal communication, July 10, 2009).

The challenge when maintaining a community-based program with group after group of students who come and want to be part of "something big" is that this can feel extractive for local communities. SIT's local Academic Directors carry a large burden in their leadership of doing the hard work — the public work needed for civic education — of being a member of the community all the time, of talking to people about their needs, of thinking proactively about their needs and how the student groups can be managed in a sensitive way to respond to the community. Many times the local staff and students are able to initiate community projects, such as a women's batik cooperative or health education resources, which require very little in terms of financial cost, but are incredibly time-intensive in terms of building relationships of trust, respect, and attention to local needs.

Training and supporting the local staff in their work with communities requires an institutional leadership that upholds reciprocity as a goal, value, and intercultural mind-set. What we often refer to as reciprocity in the SIT programs in this context is less about a specific project or exchange and more about gaining a perspective that is inclusive and committed to maintaining community connections. Hautzinger (2008) distinguishes between direct and deferred reciprocity, reminding us that while students may be the immediate beneficiaries of cultural exchanges, often the mutual returns for both hosts and visitors can come much later in time, as relationships evolve and participants become capable of responding in kind. Providing this support involves documenting best practices of community-based education and collaborative leadership, ensuring that appropriate community members are involved in projects, and extending this mind-set or perspective of reciprocity to the pedagogical model itself.

Through deep immersion in these learning experiences, students come to understand the normative aspects of global citizenship as they return home and continue to serve as witnesses to the communities and people they have come to know. Many of the SIT students have demonstrated this leadership, developing NGOs to educate the American public about Ugandan conflict and development concerns. Among many students from the University of Notre Dame who participate through an affiliation with SIT, Peter Quaranto and Michael Poffenberger returned from Uganda wanting to get involved in African justice movements. After a summer spent looking for organizations involved in Ugandan solidarity, they realized they needed to create one. The Uganda Conflict Action Network (Uganda-Can) was created to spread information and provide a voice for Ugandans seeking to inform the world about the northern Ugandan war. This organization was later renamed ResolveUganda to improve its U.S. outreach and focus on the impact of U.S. foreign policy toward Africa (P. Quaranto, personal communication, November 12, 2009). At least one element of leadership that emerges in such efforts is the ability to move between cultures and to take responsibility for action within one's own culture.

Dan Lumonya describes the connections he seeks to make between what students learn in Uganda and larger global dynamics that are also evident in the United States. Sharing his educational philosophy, he writes:

> Rwanda's genocide must be understood as a consequence of the relationships between both historical and contemporary political and economic processes: the relationships between poverty and international trade, colonialism and neo-colonialism. Similarly, our understanding of the political and social construction of genocide must go beyond the geographical boundaries of the territory of Rwanda. For example, the cycle of prejudice as a framework for understanding the social and political construction of genocide can be paralleled with the social construction of racial prejudices and stereotypes in the U.S. . . .

We constantly move from the local to the global. And finally I challenge the students to think about what they might do, and what opportunities exist in their home and community environment to do something. (D. Lumonya, personal communication, July 14, 2009)

Our initial premise of this chapter was that while civic education lies at the heart of higher education, it is in need of revitalization. This revitalization needs to link community-based education approaches such as service-learning with more active pedagogies across the curriculum. The active learning that takes place in a community-based program—in which students may be living and studying with local families, participating in local economic and social activities, interviewing and observing communities using structured methods and advised by community members, and sharing their formal knowledge with local academics and mentors who bring new perspectives to their studies—enables students to begin to build relational capacities to interact in diverse settings.

In order for civic engagement to be effective, students also must learn, through this form of direct interaction with community members, how communities respond to societal conflict and injustice. Put most bluntly, most study abroad programs do not come anywhere close to offering these types of experiences. Too many students are studying abroad without ever really leaving this country. We need to develop experiences based on principles of deep cultural immersion and learning from the local community. In the SIT Uganda programs, U.S. students have witnessed the resilience of local populations in overcoming trauma and rebuilding their lives. These students have the opportunity to learn the cultural values and norms that foster this resilience, through the social and personal relationships they build while living in Uganda. Through this active learning, they come to understand that global issues of development and reconciliation require reconstructing the social fabric of people's lives and not just the physical infrastructure of institutions, although that too is important. This is possible largely because there is an active civil society in Uganda accessible to outsiders—a critical component that is also supported when a reciprocal learning environment is developed in collaboration with local leaders (P. Quaranto, personal communication, November 12, 2009).

Our second premise was to reconceptualize leadership education in accordance with the qualities of sustained, relational, collaborative, and facilitative approaches suggested by Longo and Shaffer (2009). In the spirit of community-based knowledge, skills, and values, our model seeks to learn from and support best practices of local leadership. In this context, learning how local leadership practices are inspired and realized, as the SIT students learned from Ugandan NGOs and youth organizations, provides a way of understanding what the local obstacles to effective leadership really are, and how sustained community efforts also need to be based on and combined with locally supported efforts such as traditional justice initiatives.

Leadership education for global engagement needs to be about learning how local leadership emerges, and learning how to interact and collaborate effectively, not "taking charge" or assuming personal direction of activity. Creating a community-based learning ecology also involves training and supporting the local faculty to be community leaders. As faculty and staff work with local communities and networks, they are also facilitating the communities' own roles in representing themselves, negotiating their participation, and clarifying goals and visions. This multidimensional aspect of leadership education then becomes a basis from which program principles of reciprocity, mutual exchange, and students' commitment to ongoing engagement with their learning can be cultivated and sustained.

Our third premise concerns the need to change how we see public issues. Specifically, we argue that civic education needs to resituate civic life within a wider global civil society. This involves understanding global challenges as the "fundamental referent" (Skelly 2009, p. 22) through which students learn to situate themselves in the world. It also involves making connections between injustices and social action in one context and the analysis and motivation for action in another. For example, Dan Lumonya is able to draw parallels between the construction of ethnic identities in Africa and race relations in the United States, and to use these parallels as a lens through which to engage U.S. racial discourse. Ultimately students have the opportunity to reflect upon and to analyze the political and social construction of identity and its implications in contemporary U.S. society and elsewhere (D. Lumonya, personal communication, October 2, 2009). In the broader debates over global citizenship and cosmopolitanism, the challenges of understanding the diverse and intensely local contexts of community and citizenship can be extended to understanding how we are interconnected through multiple forms of citizenship and belonging (Stoddard and Cornwell 2003; Benhabib, Shapiro, and Petranovic 2007).

And, finally, we conclude with our fourth premise, that the connection of civic agency and public work within higher learning underlies our description of a global ecology of learning. Study abroad programs that are carefully developed through community-based learning and cultural immersion in this knowledge ecology can energize student learning while also invigorating higher education. Connecting higher education to the community, whether locally based or globally located, provides an innovative potential that comes from new sources of knowledge, comparative analysis, and challenging new moral dilemmas.

All of this work entails the moral responsibility of engaged citizens. Civic agency and leadership develop through the capacity to act based on moral judgment. The student's work cited in the case study in this chapter draws on John Paul Lederach's recent work *The Moral Imagination: The Art and Soul of Building Peace* (Lederach 2005) for the analysis of the need of the northern Ugandan Acholi people to imagine their own future (Ho 2009). Lederach's reflections on his own work building peace and reconciliation are instructive for the work of civic education for global leadership. Just as this volume calls for a shift in how we conceptualize leadership for twenty-first-century global challenges, Lederach believes that integrating the "art" of peace into the "skills" of mediation involves a shift in worldview that requires a new moral imagination, which he defines as "the capacity to imagine something rooted in the challenges of the real world yet capable of giving birth to that which does not exist" (Lederach 2005, p. ix). Our hope for our students is that a renewed vision of leadership education for civic engagement results in new hopes and new solutions to global problems that we all face together.

REFERENCES

Association of American Colleges and Universities. (2009). Bringing theory to practice. Retrieved October 25, 2009, at: http://www.aacu.org/bringing_theory/index.cfm.

Batchelder, D., and E. G. Warner, eds. (1977). *Beyond experience: The experiential approach to cross-cultural education.* Brattleboro, VT: Experiment Press, in cooperation with the Society for Intercultural Education, Training and Research (SIETAR).

Benhabib, S., I. Shapiro, and D. Petranovio, eds. (2007). *Identities, affiliations, and allegiances.* Cambridge: Cambridge University Press.

Boyte, H. (2008). Against the current: Developing the civic agency of students. *Change: The Magazine of Higher Learning* 40 (3): 9–15.

Boyte, H., and G. Mehaffy. (2008). The civic agency initiative. Retrieved October 28, 2009, at http://www.changemag.org/Photos/Civic%20Agency.pdf.

Colby, A., E. Beaumont, T. Ehrlich, and J. Corngold. (2007). *Educating for democracy: Preparing undergraduates for responsible political engagement.* The Carnegie Foundation for the Advancement of Teaching. San Francisco: Jossey-Bass.

Colby, A., T. Ehrlich, E. Beaumont, and J. Stephens. (2003). *Educating citizens: Preparing America's undergraduates for lives of moral and civic responsibility.* San Francisco: Jossey-Bass.

Gochenour, T., ed. (1993). *Beyond experience: The experiential approach to cross-cultural education.* 2nd ed. Yarmouth, ME: Intercultural Press.

Hautzinger, S. (2008). From direct to deferred reciprocity: Service- versus community-based learning in international anthropology training. *Applied Anthropologist* 28 (2): 192–203.

Ho, B.V.T. (2009). The heart of forgiveness, in light of unforgettable hurt: A multi-faceted perspective on reconciliation in northern Uganda. Independent Study Project, SIT Study Abroad, Uganda: Development Studies Program.

Hovey, R. (2004). Critical pedagogy and international studies: Reconstructing knowledge through dialogue with the subaltern. *International Relations* 18 (2): 241–54.

———. (2009). The ethnographic experience: Experiential learning via ethnographic practice. Presentation at the annual meeting of The Forum on Education Abroad, Portland, OR, February 18–20, 2009.

Hovey, R., and A. Weinberg. (2009). Global learning and the making of citizen diplomats. In Lewin, ed., 2009, 33–48.

Knight, J. (2008). *Higher education in turmoil: The changing world of internationalization.* Rotterdam, the Netherlands: Sense Publishers.

Kuh, G. D. (2008). *High-impact educational practices: What they are, who has access to them, and why they matter.* Washington, D.C.: Association of American Colleges and Universities.

Lederach, J. P. (2005). *The moral imagination: The art and soul of building peace.* New York: Oxford University Press.

Lewin, R., ed. (2009). *The handbook of practice and research in study abroad: Higher education and the quest for global citizenship.* New York: Routledge; Washington, D.C.: Association of American Colleges and Universities.

Lewin, R., and G. Van Kirk. (2009). It's not about you: The UConn social entrepreneur corps global commonwealth study abroad model. In Lewin, ed., 2009, 543–64.

Longo, N. V. (2007). *Why community matters: Connecting education with civic life.* Albany: State University of New York Press.

Longo, N., and M. S. Shaffer. (2009). Leadership education and the revitalization of public life. In *Civic engagement and higher education: Concepts and practices,* ed. B. Jacoby and Associates, 154–73. San Francisco: Jossey-Bass.

Lutterman-Aguilar, A., and O. Gingrich. (2002). Experiential pedagogy for study abroad: Educating for global citizenship. *Frontiers: The Interdisciplinary Journal of Study Abroad* 8 (Winter): 41–82.

NAFSA. (2003). Securing America's future: Global education for a global age. Report of the Strategic Task Force on Education Abroad. Washington, D.C.: NAFSA.

Ogden, A. C. (2006). Ethnographic inquiry: Reframing the learning core of education abroad. *Frontiers: The Interdisciplinary Journal of Study Abroad* 12 (November): 87–112.

Open Doors. (2009). *Open Doors 2009: Report on international educational exchange.* New York: Institute for International Education.

Saltmarsh, J. (2005). The civic promise of service learning. *Liberal Education* 9 (2): 50–55.

Skelly, J. (2009). Fostering engagement: The role of international education in the development of global civil society. In Lewin, ed., 2009, 21–32.

Stoddard, E., and G. H. Cornwell. (2003). Peripheral visions: Towards a geo-ethics of citizenship. *Liberal Education* 89 (3): 44–51.

U.S. Department of Education, National Center for Education Statistics. (2009). *Digest of education statistics, 2008.* (NCES 2009–020), Table 188. Retrieved November 21, 2009, at http://nces.ed.gov/fastfacts/display.asp?id=98.

Weinberg, A. (2005). Residential education for democracy. *Learning for Democracy* 1:29–46.

11

The Role of Higher Education in Public Leadership

Public leadership has become a central concern in higher education, but it remains a concept in flux.

The goal remains the same: build an entire generation of public leaders. But there is a new movement underway to transform what used to be seen as a dry, bureaucratic, top-down hierarchy into a vibrant, collaborative, and inclusive system of leadership that reflects the values and vision of a new generation of young people. That system eschews the still-powerful "star system" that focuses on finding and supporting a handful of future leaders. In contrast, the new model assumes that every student, no matter how young or old, has a capacity to contribute to and participate in something larger than herself or himself.

This new concept of leadership, however, requires different ways of thinking about how we *educate* for leadership. Traditionally, young people interested in becoming leaders were directed to business or management schools, where they learned public speaking, goal-setting, and budgeting. Now, as young people become more interested in leadership as public *service*, there must be new thinking about the ways in which we educate and train for those positions. This is a point to be discussed later in this chapter.

Higher education is critical to that equation. It acts as a gatekeeper into the world of public leadership and plays a crucial role in shaping student attitudes about public service of all kinds, starting with volunteering as an introduction to public leadership across the sectors. Anyone can lead a life of public leadership, be it in government, private business, or nonprofit agencies.

Too often, however, higher education sees volunteering and other forms of public leadership as something students should do in their free time. Too many career counselors view Americorps as little more than a ticket to graduate school, and public leadership as a second-choice destination compared to the exhilarating, high-prestige jobs that once existed in the private sector.

The Current Conversation

Higher education may have the right intentions, but it is still at some distance from changing direction. It tends to focus on what students can do, not on what students might do. Higher education focuses almost exclusively on short-term indicators of service such as the numbers of students who belong to clubs, participate in days of service, or take public leadership courses. All are responsible measures of important activities, but they do not indicate public leadership. The ultimate outcome ought to be social impact in addressing urgent threats that students care about, not marking time with antiquated images of service.

It is no surprise that the conversation about public leadership might be sharply divided within academic borders:

- The conversation is sharply divided between research and practice, as if research is somehow an adversary of action. Although there is high-quality research underway throughout the academic community, there are barriers between the results and needed fine-tuning of specific programs.

- The conversation is also sharply divided across academic disciplines and their schools. Even when they are housed in the same building, the disciplines seem unable to communicate as they fight over ownership of the latest fashions such as social entrepreneurship. Business schools have been at the forefront of social entrepreneurship training, leaving political science, public policy schools, sociology, anthropology, the humanities, and the hard sciences well behind or even ostracized.

- The conversation involves too many gatherings of too few people. The individuals and organizations involved in public leadership often stick to themselves, whether because they are isolated from more traditional views or because they choose to remain separate. They are old-school leaders after all — they see themselves as competitors for a relatively small number of positions that exist primarily at the very top of government.

- The conversation focuses almost exclusively on stories about lone wolves who struggle mightily against the odds to make an impact, even though we now know that collaborative creativity actually produces more success and fewer failures. As a result, collaboration is rarely discussed as a leadership tactic, in part because it produces few stars who get credit for impact.

- The conversation tends to be drawn to big goals, but not always particularly rigorous measurements and plans. Collaboration is the hot new concept, as it should be, but building successful social networks requires the same rigor that business entrepreneurs use to produce the waves of creative destruction that knock out the status quo (or at least displace it long enough to neutralize the old equilibrium that always lies in wait).

- The conversation rarely addresses the issue of failure and poor performance, perhaps because it is driven by the desire to draw more public leaders to the cause. Higher education tends to celebrate the breakthrough hero, and has few awards for teams and teams of teams. Hard as one tries, it is nearly impossible to find steady research on failures. Even as public leaders conquer the many obstacles they face, they must be constantly vigilant about potential threats to their own work.

- The conversation seems to be moving toward ever-smaller niches of action and nanoprojects, as public leaders accept the conventional wisdom that everything must be new. The same personal characteristics that create the confidence to act can also thwart the willingness to listen.

- The conversation is filled with dismissive jargon toward the old, large, "legacy" organizations that have the deep experience and authenticity that contribute to social movements. (Just imagine the civil rights movement without the NAACP Legal Defense Fund's early litigation.)

- The conversation generally focuses on communities as targets, not cocreators. Programs are driven by measures of how beneficiaries improve, but rarely by measures of how communities participate. Although there are exceptions on every campus, community building is generally underutilized as a tactic of durable impact. The main interventions tend to be programmatic drop-ins that quickly fade once funding expires.

- The conversation often neglects the potential value of creative collaboration between government, nonprofits, businesses, and unaffiliated actors who work in between the sectors. There is too much focus on form (where to build the idea and organization) and not enough on function (what to do and when to act). It does not matter where an idea emerged or who invented it, as long as it makes an impact.

- The conversation tends to understate the role of power, in part because politics sometimes involves partisanship and hardball of the kinds that produce congressional or media investigations. We all want to be nice about change, even as the status quo uses every political maneuver possible to stymie progress.

- Finally, the conversation tends to minimize essential issues of organizational structure and management. Management is not just about doing things right; it is about doing things well. Too many public leaders view organization and management as someone else's responsibility: they want to imagine, invent, and dream, not raise money for heat, light, and computers.

Simply put, we spend too much time celebrating the lone-wolf public leader, and not enough time talking about building and maintaining the movements that have produced the great breakthroughs of the past.

The Seven Myths of Public Leadership

If higher education is to play its role in cultivating public leadership, it must change the conversation that governs the curriculum, student advancement, and faculty recruitment. (Professors are public leaders, too.) But higher education must first confront its seven myths about public leadership if it is to play this role.

Public Leadership Is Only about Volunteering

Higher education often concentrates its public leadership programs on short-term, one-off volunteer efforts by students in the communities surrounding their campuses. In doing so, higher education tends to isolate the various aspects of public leadership in specialized silos such as offices of community service and career counseling.

But public leadership comes in many shapes and sizes, and should be presented as part of a life well lived. It can take place almost anywhere, including in government, charities, and businesses. It can go beyond traditional social services, such as serving meals at homeless shelters, to inventing clean technologies. And it can occur in different ways throughout a person's life.

Higher education should embrace that multidimensional definition. Presidents and chancellors might create a sustainable campaign to promote all forms of engagement, while acknowledging that public leadership often involves interdisciplinary skills that cross traditional academic boundaries.

Days of Service Are Always Positive

A day of service now and again is hard to criticize. After all, what could be better than a cleaner park, a graffiti scrub, or freshly painted schools, even if they only last for a few months? But days of service can also reinforce the episodic, sporadic volunteering that appears to be increasing among young Americans. In turn, that occasional volunteering places great stress on the organizations that young Americans want to help. Why invest in training when students only show up when they please?

Durable commitments to public leadership are essential for giving students the meaningful work they crave. It is one thing to volunteer once a year, and quite another to show up every week to read to kids or to lobby for educational reform.

Public Leadership Is a Civic Duty

As higher education designs its annual campaigns to encourage students to engage in public leadership, it often falls back on standard guilt trips about service as an obligation that must be fulfilled. After all, that is how the "greatest generation" was called to service.

However, such calls rarely work. Public leadership is better understood as a means to an end, not as an end in itself. For most students, public service is not about obligation, but about the chance to make a difference on issues such as poverty, homelessness, inequality, Darfur, and global warming. Students are not saying, "show me the money" when they think about service, but rather, "show me the impact." Colleges should structure the conversation about public leadership with a regard for issues that matter, not by treating service as a way to give students an entertaining day.

Public Leadership Is Always Rewarding

Higher education must be honest about the kind of work students can expect. Too often, institutions focus on what students can get from public leadership by way of recommendations, course credit, or future jobs, reinforcing expectations of immediate gratification.

Public service agencies cannot provide a scintillating experience for students who show up whenever they please, nor can they survive the current economic implosion without filling menial jobs. The reality is that most public service jobs involve, especially early on, at least some stuffing of envelopes and answering of phones. What is more, even as the demand for services rises, charitable giving is falling, bringing many nonprofits to the edge of collapse. That makes volunteer work more essential but perhaps less exciting. At the same time, state and local governments are imposing hiring freezes, pay furloughs, and job cuts, creating fewer opportunities for longer-term careers. Students would do well to remember that menial tasks may be the most important tasks of all.

Public Leadership Is Always Quiet

Even as some colleges wonder whether faculty should be allowed to wear campaign buttons in the classroom, their students want a stronger voice in what happens both on and off campus. Public leadership cannot be limited to "safe" service such as tutoring and mentoring, important though such work surely is.

Students also want to solve problems, not just treat them. Colleges can help by giving students the skills and small grants to bring new ideas to fruition. Some of these ideas may eventually earn support from the Obama administration's new $50 million social innovation fund. As First Lady Michelle Obama noted when she announced the program in the White House Rose Garden in May 2010, "The idea is simple: Find the most effective programs out there and then provide the capital needed to replicate their success in communities around the country."

Public Leadership Is for the Young

Those in higher education often see public leadership as something that younger students do. Whether intentionally or by accident, they too often ignore the possibility that their older students might also be ready to serve, whether through service-learning in the classroom or "encore" careers after graduation.

These older students are easily lost. Because many go to college part-time and are still working, they are rarely included in discussions about public leadership of any kind. They are not included in the advertising for volunteer work, are not part of the outreach efforts for Americorps and other postgraduate years of service, and are left on their own in career planning. Even though the Serve America Act clearly encourages older Americans to pursue encore careers, higher education has yet to build programs to attract them to service. And fewer institutions still have built the training programs that the act requires for anyone who takes an encore fellowship.

Public Leaders Stay Put throughout Life

Back in the 1970s, most graduates of the nation's top public service programs were in agreement. They started their careers in federal, state, or local government and remained in one of those sectors for their entire careers. By the early 1990s, however, students were moving across sector boundaries with ease. Some started out in business and later moved to government; others started out in government and later moved to nonprofits.

Most colleges have been slow to accept this reality. Instead, most put students in silos designed for specific destinations. Policy schools cover government and nonprofits; social work schools cover human service agencies; business schools cover consulting firms. As sector-switching has increased, however, students need skills that apply across destinations, especially the skill of managing their own sector-switching. That is why my university's social entrepreneurship program invites students from all disciplines and restricts the number of fellowships given to students from any single discipline.

These are not the only myths that frustrate public leadership, but they illustrate the growing disconnection between colleges' packaging and promotion of public service opportunities and what students value most. If an institution wants to make the list of the nation's top civic universities, it must tell students the truth about what they can expect, provide an array of destinations, and always advertise service as a way to change the world.

The New Public Leadership

These problems are perhaps most visible in the nearly 250 professional schools of public policy, public leadership, and public administration that dot the country. There has been a sea change in the destinations of graduates of these schools, but much of the curriculum remains unchanged. The new public leadership may exist in practice, but it has yet to penetrate the teaching approaches that shape lifelong careers.

In particular, these schools have not yet embraced the significant problems that government faces as baby boomers get ready to retire. This point has been well made by the Partnership for Public Service, a nonpartisan interest group created to increase the supply of talented federal applicants. As the Partnership reported in 2005, 40 percent of the Homeland Security Department's managers will be eligible for retirement in 2009, 42 percent of the Senior Executive Service is expected to retire by 2010, and the attrition rate among air traffic controllers is expected to triple by 2012 (Partnership for Public Service 2005).

Demand

Again, the federal government is a case in point. Although college seniors report that they consider taking jobs in the federal government, they tend to look at the federal government as the best place for a steady paycheck, good job benefits, and everlasting security, which are hardly the motives the nation needs in these times of great uncertainty (Princeton Survey Research Associates 2002).

The key question is not whether talented students will consider public leadership, but what might convince more of them to accept the notion of a lifetime of service. Although there is now good information on what might motivate a talented young American to give the federal government a close look, and even some information on why they might apply, the federal government has never done a study of what leads one applicant to take a federal job and another to reject it. However, young Americans view the federal government as a place to reap extrinsic rewards such as pay, benefits, and security, and much less as a destination for the intrinsic rewards that come from interesting work and making a difference.

The most compelling work on public service motivation examines the role of organizations themselves in shaping attitudes, an issue raised throughout this chapter. Arguing that motivation is shaped by organizational culture, Donald P. Moynihan and Sanjay K. Pandey (2007) come to the troubling conclusion that the longer employees stay in state government, the lower their public service motivation. Moreover, the more they balk at red tape and hierarchy, the lower their public service motivation.

These threats to public service motivation dovetail with concerns about telling the federal government's story to potential applicants. Yet, even with this acknowledged, the motivation to accept a federal job appears to be most affected by the reputation and reality of actually working for the federal service. Public service motivation may drive an applicant to a Web site and even lead to a federal application, but it may not push applicants actually to accept employment. It is not enough to make the invitation to service more inviting; the actual service must be inviting, too. Otherwise, solving the recruitment problem becomes the prelude to a retention problem. Such is the impact of the temptation to tinker (Rainey and Kellough 2000).

Moreover, the best available evidence suggests that the federal government is merely one destination in a new, highly networked world of public leadership that involves governments, businesses, nonprofits, contractors, grantees, and everything in between. Members of this new public leadership domain not only search for impact wherever they can find it but also are ready and willing to switch sectors to follow the most meaningful work. This new public leadership not only pits government against the other sectors in recruitment; it demands long-overdue concentration on the quality of work and its impact on retention.

What Motivates Service?

It is tempting to blame young Americans for the declining interest in public leadership careers. After all, they are the ones who have come to view the hiring process as slow and confusing, federal jobs as less than challenging, and public leadership as more like volunteering than traditional work. They are also the ones who have fashioned the new public leadership, switching jobs and sectors almost at will in search of challenging work, if not also in search of novelty and higher salaries.

Young Americans also have higher expectations regarding the nature of work and less loyalty to their employers. Raised in an era of downsizing, pink slips, and mergers, they may come to the new public leadership with few illusions about the nature of modern employment. They can hardly be faulted for thinking that no sector can be trusted to stand by them for long, or for holding governments, businesses, and nonprofits accountable for commitments of training, advancement, and the like. As such, they may be much more realistic regarding employment than previous generations, though there is very little parallel survey information on what earlier generations thought.

However, before stereotyping today's college seniors as self-interested sector-switchers, it is important to note that they are setting yearly records in volunteering. They have come to their current definitions of public leadership through years of service-learning in high school and their own readiness to volunteer in college. They are not at all selfish about giving time to charitable causes, and many have learned firsthand about government, business, and nonprofit work through internships and paid employment. They are hardly naïve about the promises that potential employers make, and they show a ready, indeed healthy, skepticism about the kind of work they will encounter in all three sectors of long-term service.

If the students are not the cause of declining interest, why do so many of them come to have such negative opinions regarding government employment? The answer may be their parents and the general public. General trust in government remains low, and attitudes toward government work in particular are not just skeptical but hard-edged. As already noted, the vast majority of Americans believe that federal employees take their jobs for the pay, benefits, and security, which translates into similarly negative judgments by young Americans.

Thus, young Americans are just as likely as their elders to agree that the federal government controls too much in their lives, that most elected officials are not trustworthy, and that the federal government is too powerful, all of which may reflect their coming of age during Bill Clinton's impeachment trial. Although they are more likely than their elders to say that government is really run for the benefit of all the people, the endorsement is not stunning. Moreover, they are just as likely as other age groups to say that criticism of the federal government is justified and that government does not do a better job than it is given credit for. They are equally likely to say that the big problem in government is that it runs its programs inefficiently, not that it has the wrong priorities.

Trust in government has not always been so low, however. It did surge in the early 1980s as inflation and unemployment fell, but mistrust increased with the Iran-Contra scandal in the Reagan administration's second term. More importantly for the federal government's current recruiting challenge, trust in government surged in the weeks and months following September 11, 2001, as confidence in virtually every civic institution jumped.

But what went up with a surge in patriotism following September 11 soon began to fall again. According to surveys conducted by Princeton Survey Research on my behalf in July and October of 2001 and May of 2002, the number of Americans who trusted the federal government to do what is right always or most of the time increased by 28 percent after September 11 but fell by 17 percent in the six months after (Mackenzie and Labiner 2002). Similarly, those who had a favorable opinion of the federal government also increased 28 percentage points after September 11 but fell back by 18 percentage points over the next six months. Although the number of Americans who felt very favorable toward federal government employees did move up from 12 percent to 20 percent immediately after September 11, it too fell back to 14 percent by May 2002. Similar patterns can be found in the data on confidence in nonprofit agencies.

Most important for recruiting was the percentage of Americans who thought federal employees were motivated primarily by job security, benefits, and a secure paycheck. When asked in July 2001 to pick the major influences that affect the choice of a government job, 70 percent of Americans said federal employees enter government for the job security (not helping the public), 68 percent said the salary and benefits (not the chance to make a difference), and 68 percent said having a secure paycheck (not doing something worthwhile). Only weeks after September 11, the figures had barely changed. Whereas 70 percent of Americans in the pre–September 11 survey had said that job security influenced federal employees most, 68 percent in post–September 11 interviews mentioned job security again.

At the Professional Schools

Students who graduate from the nation's top professional schools that feed public leadership broadly defined also express serious reservations about working for government (Light 1999). Bluntly put, they no longer see government as the best or only destination for a postgraduate career.

For example, the federal government had the highest attrition rate among the classes I studied. Of the graduates who started in federal government, 59 percent eventually left the government sector altogether, compared with just 38 percent of graduates who started in business, and 31 percent who started in a nonprofit organization. Asked about the most important considerations for staying in their current job, graduates across the sectors generally listed the opportunity for advancement, a chance to make a difference, job security, and public respect, but federal employees were somewhat more likely to say they were most concerned about salary. Although graduates in all sectors were generally satisfied with their work, more recent graduates were less satisfied than their peers and expressed stronger agreement that it is not wise to spend too much time in any one sector. Not only were recent graduates more likely to express interest in business and nonprofit careers, they were also more likely to think employers were less than loyal.

If the federal government took notice of this new public leadership among sector-switchers, it would provide much greater opportunity for lateral entry later in one's career. Under the government's current system, however, lateral entry at high levels is virtually impossible, in part because these jobs are rarely advertised, and in part because of an implied contract with current employees regarding advancement based on longevity. The next job on the ladder is almost always reserved for the next federal employee in line.

The New Skill Set

Higher education can consider this new multisector, sector-switching public leadership as an example of the changing options for making a difference and as a benchmark for reshaping the educational system. At least according to the graduates discussed above, their training does not necessarily measure up to the new pressures they face. The evidence is in the curricula, in which citizen engagement is rarely discussed, leadership and ethics are mostly reserved for a week or two of discussion, cultivating diversity is a continuing challenge, and innovation is mostly considered a subject for on-the-job training.

Asked what their schools did best in teaching them, for example, graduates of the top schools consistently emphasized policy analysis, statistics, public budgeting, and management. All are important areas, no doubt. But they do not touch on the new packet of skills that will shape the future. Students also receive little instruction on the need to manage the highly complex networks of state and local government agencies, nonprofits, and businesses now delivering the "extensive and arduous enterprise for the public benefit" that Alexander Hamilton considered the essential function of service and part of his design for a well-executed government.

This new skill set is not just essential for lifelong careers in government. It is also critical for students who are interested in any level of public leadership. Therefore, the curriculum for the new multitiered public leadership must include the following:

- *Students must learn about citizen action.* There is simply no excuse for the lack of systematic learning about civic movements, the role of voluntary action, the need for durable engagement, and how to harness a life of service to meaningful change.

- *Students must learn about leadership more generally.* Instead of the top-down model that graces so many course listings, courses should engage in discussions of collective leadership. Instead of the hero-centered courses that celebrate the lone wolf who struggles mightily against the odds, instruction should address collaboration, teamwork, and collective pursuits. And instead of focusing on the individuals involved in social change, courses should focus on the ideas that have made a difference in the past and the ones that might make a difference in the future on the issues about which students care most.

- *Students must learn about ethics in public leadership.* Many of the key decisions facing those in public leadership involve tough ethical choices about the design and delivery of goods and services. Courses that engage students in thoughtful analysis of these ethical challenges are essential for shaping engagement at all levels.

- *Students must learn about social innovation.* With increasing emphasis on what works and what does not work in social change, students need further course work on just how social innovation evolves. How do individuals or groups invent new ideas for solving problems? How do they spot opportunities for engagement? What are the key steps in the launch and acceleration of a new idea? And where do citizens fit in this process?

- *Students must learn about the sources and management of volunteers.* This is vital, whether volunteers arrive in their organizations on an occasional basis, as fellows, or as members of Americorps and other programs lasting one to two years. Courses should also address the philosophical questions surrounding the growing interest in private-sector social responsibility.

- *Students must learn about the new public leadership and the challenges of sector-switching.* Most will make several career changes in their working lives, moving from government to nonprofits, nonprofits to private firms, private firms to government, and so forth. Colleges must develop better sensitivity to these career shifts, including more aggressive training as their alumni make switches.

- Finally, *students must learn about the call to service* and how to guarantee a flow of talent that is motivated first and foremost by the chance to make a difference. This is more than an issue of marketing, though better advertising and tighter invitations certainly matter. Students also need to know how to change the working environment to make service of all kinds more inviting.

This kind of curriculum speaks not just to the needs of public-spirited students of all ages. It also speaks to the basic character of higher education. If higher education does not become more responsive to student needs and wants regarding public leadership, it will not only fail in a key public role, it will fail students as they chart a path into public lives.

REFERENCES

Light, P. C. (1999). *The new public service.* Washington, D.C.: Brookings Institution.
Mackenzie, C., and Labiner, J. (May 30, 2002). Opportunity lost: The rise and fall of trust and confidence in government after September 11. Washington, D.C.: Brookings Institution.
Moynihan, D. P., and S. K. Pandey. (2007). The role of organizations in fostering public service motivations. *Public Administration Review* 67 (1): 27–53.

Partnership for Public Service. (2005). Federal brain drain. Washington, D.C.: Partnership for Public Service Issue Brief PPS-05-08 (1).

Princeton Survey Research Associates. (2002). Survey on behalf of Brookings Institution Center for Public Service.

Rainey, H. G., and J. E. Kellough. (2000). Civil service reform and incentives in the public service. In *The future of merit*, ed. J. P. Pfiffner and D. A. Brook, 127–45. Washington, D.C.: Woodrow Wilson Center Press.

12

Organizing 101
Lessons I Wish I'd Learned on Campus

This new leadership movement on college campuses made me who I am. Sort of. Before my first week of freshman classes — even before orientation — and following a long day tilling dirt at a YouthBUILD site alongside my soon-to-be classmates, I found myself huddled in a homeless shelter basement discussing the merits of Monsignor Ivan Illich's famous 1969 speech to do-gooding students entitled "To Hell With Good Intentions." In it, Illich lambasts a crowd of college kids about to embark on a service trip to Mexico. He chides them for their vanity, hypocrisy, and ineffectiveness. We bright-eyed eighteen-year-olds asked ourselves: Can outsiders really make a difference in a foreign land? Is community service more about doing good or appearing to do good? If I really want to change the world, is there an alternative to service?

I was in heaven. Born in Charleston, West Virginia and raised in Plano, Texas, I had never heard of Illich and had no idea that there were other people my age who also cared about these things and wanted to ask big questions. The student-led preorientation program that had brought us together was called the Freshman Urban Program, or FUP. We called ourselves Fuppies. Heaven.

A week later, a fellow Fuppie and I were starting a citywide service group called BASIC. Two weeks after that, I was running for student government and trying to negotiate my way into Marshall Ganz's Introduction to Community Organizing course. For the next four years, for every hour in class, I spent two hours doing volunteer work. Service days. Tutoring and mentoring programs, such as PEACE Games. Harvard AIDS Coalition. Hosting the national Campus Outreach Opportunity League (COOL) Conference. The Coalition Against Sexual Violence and a campus education group called Peer Relations and Date Rape Education (PRDRE). I spent my summers working at a family shelter back home in Dallas.

But there was a problem. With each new project and each new fight, I kept coming back to Illich's reprimands and my own stomach-churning realizations.

What were we really accomplishing? Who am I doing this for? How can we make a more equal world if the charge is led by all these do-gooding people of privilege, like me?

For three weeks during my junior year, I got a taste of an alternative. During those twenty-one days I lived with about twenty-five other students in the University President's office protesting the below-poverty wages Harvard paid its service workers. Those three weeks were the result of three years of work. We collected workers' stories, researched our issue back and forth, and built a coalition of students, faculty, community members, and even alumni. We went through all the proper channels, but one by one, meeting by meeting, we were told that workers actually had it pretty good and that nothing could be done. We disagreed. And we kept fighting, with protests, teach-ins, and so forth, until finally, we decided to do something that might get us kicked out of school. And it worked. By my senior year, we had won a "living wage" of $11.35 plus benefits.

After graduation, I was able to take advantage of a school-sponsored public service fellowship that allowed me to travel to Botswana and learn how people there were responding to the AIDS pandemic. I wanted to see how another culture reacted to its problems. What I found was more of the same: Illich's do-gooding outsiders with big money and big hearts and big ideas—each with a ready explanation of why their work was different and more partnership-oriented than all other development work—working in fits and starts to fight the virus. Like so many other experiences from college, Botswana reminded me of my own privilege and left me thinking there must be a better way.

There was. When I returned to the United States, I took the advice of a fellow student who had become a community organizer and attended the Industrial Areas Foundation's weeklong national training in Arizona. Founded by Saul Alinsky, the Industrial Areas Foundation (IAF) is the nation's largest network of citizen power organizations. It was an IAF organization (called BUILD) that won the first living wage campaign in Baltimore. Another (East Brooklyn Congregations) built 4,000 homes to help revitalize New York. The Greater Boston Interfaith Organization authored and won the country's first statewide universal health care plan. The IAF helped train César Chávez, Barack Obama, and a hundred other organizers just as good as them but less well known.

The IAF training turned me upside down. I was in heaven again, except these folks not only had the right questions. They had answers. If you focused on building relationships first, you could create an organization that focused on common issues and worked across race, class, and even ideological differences. Justice work didn't have to be just service (someone doing for someone else): we could all, rich or poor, serve each other by joining forces. It didn't have to be just marketing (raising awareness of an issue): we could become more powerful and bring more people to our cause by each of us telling our stories and inviting others to tell theirs too. And it didn't have to be just narrow advocacy (a small few lobbying an even smaller few): we could hold meetings with a thousand folks across all backgrounds, asking public officials to commit to the issues that mattered to all of us.

By the end of the week, I had convinced Ed Chambers, the national director of the IAF, to hire me as an organizer in Chicago. Over the next four years, I learned a lot more about how to change the world than I had in college. Why? I went to college to learn about the world and how I could change it, but in many ways, it wasn't until I had more experience getting my hands dirty outside a campus environment that I was able to focus. The rest of this chapter is a catalog of what organizing taught me, and how universities might incorporate some of those lessons for the next generation of students.

Organizing Taught Me That All People Are Created Equal

College taught me it was my job to help people less fortunate than me. It taught me that I had the answers and the know-how to make a difference, and that answers and know-how were what mattered. While I spent that first night discussing Illich, I spent the next four years hearing implicitly and explicitly that the social justice world consisted of two types of people: the poor, unfortunate, at-risk, and uneducated; and the people (like me) who had the smarts and resources to help those people. In sociology classes, in service-learning projects, in community service groups, and even in activist endeavors such as the Harvard Living Wage Campaign or the Harvard AIDS Coalition, the dominant framework was one of servant and served, privileged and poor. Is it like this everywhere? Certainly not. But for me and many friends of mine, what we kept hearing was: You're the future. People cannot always do for themselves. The answer to the world's problems is more smart people with more resources — like you.

My inflated ego wanted to believe that this was true. If only we could get all the smart people in a room — smart people like me — we could do anything. This belief in experts, elites, and problem-oriented social change is an enticing one.

But it is also a dangerous one, as I came to see firsthand.

It leads nonprofit organizations to spend their talent, time, and energy wooing foundations and investors instead of holding themselves accountable to the world they want to help create. The shelter where I worked three summers during college (partly thanks to a service-learning grant) was no exception: the people who had the most control over our program were rich white funders. Then came the all-white "administrative" staff that was based off-site. Then came the all-black "client services" staff that was based at the shelter. And the people who had the least control over the program were, of course, the people who had the most to gain and lose: the homeless men, women, and children we called "clients." (For a provocative articulation of the ways that community service may actually be bad, see McKnight 2007.)

More innocuously, we see this belief crop up on college campuses in volunteer programs that are conceived of as an easy way for students to give back. When we direct these programs, we spend most of our time and resources trying to figure out how to make the experience as enticing and rewarding as possible for the volunteers. The underlying assumption is that one group (the servants) is more important than the other (the served).

This belief can even lead us to do more harm than good. That was the case in Botswana. Better-funded, more internationally supported anti-AIDS programs in Botswana had less success turning the tide of the disease than homegrown solutions in Uganda.

When we teach the model of servant and served, we prepare our students to have a hard time fully relating to people who have less money or who live in a different neighborhood. We prepare them to be surprised when they realize that homeless people aren't lazy or that poor parents actually care about their kids. Perhaps saddest of all, we prepare them to monopolize the ability to give. What makes relationships so great is reciprocity, give-and-take. By teaching a model of servant and served, we hinder our students' innate ability to receive and our clients' innate ability to give in meaningful ways. Thank goodness for many of the service-learning programs around the country that are experimenting with what reciprocity can mean on campus. Professors inviting community members to teach. Students joining local efforts, rather than starting new ones.

Finally, in a servant-served model we take away from both the servant and the served the ability to challenge one another. The servant is taught to make excuses (poverty, trouble at school, bad parents) for the "at-risk" kid who always shows up late, and the at-risk kid is taught always to appreciate the generosity of the volunteer's time—even if it bores him to tears.

In contrast, organizing assumes we all start off as equals. Our first encounter with each other—rich, poor, black, white, clerical, lay—is a face-to-face meeting where each of us shares his or her struggles and stories. Plans, campaigns, and programs are built out of mutual leadership by people who are addressing their own concerns together. Mutual leadership is rare, because it is harder than it sounds. I'm still learning it. My natural inclination is either simply to command (assert my interests) or to serve (elevate another's interests above my own). But I never regret the rare moments when I am able to overcome my natural tendencies and mix my interests, which I hold dear, with someone else's.

One of the organizing campaigns we worked on in Chicago was a voter registration drive aimed at influencing the next Illinois governor. The leaders of this campaign were Orthodox Jews, young Muslims, evangelical Christians, homeless mothers, ex-offenders, and junior college students. Representatives from these groups led our meetings, hosted registration drives, and chaired the public accountability session where we demanded specific action from candidates.

This sense of mutual accountability and mutual leadership is not magic, but it is countercultural. There are a couple ideas for what universities could do to move in the direction of a new leadership that values rich and poor, servant and served, as equals.

First, make students start by exploring and acting on their own self-interest. Much effort is spent trying to understand the interests—also called the needs, hopes, desires, and struggles—of the poor. In order to be equals, students can first explore and act on their own interests. Students can be the served and the servant, the organized as well as the organizer. One of the most exciting things about the voter registration campaign described earlier was the genuine surprise felt by many of the leaders (myself included) that all of our basic interests were compatible. Orthodox Jews and Muslims worked in concert, without much fanfare. White evangelical Christians lined up alongside homeless youth and liberal city college students. One way to see each other as equals is to remind ourselves that we all have the same basic drives, urges, and struggles. Rather than asking students to focus on the plight of the less fortunate, we can have them dig deep into their own interests, motivations, and problems. On the two occasions when I taught a college service-learning course, students were required to develop a project or campaign that addressed a problem that affected them or a family member personally, be it food deserts on the South Side of Chicago or the feelings of a Muslim student in London that his religion was being unfairly treated by the media. The primary instinct of most of those students was to serve, just as mine had been. But at the end of the class, many realized that by fighting for their own interests they were fighting for others, too.

And if we must serve, let's require an element of reciprocity. For instance, if we start an education program in a neighborhood, let's require that someone in that neighborhood coteach a course on campus. If we do a volunteer day in a neighborhood, let's invite local high school kids to come and clean up the school. If we send a new volunteer into a neighborhood, let's make her wrestle with what problem in her own life she is going to ask someone there to help her with.

Another favorite service-learning lesson comes from Lila Watson: "If you have come here to help me, you are wasting your time. But if you have come because your liberation is bound together with mine, then let us begin."

Let's challenge ourselves to live up to those words.

Organizing Taught Me That Not All "Community Work" Is Created Equal and That, to Be Effective, We Must Be Ready and Willing to Criticize and Be Criticized

Most of what I learned in higher education was that all community work is valuable. One popular idea when I was in school was the "continuum of service," a basic notion that activism, service, international development, philanthropy, and so on were all children of the same parent. Each in its own way was essential to the cause of justice. I fear that we echo this basic bias when we use the term *civic engagement*, which has become popular among educators and administrators precisely because it captures and endorses every conceivable impulse to do some good.

Are you interested in fighting for better health care? There's nothing wrong with posting a link to a health care article on your MySpace page. You might even call that civic engagement. But it's not the same as lobbying doctors in your neighborhood to donate more time to a free clinic or sending three buses full of friends to Washington, D.C., to flood congressional offices. Let's spend less time congratulating each other on our initial impulses to do good and more time challenging each other to risk more and do better.

There is an alternative to a culture of uncritical appreciation. Organizing taught me that high standards, tough critique, and controversy were not only healthy, but vital. Cornel West once said that justice is the closest thing to love in the public sphere. The closest thing to love I have found in public life is accountability—someone caring enough to challenge me, to tell me when I'm not making sense.

That kind of honest critique and evaluation was missing from my college experience. Even the people who disagreed with some of the work we were doing (our service programs were too broad, our campaigns were not targeted enough) kept quiet, thinking it was better to encourage all of our impulses than to share the critical wisdom of their experience.

This point was driven home to me again when I returned from four months in Botswana. I was struck by all the praise I got. "It's so great that you did that." "You must have really made a difference for those people." For the most part, people were just being nice, being polite. But there I was, twenty-three years old, convinced that in the last four months I had done more harm than good inserting myself in another country's processes, only to leave. I was hungry for someone who would shoot straight with me, someone who could help me parse the good from the harm, help me do better next time. And that was nearly impossible to find.

In contrast, in four years of organizing, I was constantly reminded about what I was doing wrong. I was expected to be conversant about my own faults, the faults of the leaders I worked with, and what we were doing to fix those. After every large meeting and after every action, we evaluated for fifteen minutes or more so that we would do better the next time we acted together.

And what better role for academia to play in social change? To be critical, to be harsh, to be unrelenting in our pursuit to do better for our world, to hold our students and ourselves up to the world as it should be and ask why we are not there yet. I'm encouraged by the many practitioners who are already melding the critical tradition of the academy, including some of those described in Part Two of this book, with the practical organizing tool of evaluation.

What might this look like?

- Conduct regular evaluations. How hard would it be to build regular evaluations into all of our programming? On the bus ride home from every service project, we could ask, what will we do better tomorrow? At the end of every voter registration outing, we could ask, what strategies worked best? At the end of every course, we could ask, what's one thing we learned from this student, and what's one thing we think this student could continue to work on? Let's make evaluation a habit.

- What might happen if we invited Republican and Democratic clubs (never short on opinions) on campus to debate the effectiveness of various civic engagement programs at our schools? It's not hard to imagine similar discussions led by religious studies majors or ethics professors or local public officials. There's a youth civic engagement program here in Chicago called Mikva Challenge, which at the end of the year invites community leaders to judge the community action programs that various high schools have been working on. If high school students from mostly "low-income" schools can embrace this criticism, certainly college kids can too.

- What would happen if we required that all service-learning programs and courses ended with a student's public defense of the good that she achieved and the things she could have done better? Imagine a room in which a student who set up a mentoring program at a local middle school is challenged by his classmates at the end of the term: What have you done to make sure this program will be around in five years? How did you incorporate the ideas we discussed from Freire's *Pedagogy of the Oppressed*? In what ways are the mentees leading and teaching the mentors? How are you measuring the program's success?

Doing good can become a sort of safe haven, something we do when we want to avoid criticism. At times in my life, social justice work has played that role for me. Volunteering and activism were things that I knew would make people proud of me and think highly of me—regardless of the outcomes. I sympathize with the urge to applaud our students for merely wanting to do something for the public good. But some things are more important than wanting to do good.

Organizing Taught Me That Good Leadership Is Relational

Some argue that my generation is redefining leadership to mean a much broader range of things: everything from blogging to volunteering to designing a Web site for a nonprofit to participating in a fundraiser. This line of thinking holds that the academy should embrace this new, broader definition of leadership. I strongly disagree. Referring back to my previous point, I think the academy is already too accepting, too uncritical, and too reactive to students.

When it comes to defining leadership, the organizing community has a different concept: leadership means having relationships and mobilizing those relationships for public action. The way we get relationships is through listening and action, by proving to the people around us that we do what we say we are going to do. Leadership is hard to do. It involves knowing what matters to the people around you, knowing what they are ready for, sharing power and recognition whenever possible, navigating personalities. It is the quality of building and maintaining relationships that makes someone a leader—not charisma, not volunteerism, not having a skill. If we fail to lift up a model of leadership that is relationship-based as opposed to skill-based, we will end up teaching our students that it is enough merely to contribute skills to the social good, rather than to invest the time, energy, and humanity that it takes to really lead.

How we define leadership is going to be an important question for our generation. While we are gifted with a thousand new ways to speak up, there is a decreasing likelihood of being heard. The difference between those who achieve great things in this generation and those who do not will come down to using new social tools to cultivate and enhance genuine, old-fashioned relationships rather than to replace them.

I learned this lesson the hard way as an organizer, and I am still learning it. Many times I would find myself two weeks away from an important strategy session. I knew that having a strong showing of people from all over the city was going to help our cause. And I knew that the single best way to ensure turnout was to call up all the people I wanted to be at the session and to meet with each of them beforehand—to talk through their interests, to hear what they wanted out of the session, and to challenge them to take a specific role on the agenda. In short, I knew that the way to get people excited was to really *relate* to them. I knew all those things, but more often than not, I took the easy way out and sent a big e-mail or posted something online or left a voice message.

Here are some ways we can help redefine leadership on campus as fundamentally *relational*. First, encourage relational meetings. The main tool that organizers and community leaders use to identify, train, and engage new leaders and followers is called a relational meeting: a one-on-one encounter between two people who want to learn each other's struggles and stories and find out if and how they could fight alongside each another. To build the community organization we started in Chicago, we first conducted 2,300 relational meetings with potential young leaders across the city. Before the organization was founded, before we ever acted, we used these meetings to ask: What matters to us? Where do we come from? What would we be willing to fight for? What keeps us from fighting for these things? How can we build across race and class differences? Who are the other people we should talk to? Relational meetings do not just form the foundation of organizations and campaigns. They are also the tool we use to plan actions, to challenge each other to take on bigger responsibilities, and to evaluate our mistakes. What is better than a face-to-face meeting to permit us to be vulnerable and honest and imaginative? When we start with curiosity and mutual interest, as opposed to salesmanship or service, we are more likely to build rich relationships.

Here is how relational meetings could be incorporated on campuses. Do you want to find out what issues are most important to students in your club? Give your team a goal of fifteen relational meetings at which they ask members what matters to them and what they would be willing to do to act on those things. Do you want to start a new service project? Meet one-to-one with twenty-five parents and twenty-five students in the neighborhood where you want to work and ask those same two questions: What do you want to see happen? What could we do together to get there? Do you want a student to research a local issue? Rather than assigning a paper analyzing newspaper articles and sociological studies, ask them to meet with ten people affected by that issue. Do you want to evaluate why your campaign didn't go as planned? Meet one-on-one with all of your fellow leaders to really dig into their experiences, learn what could have been better, and get people excited about next time.

Organizing Taught Me How Much Mentors Matter

My organizing mentor told me, "I don't fire people for making mistakes. I fire people for NOT making mistakes." And he meant it.

Every week, I submitted to him a report with the following headings:
- Rumblings (unformed reflections and struggles I was having)
- Lessons learned (mistakes I had made and what I was taking from those mistakes)

- People (whom I was working with, what mattered to them, what I could teach them, what I could learn)
- Victories (things I had accomplished or was planning to accomplish soon)

Every week, we met for half an hour or longer and discussed the report. He told me when I was full of shit. He told me when I wasn't risking enough. He said, "What are you going to say to this person? Let's play it out." Those meetings gave me the confidence to keep making mistakes. They forced me to keep the big questions front and center. Combined with my reports, they taught me to write and communicate better. And more than anything, they taught me how to mentor others.

I think this is actually the way we learn most things. What sticks with us we can trace back not to a lecture or a book but to an individual colleague or mentor who gave us some of their time. Organizing upholds the value of one-on-one, critical, report-driven mentorship. The academy, for the most part, doesn't seem to share this view.

Most organizations don't make the time for effective mentoring. Instead, mentoring happens in stolen moments here and there, if it happens at all. Organizations rationalize that mentoring doesn't help their bottom line, or they don't think about mentoring at all. The executive director is too busy. Having seen what mentoring did for me (in the role of both mentee and mentor), those arguments don't make any sense to me. But universities could be the perfect place for mentoring. Where else is there time and structure and wisdom to establish serious mentoring relationships? Obviously, mentoring already happens to varying degrees on every campus, but we can always do more to make mentoring a more prominent tool for propagating a new leadership model.

Yes, professors and administrators are busy. Yes, students think they have better things to do. (In four years of school, I spent maybe two and a half hours total in a professor's office during weekly office hours.) But if we believe that this kind of time is valuable, why not take it? Here are a few ways we could build mentoring into our campuses and curricula:

- *Give course credit.* Why not give students a credit hour (or more) for a weekly meeting that they have with a professor or professional mentor, to whom they must submit a weekly report of their successes and failures?

- *Require mentorship* for any new independent study, student group, or service-learning course. Students would be required to seek out formal mentors before they started realizing their dreams of helping people.

- *Pay professors to do it.* If we value this one-on-one time with the next generation of leaders as much as we value time spent writing journal essays or preparing for lectures, let's pay for it.

- *Ask our community partners to pony up.* If we value the services we provide our surrounding neighborhoods and nonprofits, let's ask that in return local leaders give an hour each week to a formal mentoring relationship with a student.

A word of caution: it will take a lot of work to elevate the practice of mentoring. Professors see mentoring as something they are already doing, because they impart a little advice here and there. Students will say they can already talk to somebody if they need to. A conversation during a crisis or a nice exchange after a service project is not the kind of dedicated, regular, difficult, report-based mentoring that I'm suggesting. Most efforts to formalize mentoring fail because we demand too little of mentors and mentees: a get-together for coffee once a semester, a shoulder to cry on in an emergency, that sort of thing.

If we really value mentoring, let's demand more from mentors and mentees alike.

Organizing Taught Me to Seek Tension

The best leadership education I got in college happened so far outside the university structure that it led to my arrest on one occasion and to disciplinary action by the university on another. I was a proud member of the Harvard Living Wage Campaign, which resorted to civil disobedience when every other method we had tried had failed. This experience taught me the importance of tension. What we lacked in terms of leadership, mentorship, evaluation, and equality, we made up for in a willingness to make trouble when it was warranted, and that made the difference.

Organizing retaught me this lesson over and over: two hundred young people ready to boo or applaud a public official's answer to our questions; asking an angry kid why he was not putting his anger into actually making things different; evangelical Christians, college students, service providers, and homeless youth sleeping outside a mayor's office to protest inadequate funding to address youth homelessness. Tension made the difference.

Tension and relationality are not incompatible. On the contrary, they are something of a yin and yang. It is in the slow process of developing relationships of trust that we earn the right to introduce tension. The tension of mutual accountability makes relationships stronger. These strong relationships then allow us to stand side by side and introduce tension in the public sphere. Finally, there is nothing like the experience of risky, collective action to reinforce our relationships.

But what would it mean for a university to invite conflict? To teach tension?

Recently, Iranians challenged a fraudulent election and risked their lives to take to the streets in record numbers. University students and academics led the marches. In 2007, Venezuelans defeated Hugo Chávez's antidemocratic referendum 51 to 49 percent, and universities led the way. Tiananmen Square. The antiapartheid movement. Students for a Democratic Society (SDS). Even the modern conservative resurgence has employed universities as fertile ground for dissent. Then we have the Highlanders, the Catholic Worker houses, and so on, instances when movements turned education into a means of conflict and movement.

Perhaps the most crucial strategic moment during the Harvard Living Wage Campaign's twenty-one-day sit-in occurred about one week into it, when the president of the university called an emergency meeting of the faculty. From what we heard, after the president finished stating why the university would not react to us protestors, one by one professors stood up to voice their support for what we were doing. That act of solidarity took the wind out of the administration's sails. Two days later, for the first time, they opened negotiations with us.

How do we teach tension?

- Invite more radicals, organizers, and extremists of different stripes to our campuses. More people such as Max Rameau in Florida who is (illegally) placing homeless people in foreclosed homes. Or neoconservatives who believe that military intervention is the best kind of intervention. Or undocumented immigrants who are fighting for equal rights. Or Christian fundamentalists who believe we do our schools a disservice by banning prayer and religious practice. Let's make our campuses homes for dissent.

- Open up our administrative structures (boards of trustees, boards of directors, hiring processes, investment decisions, and so forth) to student scrutiny and leadership.

- Expand on the work of folks such as Marshall Ganz who have designed service-learning-style courses that are more about social action than social service. In Ganz's class, we were each required to turn a personal passion into a concrete act of social action. One week, we were reflecting on our hopes and fears. The next, we were learning various avenues for building relationships. In later weeks, step by step, we learned how to tell our story, researched our obstacles and opponents, mapped the relevant power relationships, and decided on a strategic course of action (that was sometimes confrontational) to get what we wanted. This was not tension for tension's sake. This was a recognition that tension is often what is needed to make real change.

How do we teach tension? I'm not sure there's an easy answer to that question. Let's keep asking it.

REFERENCES

Illich, I. (2007). To hell with good intentions. In *Education for democracy*, ed. B. R. Barber and R. M. Battistoni, 456–60. Dubuque, IA: Kendall Hunt Publishing.

McKnight, J. (2007). Why servanthood is bad. In *Education for democracy*, ed. B. R. Barber and R. M. Battistoni, 461–66. Dubuque, IA: Kendall Hunt Publishing.

Conclusion

"I think we are at the end of a difficult generation of business leadership, and maybe leadership in general," said Jeff Immelt, Chairman and CEO of General Electric, when reflecting on the first decade of the twenty-first century in a December 2009 speech at West Point. "Tough-mindedness, a good trait—was replaced by meanness and greed—both terrible traits. Rewards became perverted. The richest people made the most mistakes with the least accountability." He concluded, "In too many situations, leaders divided us instead of bringing us together" (Immelt 2009).

No one can predict the future, but it may be safe to assume that the era in which leadership is viewed as the purview of a just a handful of people with certain predetermined traits, largely individualistic, is coming to a close. What replaces it is anyone's guess.

Periods of uncertainty, however, can be fertile ground for seeding change, which is why we believe that there could be no more auspicious time than now to experiment with new forms and approaches to leadership, many of which have been described in the pages of this volume. Clearly, we have little to lose, given the unprecedented amount of failed leadership, from the economic collapse and a global environmental crisis to pervasive poverty and widening inequities between the haves and the have-nots, that we have faced in recent decades. Perhaps we don't even need leaders per se; as Ella Baker argued during the civil rights movement, "Strong people don't need strong leaders" (Ransby 2003). Rather, we need to shift our ideas about what exactly leadership is and, most important, what we expect from leaders—and from ourselves in relation to them. This book can be seen partially as a first step toward reframing those issues in response to the failure of "old" leadership—and as offering an alternative.

Although this book focuses on the new leadership concept in the context of higher education, that is clearly only one of many domains and sectors that we believe are essential to understanding, advancing, and embodying new forms of leadership in our country and internationally. In fact, the most powerful models for bottom-up, relational, collaborative, public leadership are bubbling up in communities outside the academy, as well as in businesses, nonprofit groups, legislatures, and political campaigns (Leighninger 2006; Longo 2007; Mathews 2009). That doesn't let higher education off the hook, however.

We believe that higher education, as the nation's foremost crucible for knowledge and new ideas, has a critical and unique role to play in leadership education and practice that points us in a different direction. Higher education is also uniquely positioned to educate the next generation of leaders who will be confronting some of the most daunting challenges of our time, challenges that require a set of skills that deviate from those traditionally associated with leadership. So how colleges and universities teach leadership studies is vitally important. As the world becomes smaller and more connected, leaders will also have to be more adept at transcending the self, reaching out, and working with others in a larger community or external setting. Colleges and universities, many of which already require service-learning or community-engaged research from students, can build on these efforts by linking them with a deeper model of leadership education that emphasizes civic engagement as fundamental to leadership. In short, higher education is an ideal place to educate a new generation for responsible leadership, while it also addresses the interdependent challenges in our world.

As we have seen, there are many promising examples of education for the new leadership. With new technologies and a Millennial generation impatient with the old top-down model in which one charismatic person shows us the way, change is occurring in our models of leadership. And higher education has an array of innovative programs that link leadership and civic engagement. But there is much more that higher education can do, we believe, as do the authors of the chapters of this book.

What more? Rather than just presenting our own ideas, we have decided to practice the new form of leadership by asking each of our authors to respond to this question: What are the most important things that higher education should do to advance a new form of leadership education, one that reflects the approach described in this book? What follow are some suggestions that we hope will lay the groundwork for future research, conversations, and action.

Leadership and Civic Engagement: A Comprehensive Approach

We believe that higher education must think comprehensively about a new approach to educating the next generation of leaders. This means starting early and continually moving beyond the boundaries of the campus by connecting with K–12 education, community institutions, and non-college-bound youth. Higher education must demonstrate an institutional commitment to collaborative, interdisciplinary knowledge, integrating this approach seamlessly into the curriculum and assessing progress. In this approach, there is an understanding of the importance of infusing student voice into the culture of higher education, as well as giving students the opportunity to practice democratic leadership during their time on campus. Finally, a comprehensive approach doesn't end at graduation but instead draws upon the resources of alumni to create postgraduate opportunities in public leadership.

Reaching Out: Partnering with K–12 and Community Institutions

When recognizing that the new leadership model stresses inclusivity and participation in civic and political life, colleges and universities need to reach out to and involve K–12 schools and community institutions in their activities. Reciprocal partnerships with schools and communities, in which each partner has something to contribute and something to gain, are a practical example of the kind of leadership we encourage in this book. At the University of Pennsylvania's Netter Center for Community Partnerships, for example, student leadership helped to catalyze a community-based health clinic at the Sayre Middle School in West Philadelphia, as described in chapter 3. Begun in 2003, the partnership has since enabled students and faculty from medicine, nursing, dentistry, social work, design, and arts and sciences to collaborate with local schools and community members to address pressing health concerns. Likewise, in chapter 9 Decker Ngongang has demonstrated that "the most important investment" for community college leadership programs is community resources and partnerships.

These partnerships are important for myriad reasons. First, they offer students the opportunity to step outside themselves and their immediate environments to learn about and ultimately work in partnership with people and communities that may be wholly different from themselves. This collaboration is key to leadership in a global world. Second, they give young people who may not have access to the college environment the chance to see what it is like and, perhaps, develop academic aspirations that may not have previously existed. Third, they send a powerful message to the community that higher education institutions care about the civic mission on which they were founded and see themselves as part of the community—in spirit and in practice. Finally, they are opportunities for young people in those communities—both college students and non-college-bound youth—to learn new ways of practicing leadership through courses, online learning, internships, research, and other activities designed to engage a diverse swath of the population.

Specific recommendations in this area include the following:

- *Developing intergenerational civic leadership programs* with K–12 schools such as Public Achievement at the University of Denver (and in dozens of communities around the world), as described in chapter 7. In these programs, college students act as "civic coaches," gaining leadership skills by mentoring youth through a collaborative process of identifying, understanding, and then addressing challenging public issues.

- *Creating service and community leadership scholarships* such as those originally developed at Bentley University, which reward students involved in community service during high school with funds for college and then ask them to make a commitment to be part of formal programs that offer civic leadership opportunities both on and off the traditional campus. The scholarships should also be used to support students from diverse backgrounds and to recognize students who practice the kind of collaborative leadership that can then catalyze the civic involvement of their peers (see Zlotkowski, Longo, and Williams 2006).

- *Enhancing the leadership education opportunities* of people who don't attend college by conducting research that benefits noncollege youth, advocating for favorable public policies that support leadership development among noncollege youth, creating programs or courses that partner students and faculty with noncollege youth, and offering resources and access, especially through community colleges

Institutional Commitment

As stated in the Introduction, unless this approach to leadership education, along with the values of collaboration, inclusiveness, and community problem solving inherent in it, is embraced and supported by the entire institution, it is unlikely that it will gain traction over the long term, and it will be seen as tangential at best, and superfluous at worst, to students' higher education experience. In short, it is not enough for only students to champion this approach; it must be reflected in the words and, more importantly, actions of everyone at the university, from the trustees and the president to the deans and the department chairs.

Therefore, leadership education should no longer be siloed but instead be melded into a rich, comprehensive approach to helping people, especially young people, gain the skills, knowledge, and experience they need to become leaders in an interdependent, global society. This won't be easy, given that universities and colleges tend to isolate or separate themselves from their surrounding communities and that, internally, academic affairs and student affairs departments are walled off from one another. There also continues to be a strong emphasis on the disciplinary approach to education, despite growing evidence that interdisciplinary frameworks are becoming—and will continue to become—more important in addressing increasingly complex issues that warrant examination on a number of levels and from a number of perspectives.

Concrete recommendations for institutions to consider include the following:

- *Housing leadership programs jointly in academic affairs and student affairs departments.* As explained in chapter 4, to educate "the whole person" for leadership, the expertise of both academic affairs and student affairs is necessary. As Kathleen Knight Abowitz and her colleagues have noted, while academic affairs tends to contribute content knowledge from a variety of disciplines, student affairs offers an understanding of student development and a wealth of experience building learning communities. To ensure an appropriate level of institutional commitment to this kind of partnership, institutions should consider jointly housing their centers for leadership and civic engagement within academic affairs and student affairs departments, as was done with the institute at Miami University of Ohio.

- *Practicing interdisciplinary problem solving locally and globally.* In chapter 3, Matthew Hartley and Ira Harkavy have called on higher education to reconsider its disciplinary model and instead inculcate knowledge and practice through a "problem-solving" lens, through which a problem becomes the primary focus and then different angles or viewpoints are brought to bear on it. Adam Weinberg and his colleagues have offered a similar approach to global education in chapter 10. This approach warrants much more attention, and we believe that a promising place to start is with leadership education programs, since their aim is to help potential and upcoming leaders become better problem solvers. In doing so, higher education also needs to find ways to test this approach at the local and global levels, as well as to find ways to link these so that students (and others) understand the relationship between them. This could be achieved through programs such as those at the Netter Center for Community Partnerships at the University of Pennsylvania, the SIT Study Abroad programs, and yearlong senior capstone courses that apply study abroad experiences to local problems.

- *Evaluating the impact of leadership programs on the participants themselves and on the student body as a whole.* As with the efforts at Tufts University's Tisch College of Citizenship and Public Service, described in chapter 8, we can't be satisfied with documenting that students are civically engaged and that they demonstrate leadership. Instead, we need to use evaluation techniques that measure how much value the institution actually adds. Longitudinal surveys are one such technique, but qualitative methods also work if they are structured appropriately. There must also be more effort to meld, rather than separate, leadership and civic engagement as the focus of these kinds of studies, so that the new leadership education models may be evaluated more comprehensively.

Curricular Connections

Inherent in an institutional commitment is the recognition that leadership education, along with service-learning or other forms of experiential education, is integral to, rather than at the margins of, curricula. Although leadership education can be viewed as a separate set of courses or programs, we believe that the approach outlined in this book works best when it is integrated into required course work in subjects or disciplines across an institution. Engineering students, for example, could be required to design projects in partnership with the community, while education students could work in local schools. Students learning research methodologies could be asked to pick something in their communities to research and then conduct that investigation with local nonprofits.

Achieving this, however, requires commitment and interest from faculty. Today, although there are many faculty members at colleges and universities involved in service-learning, civic engagement, leadership development, and other programs and curricula that are bringing new pedagogies and practices to the academy, a large swath of faculty members continue to view these efforts as nice things to do but not necessarily essential to students' academic development and goals. This is an issue that initiatives such as Imagining America's Tenure Team Initiative on Public Scholarship seek to address (Ellison and Eatman 2008).

Some concrete recommendations include the following:

- *Creating sustained, developmental, cohort-based curricular programs* on student leadership through civic engagement. The evidence seems to indicate that developing programs that invite long-term relationships with faculty, fellow students, and community partners is more likely to lead to the kind of civic learning we are hoping to achieve. Almost all of the programs highlighted in this book were designed as multisemester courses, including those at Stanford, the University of Massachusetts Amherst, and Providence College (described in chapter 6), as well as those at Duke (chapter 1), Georgetown (chapter 5), and Tufts (chapter 8).

- *Encouraging more faculty to incorporate this approach into their work.* As noted, higher education institutions need to consider creating stronger incentives that will encourage more faculty to participate in these efforts and to participate in different ways. Among these are research fellowships that offer faculty the opportunity to engage in community-based research that involves students as partners; training and professional development activities (for instance, symposia, workshops, and stipends for course development); institutional rewards and recognition for outstanding programs or courses that reflect the new leadership approach; and including these efforts as part of tenure decisions. Faculty members will also need to model the engagement they would like to see in their students by becoming more engaged themselves in community-based work and serving as coaches or facilitators of civic learning for students as the latter become more involved in coteaching and joint research efforts.

- *Teaching a new skill set.* Throughout this book it has become clear that the new leadership approach is also about developing a new skill set for students. Based on the needs they see in society, Paul Light in chapter 11 and Stephen Smith in chapter 12 have outlined some of the leadership and organizing skills higher education will need to develop in students. This skill set needs to be understood and embraced by faculty, trustees, and institutional leadership so that it gains more traction and, ultimately, comes to be seen as integral to developing new leaders for a new century.

Student Voice

Because central tenets of the new leadership model described in this book include authenticity, transparency, and "walking the talk," attempts to establish a leadership education program or curricula without intentional involvement of students in the development and implementation of those efforts would be antithetical to the model. To that end, students should be encouraged to take part in creating new leadership programs and courses, in overseeing their progress, and in recommending improvements. Most importantly, students should be viewed as bona fide partners in these efforts. In short, students need to be seen as partners working with faculty, not for faculty, as described (and practiced) by Edward Zlotkowski, Katelyn Horowitz, and Sarah Benson in chapter 2 and by the writing team from the University of Denver in chapter 7.

Specific recommendations for infusing student voice include the following:

- *Developing more opportunities for students to get credit, fellowships, and payment* for providing leadership in service-learning courses on campus by, for example, serving as teaching assistants who lead discussions in the classroom about students' community work or as community assistants who act as liaisons between community institutions and students in service-learning courses. We should also rethink undergraduate research funding and expectations and specifically require that the research funding that colleges and universities provide to undergraduate students include a public dimension.

- *Creating a national student network.* Through this network, students could develop campus-to-campus consulting teams and program development materials using the "students as colleagues" concept that students have agency in their education for working with faculty and others on civic engagement projects. This network would also be able to promote the new leadership model on campuses, compile examples of ways in which student leaders have played significant roles in higher education, and provide practical support for campuses at every stage of development.

- *Developing a Millennial leadership training institute.* A training institute for students could provide a follow-up to the original national symposium that catalyzed this book. The training institute could help to develop and expand the ideas and practices defined in this book by bringing teams of students, with student-selected faculty and staff from their campuses, together to foster leadership and civic engagement on and across campuses.

After Graduation

Just as leadership education doesn't begin when students come to freshman orientation, it doesn't end with graduation. Alumni have the potential to be an excellent resource for advancing this new leadership education approach on college campuses. Many alumni have had their own experiences as leaders in their communities and across the globe — experiences that students would most likely find inspirational and educational in developing their own leadership skills and knowledge. Alumni also often have extensive networks that can be helpful to students embarking on new leadership careers.

But colleges and universities also have to develop opportunities for their graduates to devote their lives to public leadership, especially in the nonprofit and government sectors, as Paul Light notes in chapter 11. Some recommendations for including graduates in leadership education include the following:

- *Using alumni.* Colleges and universities should consider going beyond asking alumni for their money to asking them for their knowledge and then bring that knowledge to bear in the classrooms and in the communities where the institutions are working. Several of the authors of this book, including Carol Bellamy, Elizabeth Hollander, Kathy Kretman, Paul Light, Decker Ngongang, Stephen Smith, and Jonathan Zaff, have served as leaders in the public sector, as have thousands of their peers, suggesting the potential to bring fresh new perspectives, as well as new resources and talents, to leadership education.

- *Offering postgraduate fellowships and loan forgiveness for public leadership.* Finally, we need to provide more postgraduate opportunities that enable students to continue to act as public leaders in their work as teachers and nurses, as community organizers and civil servants. This is a desire illuminated in recent graduates' narratives, such as that of Decker Ngongang (in chapter 9), describing how he wanted his civic work to be more than an extracurricular activity, and that of Stephen Smith (in chapter 12), describing the passion he puts into his work as a community organizer. We also need to help those with public service career aspirations to gain the skills and resources they need to work in, start, and sustain strong nonprofit organizations that address difficult issues. That may require creating new internship and mentoring programs, offering forgiveness of student loans, and providing more financial aid for students engaged in nonprofit work.

Risk and Experimentation

We don't yet know what the new leadership model will look like exactly, because it is still being developed through an iterative process that presents both risks and opportunities. One risk is that mistakes may be made along the way—a risk that some higher education institutions may want to avoid. We believe that such a stance is antithetical to institutions whose primary purpose is knowledge acquisition, the foundation of which is the embrace of new ideas and challenges, as well as the chance to innovate and experiment with them. In fact, it is not a stretch to suggest that the stakes are too high for higher education *not* to develop new ways of educating students and creating knowledge, given the rapid and complex changes taking place in our globally connected world, which are demanding new ways of thinking and doing. The question is whether higher education will continue not only to adapt but also to lead. When colleges and universities do so, they send a powerful signal to their students, faculty, trustees, and the larger communities in which they operate that they are willing to step into new waters and demonstrate what courage and leadership look like. This seems like a worthy experiment whose time has come.

REFERENCES

Ellison, J., and T. Eatman. (2008). Scholarship in public: Knowledge creation and tenure policy in the engaged university. Retrieved May 31, 2010, from: http://www. imaginingamerica.org/TTI/TTI_FINAL.pdf.

Immelt, J. (December 9, 2009). Renewing American leadership. Speech at U.S. Military Academy at West Point, Distinguished Leaders Series. Retrieved May 31, 2010, from: http://files.gereports.com/wp-content/uploads/2009/12/90304-2-JRI-Speech-Reprint1-557.qxd_8.5x11.pdf.

Leighninger, M. (2006). *The next form of democracy.* Nashville, TN: Vanderbilt University Press.

Longo, N. (2007). *Why community matters: Connecting education with civic life.* Albany: State University of New York Press.

Mathews, D. (2009). Afterword: Ships passing in the night? In *A different kind of politics: Readings on the role of higher education in democracy*, ed. D. W. M. Barker and D. W. Brown, 93–104. Dayton, OH: Kettering Foundation Press.

Ransby, B. (2003). *Ella Baker and the black freedom movement: A radical democratic vision*. Chapel Hill: University of North Carolina Press.

Zlotkowski, E., N. Longo, and J. Williams, eds. (2006). *Students as colleagues: Expanding the circle of service-learning leadership*. Providence, RI: Campus Compact.

||||||||||||||||||||||||||||||||||||||||||||||||||||||||||||||||||||||||||

ABOUT THE CONTRIBUTORS

||||||||||||||||||||||||||||||||||||||||||||||||||||||||||||||||||||||||||

Volume coeditor **Cynthia M. Gibson** is senior vice president of The Philanthropic Initiative, a Boston-based firm that designs, implements and evaluates philanthropic programs for individual donors, families, foundations, and corporations in the United States and internationally. Previously, she was principal of Cynthesis Consulting, which provided strategic planning, evaluation, and communications services to a wide range of non-profit and philanthropic organizations, including higher education institutions and associations. Gibson was also a program officer at Carnegie Corporation of New York in the areas of youth civic engagement, democracy, and nonprofit management. She is the author of numerous publications on these and other topics.

Volume coeditor **Nicholas V. Longo** is director of the Global Studies program and associate professor of Public and Community Service Studies at Providence College. Previously, he was the founding director of the national student civic engagement campaign, Raise Your Voice, for Campus Compact from 2002 to 2004 and then was director of the Harry T. Wilks Leadership Institute at Miami University. He is also the author of *Why Community Matters: Connecting Education with Civic Life* (SUNY Press, 2007) and coeditor of *Students as Colleagues: Expanding the Circle of Service-Learning Leadership* (Campus Compact, 2006).

Kathleen Knight Abowitz is a professor of Educational Leadership at Miami University in Oxford, Ohio. As a teacher and scholar of democratic and community-based education, she is a collaborator with the Wilks Leadership Institute at Miami. Abowitz teaches courses in the philosophy of education, educational foundations, cultural studies, and leadership; her scholarship investigates questions of public life and citizenship with regard to both K–12 and postsecondary education.

Charla Agnoletti is a recent graduate of the University of Denver who coached Public Achievement for four years in the Denver Public Schools. She is currently a teacher with Teach for America.

Rick Battistoni is a professor of Political Science and Public and Community Service Studies at Providence College. Formerly the director of the Feinstein Institute for Public Service at Providence College, Rick also developed and directed civic engagement efforts at Rutgers University and Baylor University. A scholar in the field of political theory with a principal interest in the role of education in a democratic society, he is the author of several publications, including *Civic Engagement Across the Curriculum: A Resource Book for Faculty in all Disciplines.*

Carol Bellamy was recently appointed chair of the Board of Governors of the International Baccalaureate Organization. From 2005 to 2009 she was the C E O and president of World Learning, a private, not-for-profit international education and development organization based in Vermont and Washington, D.C. She has previously held positions as the executive director of U N I C E F, director of the United States Peace Corps Organization, and president of the New York City Council, among other positions in private-sector finance and law.

Sarah Benson is a student and marketing major at Bentley University. She has been involved with the Bentley Service-Learning Center as a Project Manager and member of several committees since her freshman year.

Alma Blount is director of the Hart Leadership Program in the Sanford School of Public Policy at Duke University. She has been teaching Duke undergraduates about adaptive leadership since 1994.

Eric Fretz is an assistant professor of Peace and Justice Studies at Regis University in Denver, Colorado. His writings include articles on civic engagement in higher education and the use of democratic practices in the classroom.

Hannah Goedert is a student and a Public Achievement coach at the University of Denver.

Ira Harkavy is associate vice president and director of the Netter Center for Community Partnerships at the University of Pennsylvania. Among Harkavy's recent publications are *Dewey's Dream: Universities and Democracies in an Age of Education Reform* (Temple Press), which he coauthored with Lee Benson and John Puckett, and *The Obesity Culture: Strategies for Change. Public Health and University-Community Partnerships* (London, Smith-Gordon), coauthored with Francis E. Johnston.

Matt Hartley is an associate professor of Education at the University of Pennsylvania's Graduate School of Education, where he currently serves as the chair of the higher education division. His research and writing examine the ways in which colleges and universities conceptualize and strive to realize their educational missions. A significant thread of his research focuses on the civic purposes of higher education and the responsibilities of colleges and universities in a democracy.

Elizabeth Hollander currently serves part-time as a senior fellow at Tufts University's Tisch College of Citizenship and Public Service. From 1997 to 2006 she was executive director of Campus Compact. Prior to that she had a career in urban development in Chicago.

Katelyn Horowitz is a student in the honors program at Bentley University. She is majoring in accounting and as a service scholarship student has had extensive experience as a Project Manager.

Rebecca Hovey is the dean for International Study at Smith College. She previously served as dean of S I T Study Abroad from 2001 to 2008. She holds a PhD in city and regional planning from Cornell University.

Stephanie Raill Jayanandhan graduated from Miami University in 2009. She is currently exploring the intersections of financial literacy and public participation.

Kei Kawashima-Ginsberg is the lead researcher at CIRCLE and is particularly interested in providing various organizations and communities with research to help increase civic and political engagement among diverse populations of youth. With a background in program evaluation, Kawashima-Ginsberg often assists practitioners in planning and implementing an evaluation of various initiatives and programs. As a staff member at the Jonathan M. Tisch College of Citizenship and Public Service at Tufts University, Kawashima-Ginsberg provides consultation to staff and community partners about university-community collaboration and community-based research.

Arthur S. Keene is a professor in the Anthropology Department at the University of Massachusetts, where he has taught for the last thirty years. He is cofounder and codirector of the UMass Citizen Scholars Program and founder and faculty director of the UMass Alliance for Community Transformation, the organization that coordinates academic alternative spring breaks at UMass. His current research project, entitled The Ethnography of Us: How Millennials Learn, engages teams of student ethnographers to explore the culture of undergraduate learning at UMass Amherst.

Kathy Postel Kretman is the director of Georgetown University's Center for Public and Nonprofit Leadership. She also serves as research professor at the Georgetown Public Policy Institute, where she teaches courses on public leadership, philanthropy, and nonprofit management. She has designed and delivered leadership programs for education institutions, foundations and nonprofit organizations since 1994.

Peter Levine is director of research and director of CIRCLE (Center for Information and Research on Civic Learning and Engagement) at Tufts University's Jonathan M. Tisch College of Citizenship and Public Service. He is the author of *Reforming the Humanities* (2009), *The Future of Democracy* (2007), and several other books.

Paul C. Light is Paulette Goddard Professor of Public Service at New York University's Wagner School of Public Service. Before joining NYU, he was vice president and director of governmental studies at the Brookings Institution and founding director of its Center for Public Service. He has published extensively on American government, the presidency, government reform, nonprofit performance, and organizational excellence. Light is the author of twenty books, including *Making Non-Profits Work* and *Pathways to Non-Profit Excellence*. He is a graduate of Macalester College and holds an MA and PhD from the University of Michigan.

Sarah McCauley is the student civic engagement coordinator at the Center for Community Engagement and Service Learning at the University of Denver.

Tania D. Mitchell is associate director for undergraduate studies and director of service learning in the Center for Comparative Studies in Race and Ethnicity at Stanford University, where she directs the academic program in public service, community development, and community-based research. She has been recognized as an Emerging Scholar by the International Association for Research in Service Learning and Community Engagement (IARSLCE) and as an Engaged Scholar by Campus Compact. Mitchell's teaching and research interests include service-learning pedagogy, college student development, and social justice.

Emelye Neff is a student and Public Achievement coach at the University of Denver.

Decker Ngongang is vice president for programs at Mobilize.org, where he is responsible for managing program operations and development. Before joining Mobilize.org, he was executive director of Generation Engage, having started with the organization as a Charlotte grassroots outreach coordinator who worked with local organizations to engage young adults in civic participation. In 2003 he received a BA from North Carolina State University and served as Senior Class President and a member of the Alumni Association Board of Directors. Born in Charlotte, North Carolina, he now resides in Washington, D.C.

Sarah J. Nickels is a doctoral student at the Graduate School of Social Work at the University of Denver.

Nicole Nicotera is associate professor at the University of Denver, Graduate School of Social Work. Her research and scholarship focus on measuring civic development in children, interventions to enhance civic leadership and positive youth development, the influences of neighborhood collective socialization and social cohesion on young people, and issues of unearned privilege and oppression in social work practice, education, and research.

Duncan Pickard is a 2010 graduate of Tufts University who was a history major and Tisch Scholar of Citizenship and Public Service. He is from Oak Bluffs, Massachusetts.

Taylor Rowe is a student and Public Achievement coach at the University of Denver.

Stephen Smith likes building new things, fighting for justice, mentoring new leaders, and being married. He resides in Chicago, where he is the organizing director of the Illinois Coalition for Immigrant and Refugee Rights. His book *Stoking the Fire of Democracy: Our Generation's Introduction to Grassroots Organizing* is now available through ACTA Publications.

Russell Takeall is a student and Public Achievement coach at the University of Denver.

Virginia Visconti is the director of the Public Service Research Program at the Haas Center for Public Service at Stanford University. She oversees the Public Service Scholars Program and Community-Based Research Fellows Program and teaches community-based research courses through the Urban Studies Program. Her work explores the epistemological and methodological implications of engaged scholarship and critically examines what it means to practice research as a form of service. Visconti holds a dual major PhD in social/cultural anthropology and education policy studies from Indiana University Bloomington, an MAT in English, also from Indiana University, and a BA in English from the University of Illinois at Urbana-Champaign.

Adam Weinberg is the president and CEO of World Learning, where he oversees education programs in over eighty countries. From 2006 to 2009, he served as executive vice president at World Learning, where he was also the provost of SIT Study Abroad. Before coming to World Learning, Weinberg held a number of faculty and administrative positions at Colgate University, including vice president and dean of the college. Weinberg has worked in and written extensively about civic education, focusing on ways to develop organizations and projects that connect universities and communities through public work.

Sarah Woiteshek is the assistant director of the Wilks Leadership Institute at Miami University. She graduated from Longwood University with a Bachelor of Science degree and Miami University with a Master of Higher Education and Student Affairs degree. Her professional interests include community-based learning experiences and public leadership studies.

Jonathan Zaff is the vice president of Research and Policy Development at America's Promise Alliance. He is also a scholar-in-residence at the Institute of Applied Research in Youth Development and a senior scholar at the Tisch College of Citizenship and Public Service, both at Tufts University. His research focuses primarily on studying the content of social contexts that promote positive outcomes among youth, particularly with regard to academic achievement and civic engagement.

Edward Zlotkowski is a professor of English at Bentley University and the founding director of the Bentley Service-Learning Center. With Nicholas Longo and James Williams, he coedited *Students as Colleagues: Expanding the Circle of Service-Learning Leadership* (Campus Compact, 2006).

INDEX

National Society of Internships and Experiential Education (NSIEE), 74

national student network, 253–54

National Survey of Student Engagement, 90

NCOC (National Conference on Citizenship), 6, 193

Neff, Emelye, 152, 161–63

negative student attitudes, 60

Net Gen, 5

Netter Center for Community Partnerships, 15, 249, 251

A New Engagement? Political Participation, Civic Life, and the Changing American Citizen (Zukin et al.), 45

new leadership, 3–23, 247–55; and civic identity, 116–18; in higher education, 8–10; overview, 3–8; through civic engagement, 10–14

Newman, Frank, 72–73

newspaper industry, potential demise of, 9

Ngongang, Decker, 19, 188, 249, 255

NGOs (non-governmental organizations), 210, 213, 216–17

Nicaraguan Garment Workers Fund, 128

Nickels, Sarah J., 152

Nicotera, Nicole, 152

noncollege youth, 250

non-governmental organizations (NGOs), 210, 213, 216–17

North High School (Denver, CO), 152

North Korea youth refugee resettlement program, 34–36

Obama, Barack, 226

Obama, Michelle, 226

obstacles to change, 79

Office of Public Engagement, 88

Ohio Agricultural and Mechanical College, 70

Ohio State University, 70

older students, 226

Omidyar, Pierre and Pamela, 171

one-to-one relational meetings, 158, 160, 166

organizational competency, 144

organizational illiteracy, 61

organizing skills, 4, 28, 46, 253

orphanage for children with HIV, Bangalore, India, 42–43

Padron, Eduardo, 193

Pandey, Sanjay K., 227

Park, Miss, 34–35

Parks, Rosa, 11

Parks, Sharon, 27–28

participatory leadership, 12–13

participatory research, 212

Partnership for Public Service, 227

paying attention, power of, 97

PBL (Problem-Based Learning), 79

peer-reviewed journals, 76, 77

People-to-People program, 54

perseverance, 26

personal competencies, 144–45

personal energy investment, 55

personal narrative essays, 33

Pew Charitable Trusts, 78

philosophy of service, 143

Pickard, Duncan, 18, 169, 182–86

place-based knowledge, 93–94

Poffenberger, Michael, 216

Point-of-View Essays, 39–40

police harassment against youth and minorities, 159–61

Policy Research Portfolios, 39–40

political activism, 71, 73

political and civic engagement, compared, 5–6, 46

political disengagement and disaffection, 71

political knowledge, 93–94

politics, defined, 154

positional leadership, 12

Post-Conflict Transformation Program (Uganda), 210–11

postgraduate fellowships, 254

power: Agnoletti on, 155–56; challenges to, 135–36; and community-based leadership, 94; and conflict, 164; defined, 154; of group membership, 97; Rowe on, 159–60; and tension, 164; understanding through writing process, 150–51; understated role of, 223

power mapping, 18, 144, 151, 159, 166

power relations knowledge, 94

power sharing, 61

practice, power of, 97

praxis, 125, 133, 142

President's Commission on Higher Education (1974), 191

"Principles of Best Practices for Combining Service and Learning in 1989," 75

privilege walks, 157–59

Problem-Based Learning (PBL), 79

Problem-Solving Learning (PSL), 69, 79–80

problem-solving skills, 14–15, 26, 36, 98, 251

professional schools, 230

Project Coordinators, BSLC, 53–54

Project DC: Research Internship on Urban Issues, 109

Project Managers, BSLC, 52–54

Project Pericles, 173

Providence College, 4, 17, 126–29, 132, 133–34, 138, 143, 252

PSL (Problem-Solving Learning), 69, 79–80

PSP. See Public and Community Service Studies Program (PSP, Providence College)

public, defined, 84–85

Public Achievement program (DU), 150–53, 249

public action, 167

Public Allies, 8

public and community-based leadership education, 15–16, 83–102, 251; content knowledge focus of, 93–95; fitting into existing academic departments, 91–93; importance of, 88–91; optimal enactment in today's colleges and universities, 91–100; overview, 83–88; pedagogies, best suited for, 97–100; skills content of, 95–97

Public and Community Service Studies Program (PSP, Providence College), 17, 126–29, 132–34, 138, 143

public health and health systems management, 110

Public Higher Education Network of Massachusetts (PHENOM), 131

public land grant colleges and universities, 70

public leadership, 39–40, 84, 110, 247, 249, 254. See also higher education's role in public leadership; public and community-based leadership education

public problem-solving, 14, 26

public service, 20, 73–74, 103, 110. See also specific colleges, universities, and topics related to public service

public service plans, 120–21

Public Service Scholars Program (Stanford University), 17, 118–22, 133, 137

public skills, 165–68

public sociology, 77

public speaking skills, 145

public voice, 46

Puerto Rico history project, 125

Putnam, Robert, 45, 88